Selected Poems and Prose

GOTTFRIED BENN was born on 2 May 1886 ⸱
in Westpriegnitz, North Germany). He ⸱
to study philology and theology, h⸱
study of military medicine at t.
Berlin. His first small collection of p⸱
published as a pamphlet in Berlin in   .ᴗation:
Benn became known as a leading figur⸱   .ment called
literary Expressionism. During the First   .ır he worked as an
army doctor in a hospital in Brussels. In 1⸲ , ne was discharged and
returned to Berlin, where he opened the private practice for skin and
venereal diseases which was his often meagre source of income for
most of the rest of his working life. In 1932 he was elected to member-
ship of the Literary Section of the Prussian Academy of Arts, and
remained in place after the Nazis' rise to power. Although he never
joined the NSDAP, his prose writings from the period incorporate
Nazi terminology and support elements of Nazi ideology. He rejoined
the army in 1935, but was attacked by the SS as an exponent of
'degenerate' Expressionist art and forbidden to publish while still a
serving soldier. After the war Benn began to publish new work and
his reputation as a poet rose quickly in West Germany. He died in
July 1956.

Educated in Cardiff and London, DAVID PAISEY wrote a study of
diction in Gottfried Benn's poems to 1927 as part of a London
University MA, in the course of which he met Benn once in Berlin.
After learning Russian during National Service, he worked as a
German specialist in the British Museum Library, later the British
Library, where he produced its catalogue of German books of the
seventeenth century. He has written extensively on the history of the
book in Germany and matters Anglo-German.

Fyfield*Books* aim to make available some of the great classics of British and European literature in clear, affordable formats, and to restore often neglected writers to their place in literary tradition.

Fyfield*Books* take their name from the Fyfield elm in Matthew Arnold's 'Scholar Gypsy' and 'Thyrsis'. The tree stood not far from the village where the series was originally devised in 1971.

> *Roam on! The light we sought is shining still.*
> *Dost thou ask proof? Our tree yet crowns the hill,*
> *Our Scholar travels yet the loved hill-side*

from 'Thyrsis'

GOTTFRIED BENN

Selected Poems and Prose

Edited and translated by
DAVID PAISEY

FyfieldBooks

CARCANET

First published in Great Britain in 2013 by
Carcanet Press Limited
Alliance House
Cross Street
Manchester M2 7AQ

www.carcanet.co.uk

A CIP catalogue record for this book is available from the British Library

ISBN 978 1 84777 150 6

The publisher acknowledges financial assistance from Arts Council England

Supported by
ARTS COUNCIL
ENGLAND

Typeset by XL Publishing Services, Exmouth
Printed and bound in England by SRP Ltd, Exeter

Contents

POEMS

Translator's Preface

This is a personal selection from the much larger work of Gottfried Benn, presented in two roughly chronological sequences, of verse and prose respectively, so that developments over time can become apparent. In bulk he produced several times more prose than verse, but I have selected much less of the former for translation. The dates supplied here are of first recorded appearances of texts, either in manuscript or print, as established in the four-volume collected edition published by Limes Verlag (Wiesbaden) in 1958–61, edited by Dieter Wellershoff; later authorial amendments have been incorporated. Note that the date supplied at the head of each text is not part of the original: where no dated manuscript survives, composition may have preceded the year of first publication. I have left the texts largely without commentary, to allow readers to form their own opinions. A brief biographical note follows, which may help to put particular works into context, notably those of the Nazi period. There is a huge critical literature on Benn in German, but I see no point in listing any parts of it for readers who know no German. Benn's original texts can all be found in the latest collected edition by Klett-Cotta Publishers in Stuttgart. I did not think it necessary to print a bibliography of their first and subsequent appearances during his lifetime.

People say poetry cannot be translated – Benn said so himself – and my efforts may be futile, but I think there may be some merit in trying to convey something of the quality of a great poet to Anglophone readers who cannot read him in the original. Nevertheless the inclusion of the German originals of all the poems selected may encourage some interaction with the poet's own words. In my renderings of the poetry, which Benn intended to be read on the page rather than spoken, I have tried to reflect the scope of his characteristic diction, as well as his original metric structures, rhyme-schemes (with the occasional expedient of assonance), and often even the punctuation. I have allowed myself more latitude in translating the free verse. The prose is more easily rendered into English, and I have aimed at literal versions which respect the rhetorical structures – sentence length and so on – of the German originals, some of which were intended to be spoken. The early experimental narratives are pioneering examples of Expressionist prose, but the other works are mostly quite straightforward. I have translated two from the Nazi period in full, one because it is a superb piece of rhetoric, the other because its toxicity is extreme. I have omitted a substantial study entitled *Goethe and the Natural Sciences* (1931) because it takes for granted educated German readers' familiarity with the life and works of Goethe and would require much annotation. The eyewitness account of the trial and execution of Edith Cavell in 1915 (1928) is included for its English interest. Most of the remaining prose here consists of excerpts from longer texts, chosen sometimes for their beauty, sometimes for their information content and interest, notably those which refer to poetry, especially Expressionist poetry. There are many fine poems I have not translated, but, apart from remaining narratives and the Goethe essay, I think I have included the best (and worst) of the prose.

I should like to dedicate these translations to the memory of Leslie ('Moses') Reed (1920–84), in September 1947 my meticulous first teacher of German in Whitchurch Secondary School, Cardiff. I am grateful to Professor Leonard Forster (1913–97) who encouraged me to work on diction in Benn's poems up to 1927 at University College London and in Berlin, where I met Benn briefly in July 1955. My thanks also to Michael Schmidt (another Benn enthusiast) and Helen Tookey of Carcanet, Alun and Julie Emlyn-Jones, and to Massimo Danielis, who created the aquatint engraving *Benn: Ein Wort* in 2012 for the cover of this book.

Biographical Introduction

In a letter Gottfried Benn wrote to his long-standing correspondent in Bremen Friedrich Wilhelm Oelze on 11 September 1950, he said: 'My private life is really completely opaque, a continuum of gaps and losses, no-one could make a story of me, perceive and portray any coherence. A strange parallel to my so-called oeuvre, which consists only of break-ups and break-downs, and has no line which can be read'. Nevertheless a brief biography follows, with particular attention to a period in the 1930s which caused Benn, and causes his readers, severe problems.

Gottfried Benn was born on 2 May 1886 in Mansfeld (a village in Westpriegnitz, North Germany), as the second child of a Lutheran pastor and his French-Swiss wife. He spent most of his childhood in Sellin (now Zielin, West Poland, another village in what was then the German Neumark), where he was allowed to join the son of the local manor as he received instruction from a private tutor; the two went together to secondary school (Gymnasium) in Frankfurt on the Oder. In adulthood he liked to point out how many important German writers had grown up in Lutheran parsonages, but his father was very authoritarian, and Gottfried clashed with him bitterly for refusing his mother medical relief during her painful death from cancer in 1912.

He went to Marburg University to study philology and theology, as his father wished, but after two years, in accordance with his own wishes, changed to the study of military medicine at the Kaiser-Wilhelm-Akademie in Berlin, for which there was a state subsidy. His intended career as a regimental doctor in peacetime was cut short by kidney damage suffered during manoeuvres. He undertook further training as an auxiliary doctor in Berlin hospitals, including the Westend Hospital in Charlottenburg, and in particular on a dissection course in Moabit. He later confessed[1] that he had been removed from psychiatric work because he found it impossible to take any interest in individual patients' case histories, to the extent that doing so led to severe physical symptoms in himself. His first small collection of poems, *Morgue and Other Poems*, was published as a

---

1 In *Epilog* (1922).

pamphlet in Berlin in 1912 and created a sensation: Benn became known as a leading figure in the new movement called literary Expressionism.

After his further professional experience and a trip to America as a ship's doctor, he found himself in the army again at the beginning of the First World War. He took part in the battle for Antwerp, then spent much of the war in Brussels, where he was given the job of doctor in a hospital for prostitutes; this was a very productive period in literary terms. In 1917 he was discharged as a result of some kind of nervous breakdown, and returned to Berlin. Here he opened the private practice for skin and venereal diseases which was his often meagre source of income for the rest of his working life in that city, with the exception of the period from 1935 to 1945, when he was again employed by the army, this time as a medical administrator. Throughout his life, poetry was of primary importance to him, though he wrote in other genres too; medicine merely paid the bills.

Although intellectually and socially he was very much a loner, he married three times,[2] and, particularly in the unmarried intervals, had a number of sometimes overlapping and far more than casual sexual relationships, possibly the first being with the very fine poet Else Lasker-Schüler.[3] His first marriage was cruelly cut short by his wife's early death, and, as he did not like young children, he did not feel able to bring up his daughter Nele himself, so she lived with friends in Denmark, and was adopted there in 1946. In 1929 a young actress with whom he was having an affair committed suicide, knowing he did not consider her his equal intellectually. There are tender references in a few poems to his second and third wives, but despite their importance to his daily life, neither played a part in his creative work. Only one of his male friendships can be said to have been close for a time, that with Erich Reiss,[4] a Berlin publisher who

2 He married: firstly in 1914 Edith Osterloh, who died in 1921 (their daughter Nele was born in 1915); secondly in 1938 Herta von Wedemeyer, who committed suicide during the chaotic final weeks of the Second World War when, alone, she despaired of leaving the Soviet zone of occupation for the American one; and thirdly in 1946 the dentist Dr Ilse Kaul, who outlived him.
3 Else Lasker-Schüler (1869–1945), a Jew who would emigrate to Jerusalem to avoid Nazi persecution. Benn delivered a moving eulogy to her in Berlin in 1952, long after her death.
4 Erich Reiss (1887–1951) was a Jew, and his business, begun in 1908, was liqui-dated by the Nazis in 1936. He was sent to Sachsenhausen concentration camp,

had produced some of his early works; around 1930 the two met regularly in the evening to drink in Benn's favourite pub. Benn's long correspondence with F.W. Oelze, already mentioned, maintained a polite distance at the personal level, after Benn's extreme wariness at first and a hiccup in 1936, but it did provide him with a degree of support (though hardly at the intellectual level Oelze unsuccessfully aimed for), and, more importantly, assistance with preserving his manuscripts through the war of 1939–45 and its immediate aftermath.

Benn's early poems of extreme suffering amongst the lowest levels of society seem driven by a wild but unexpressed compassion, and some of the early prose suggests a highly vulnerable sensitivity which was to be hidden under various assertive defence strategies. However, he soon turned his attention to his thereafter constant theme of the fractured human self in a tragic world of post-Nietzschean nihilism, where human existence and experience is potentially meaningful and transcendent only in so far as it produces art. States of intoxication, rushes of blood to the brain and other organs, commingling of cultural and anthropological memories, all these could help provide the conditions necessary for the production of poetry and in part its subject. Benn's poems are monologues, acts of defiance erected against the void: but 'the poem is the mind's unpaid work … one-sided, without effect and without a partner'.[5] The poems trace a great arc across his life and are undiscursive: they can stand for themselves.

His prose, by contrast, with the exception of some early experimental pieces with a narrative-autobiographical kernel, is full of assertions and arguments, though it too tends to the conclusion the poems simply incorporate. Much of it is rhetorically refined and mellifluous, but it should not be read in isolation from its social and political circumstances. He was elitist, and a racist foretelling the end of the white race.[6] It is perhaps easy to see the attraction of parts of National Socialist ideology for him, but difficult to understand the stupidity of such an apparently rigorous thinker leaving his isolationist comfort zone to welcome the Third Reich in print, as he did

from which he was released in 1938 thanks to appeals from influential supporters (not including Benn, who at that time would have had no influence with the authorities), and emigrated to the USA via Sweden. His warm and chatty letters to Benn from 1946 to 1951 have been published.
5 In *Summa summarum* (1926).
6 In Benn's view, the threat came mainly from the East.

in prose collections of 1933 and 1934; politics had hitherto been for him a sphere outside the permanent haven of art, and certainly never its possible concurrent. Perhaps there is a millenarian in every lyric poet, but for a time Benn saw the political upheaval as an anthropological mutation capable of countering European nihilism; perhaps also he was blinded by the possibility of acceptance in the nationalist community, as opposed to the indifference to the individual of modern society.[7] He had also been flattered in 1932 by the public recognition implicit in his election to membership of the Literary Section of the Prussian Academy of Arts. But the uncharacteristically convoluted prose of his 1932 inaugural speech to that body reveals how nervously he was trying to impress; as spoken it must have been near-incomprehensible. Despite misgivings, he remained among the rump of members who had not resigned, emigrated or been dismissed at the beginning of the Nazi regime in 1933, as had several whose places were filled by more of its literary supporters, and from 15 February to 8 June 1933 was its acting chairman. He was criticised for remaining in Germany by various writers who had emigrated, notably his friend Heinrich Mann, and defended his position in print.

What today seems his worst moral failing of this or any period is his acceptance of Nazi policy towards Jews. His essay 'Doric World'[8] considered, as a model for the 'total state' of Nazi Germany, the severe, militaristic, slave-based and to us morally transgressive state of ancient Sparta, because it had bred what he considered the beginnings of high art. And 'Eugenics I'[9] of the previous year had supported state-run eugenics, and by implication the beginnings of the Holocaust, since it contains the chilling proposition that modern man 'becomes great through the concept of the enemy, only the man who sees enemies can grow': from the start, the Nazi state had insistently proclaimed Jews its prime enemy. Benn's absorption and repetition of Nazi theory in prose examples from 1932 to 1934 extends even to

7 Ferdinand Tönnies' *Gemeinschaft und Gesellschaft* (1887) is the classic formulation of this sociological opposition, still very current in Benn and his contemporaries. Nazi community was, of course, exclusive.
8 'Dorische Welt' (1934).
9 'Züchtung I.' (1933). Eugenics, systematised by Francis Galton (1822–1911), remained a much-studied subject until some time after the Second World War, when its Nazi associations discredited it. University College London maintained a lecture room named Eugenics Theatre for well over a decade after 1945.

the micro-level of vocabulary, which no English translation can reveal:[10] and the climax of 'Eugenics I' uses the extreme rhetoric later characteristic of Goebbels in his prophetic rants: '*brains* must be bred, great brains to defend Germany, brains with canine teeth, teeth of thunderbolts'.[11] Benn did not act like an anti-Semite, as we have seen in his friendships with Else Lasker-Schüler and Erich Reiss, and wrote to one of his concurrent mistresses on 4 December 1935: 'My favourite milieu has always been the Jewish, and next to it the aristocratic one'. But he had nevertheless decided to adopt the Nazi position, or at least not to criticise it, and wrote to the same correspondent two weeks later: 'Yes, the Jews, that inexhaustible subject! One should *really* have nothing to do with *any* of them, taking an absolutely strict line. But then along comes someone like E[rich] R[eiss] with a gift of chairs and two books published by Piper, and that is nice'.[12]

Whatever his personal feelings, he did not publicly oppose Nazi policy towards the Jews, nor, even after the war, did he disown or apologise for his earlier arguments in favour of other aspects of the Third Reich, arguments which had been long in gestation. His fault was not a *Lord Jim* leap, a momentary error bitterly regretted and expiated over many years.[13] In 1949, Benn heard that the Jewish émigré novelist Alfred Döblin,[14] with whom he had been friendly before 1933, and who returned to Germany in November 1945 as a French Cultural Officer in Baden-Baden, despite his admiration for some of Benn's works, had called him 'a scoundrel';[15] morally this seems to me entirely just.

---

10 For instance, the words *Führerbegriff*, *Volkheit*, *volkhaft* and *arthaft*, not hitherto part of Benn's diction, can be found in 'After Nihilism', 'Eugenics I', 'Expressionism' and 'Doric World', but not in the poems.

11 Compare Goebbels: 'Only a brazen species will be able to assert itself in the storms of our time. It must have guts of iron and a heart of steel' (quoted in the notes to Victor Klemperer, *Tagebücher 1944*, ed. Walter Nowojski and Hadwig Klemperer, 4th ed. (Berlin, 2006), p. 85. Victor Klemperer's *LTI* [*Lingua Tertii Imperii*], first published in 1946, has documented Nazi linguistic practices.

12 Benn's letters to Elinor Buller of 4 and 17 December 1935.

13 Joseph Conrad's novel *Lord Jim* (1900) was known to Benn in translation.

14 Alfred Döblin (1878–1957), now best known for his novel *Berlin Alexanderplatz* (1929).

15 'Ein Schuft'; see Benn's letter to F.W. Oelze, 23 March 1949. In his memoir *Doppelleben* (1949), Benn wrote that he could not see why Döblin had described him thus.

Benn never joined the Nazi Party (NSDAP), and after the war was to have no difficulties during the de-Nazification process of the occupying powers. The more he was exposed to the organisations and ideas of Hitler's Germany immediately after his welcome of 1933/34, however, the more they revealed strong currents of opposition to his avant-garde past and far from orthodox present, and he felt himself under threat. Keeping his head down did not seem by itself a sufficient strategy for self-preservation, and in 1935 he decided to rejoin the army, calling this step 'the aristocratic form of emigration'.[16] He left Berlin for an administrative post in Hanover at the end of March 1935, and continued in this post in Berlin again from 1937, and from 1943 to 1945 in Landsberg an der Warthe (now Gorzów in Poland).

He had reckoned without the non-intellectual side of the Nazi regime, however, and, in response to the publication in March 1936 of his *Selected Poems*, was subjected to a virulent anonymous attack in the 7 May issue of *Das Schwarze Korps*, the weekly newspaper of Heinrich Himmler's SS, which took exception mainly to the shocking explicitness of some early works, and said he qualified as 'a successor of those who have been thrown out of the house because of their unnatural piggery'.[17] To counter this implied threat of dismissal from the army, and possibly worse, Benn succeeded in raising support from his commanding officer in Hanover, Major-General von Zepelin, and from Hanns Johst,[18] President of both the Literary Section of the Academy of Arts and of the Reichsschrifttumskammer (Chamber of Literature, founded by Goebbels in 1933), of which Benn had been a member since December 1933. However, on 15 May 1936 he was forbidden to publish anything while still a serving soldier, and on 28 April 1938 was to be excluded from the Chamber of Literature.

Benn continued writing while under this ban, which did not prevent further National Socialist attacks on Expressionism and its literary products, including Benn. He had a particularly virulent

16 So in *Zum Thema Geschichte* (probably 1943) and *Doppelleben* (1950), part 2.
17 The reference is to the homosexual Ernst Röhm and his supporters in the paramilitary SA, many of whom were murdered in the 'Night of the Long Knives' on 30 June 1934. The passage on Greek homosexuality in Benn's 'Doric World' (1934) is purely factual, and there are few other hints of any bisexual interest.
18 Hanns Johst (1890–1978), a writer whose play *Schlageter* (performed on Hitler's birthday in 1933) contains the famous line: 'When I hear the word *culture* I release the safety-catch on my Browning'.

opponent in Wolfgang Willrich,[19] but in September 1937 Heinrich Himmler wrote to Willrich that the institutions for which he was responsible had been forbidden to take any part in actions against Benn, thanks to his unobjectionable behaviour since 1933.[20] Benn was incautious enough to have 22 recent poems privately printed in August 1943, and sent them to seven people only.[21] One of these poems ('Monologue', written in 1941) contained some withering criticism of National Socialism and its policies of enslavement, which could have cost him his life had it become public. Including a Shakespearian lament for the loss of measure, and denunciation of individual Nazi leaders, mainly for their vulgarity, it mourns the tragedy of inaction he had chosen.

After the war, and then long-drawn-out difficulties in finding publishers for his new works, his reputation in West Germany rose quite quickly, based largely on the rhyming, strictly metrical poems he was still writing, which found admirers and imitators among some poets of the younger generation. He also had considerable success with new works in prose, though he never returned to the experiments of his early years. Alexander Lernet-Holenia, one of the friends to whom Benn sent a copy of his privately printed poems of 1943, had told Benn in 1942 that he was the greatest lyric poet for 100 years, but needed to invent a new third style after his 'cancer shed' early poems and his eight-line stanzas of the 1920s:[22] I believe he never did so. In both prose and verse he revisited familiar themes and arguments. When I visited him on 20 July 1955, he was very kind to a painfully inexperienced student, and obligingly wove into his conversation many of the formulations I knew well from his publications. In his post-war letters he tells how his wife had asked him to stop writing poems about roses and melancholy, and I believe most of the works of that final period bear the mark of depression. The often repetitious prose seems to me a falling-off, and the verse to shrink in scope to a concentration on art as the sole product capable of transcendence, to poems about writing poems. He thought no

19 Wolfgang Willrich (1897–1948), a member of the SS and author of *Clearing Out the Temple of Art* (*Säuberung des Kunsttempels*, 1937).
20 Quoted by Joachim Dyck in *Der Zeitzeuge. Gottfried Benn 1929–1949* (Göttingen, 2006), p. 235.
21 Listed by Dyck, *Der Zeitzeuge*, p. 300.
22 Alexander Lernet-Holenia (1897–1976), Austrian writer, whom Benn had known since 1930; see Benn's letter to Oelze of 24 April 1942.

writer could hope to produce more than a handful of perfectly achieved lyric poems in a lifetime, but for me there are more than enough in his work to rank him among the greatest German poets of the twentieth century, however seriously flawed he was as a man. He died on 7 July 1956.

POEMS

Finish

I

Das Speiglas – den Ausbrüchen
so großer grüner warmer Flüsse
nicht im entferntesten gewachsen –
schlug endlich nieder.
Der Mund fiel hinterher. Hing tief. Sog
schluckweis Erbrochenes zurück. Enttäuschte
jedes Vertrauen. Gab Stein statt Brot
dem atemlosen Blut.

II

Der kleine Klumpen roch wie ein Hühnerstall,
schlug hin und her. Wuchs. Ward still.

Die Enkelin spielte das alte Spiel:
Wenn Großmutter schläft:
Um die Schlüsselbeine war es so eingesunken,
daß sie Bohnen drin versteckte.
In die Kehle paßte sogar ein Ball,
wenn man den Staub rausblies.

III

Es handelte sich für ihn um einen Spucknapf mit Pflaumenkernen.
Da kroch er hin und biß die Steine auf.
Man warf ihn zurück in sein Kastenbett,
und der Irre starb in seiner Streu.

Gegen Abend kam der Oberwärter
und schnauzte die Wächter an:
Ihr verdammten Faultiere,
warum ist der Kasten noch nicht ausgeräumt?

Schluss

I

The spittoon-glass –
not remotely a match
for such great green tepid floods –
crashed down at last.
The mouth dropped after it. Hung deep. Sucked
back vomit convulsively. Disappointed
any trust. Gave stones for bread
to the breathless blood.

II

The little bundle smelled like a chicken-coop,
beat to and fro. Grew. Fell still.

The granddaughter played the old game:
when grannie's asleep:
around the collarbones there were such hollows
she hid beans in them.
In the throat you could even fit a ball,
if you blew the dust out.

III

His thing was a spittoon with plumstones.
He crawled over and bit them open.
They threw him back in his bunk,
and the madman died in his straw.

Towards evening the head keeper came
and gave the attendants an earful:
You lazy damned beasts,
why is this box not cleared out yet?

3

IV

Seit Wochen hielten ihr ihre Kinder,
wenn sie aus der Schule zurückgekommen waren,
den Kopf in die Höhe:
Dann ging etwas Luft durch und sie konnte schlafen.

Dabei bückte sich eines einmal unversehens
und der Kopf fiel ihm aus den Händen.
Schlug um. Hing über den Schultern
tiefblau.

V Requiem

Ein Sarg kriegt Arbeit und ein Bett wird leer.
Wenn man bedenkt: ein paar verlorene Stunden
haben nun in die stille Nacht gefunden
und wehen mit den Wolken bin und her.

Wie weiß sie sind! Die Lippen auch. Wie Garben
aus Schnee, ein Saum vom großen Winterland
tröstenden Schnees, erlöst vom Trug der Farben,
Hügel und Tal in einer flachen Hand,

Nähe und Ferne eins und ausgeglichen.
Die Flocken wehn ins Feld, dann noch ein Stück,
dann ist der letzte Funken Welt verblichen.
O kaum zu denken! Dieses ferne Glück!

The eight-line section IV is not present in the Klett-Cotta collected edition
mentioned in the preface.

4

IV

For weeks her children had been looking after her
when they came home from school,
holding her head up,
then there was some air-movement and she could sleep.

One of them bent over unintentionally
and the head fell out of its hands.
Turned round. Hung across her shoulder
deep blue.

V Requiem

A coffin gets to work, an empty bed.
When you consider: a couple of hours wasted
to silent night now find themselves translated
and floating in the cloudscape overhead.

How white they are! The lips as well. Like smudges
at the edge of snow across the winter land,
comforting snow, redeemed from deceitful colours,
hill and valley held in an open hand.

Near and far are one in perfect balance.
The flakes blow over fields, then rapturous
blow on, the world's last flickering mere absence.
O scarcely dreamt! The distant happiness!

Schöne Jugend

Der Mund eines Mädchens, das lange im Schilf gelegen hatte,
sah so angeknabbert aus.
Als man die Brust aufbrach, war die Speiseröhre so löcherig.
Schließlich in einer Laube unter dem Zwerchfell
fand man ein Nest von jungen Ratten.
Ein kleines Schwesterchen lag tot.
Die andern lebten von Leber und Niere,
tranken das kalte Blut und hatten
hier eine schöne Jugend verlebt.
Und schön und schnell kam auch ihr Tod:
Man warf sie allesamt ins Wasser.
Ach, wie die kleinen Schnauzen quietschten!

Nice childhood

1912

The mouth of a girl who had lain long in the reeds
looked kind of nibbled.
When we sectioned the thorax, the gullet was full of holes.
Finally, in a pocket under the diaphragm
we found a nest of young rats.
One little sister lay dead.
The others lived on liver and kidney,
drank cold blood and had had
a nice childhood here.
Their death was nice too, and quick:
we threw them all in the water.
Ah, how the little muzzles squeaked!

Kreislauf

Der einsame Backzahn einer Dirne,
die unbekannt verstorben war,
trug eine Goldplombe.
Die übrigen waren wie auf stille Verabredung
ausgegangen.
Den schlug der Leichendiener sich heraus,
versetzte ihn und ging für tanzen.
Denn, sagte er,
nur Erde solle zur Erde werden.

Circulation

The solitary molar of a whore
who had died a missing person
had a gold filling.
As if by mutual consent,
all the others had left.
The morgue attendant knocked it out
and pawned it to go dancing.
Because, he said,
only dust should come to dust.

Blinddarm

Alles steht weiß und schnittbereit.
Die Messer dampfen. Der Bauch ist gepinselt.
Unter weißen Tüchern etwas, das winselt.

»Herr Geheimrat, es wäre soweit.«

Der erste Schnitt. Als schnitte man Brot.
»Klemmen her!« Es spritzt was rot.
Tiefer. Die Muskeln: feucht, funkelnd, frisch.
Steht ein Strauß Rosen auf dem Tisch?

Ist das Eiter, was da spritzt?
Ist der Darm etwa angeritzt?
»Doktor, wenn Sie im Lichte stehn,
kann kein Deibel das Bauchfell sehn.
Narkose, ich kann nicht operieren,
der Mann geht mit seinem Bauch spazieren.«

Stille, dumpf feucht. Durch die Leere
klirrt eine zu Boden geworfene Schere.
Und die Schwester mit Engelssinn
hält sterile Tupfer hin.

»Ich kann nichts finden in dem Dreck!«
»Blut wird schwarz. Maske weg!«
»Aber – Herr des Himmels – Bester,
halten Sie bloß die Haken fester!«

Alles verwachsen. Endlich: erwischt!
»Glüheisen, Schwester!« Es zischt.

Du hattest noch einmal Glück, mein Sohn.
Das Ding stand kurz vor der Perforation.
»Sehn Sie den kleinen grünen Fleck? –
Drei Stunden, dann war der Bauch voll Dreck.«

Appendix

Incision-ready, everything is white.
The scalpels steam. The belly's painted.
Under sheets a whimpering thing waited.

'Herr Professor, the time is right.'

The first incision. Like slicing bread.
'Clamps, please!' A spurt of something red.
Deeper. The muscles: shining, fresh and wet.
Is that a bunch of roses on the bed?

Is that pus that's spurting so?
Is the intestine snagged below?
'Doctor, you're standing in my light,
the peritoneum has vanished from sight.
Anaesthetic, I can't operate
if the belly is walking to the Brandenburg Gate.'

Silence, muffled and deep, only broken
by dropped scissors that cause a minor explosion.
And the sister, an angel in blue,
proffers sterile swabs to the crew.

'I can't find a thing in this dirt, OK!?'
'Blood turning black. Take the mask away!'
'But – God in heaven – what are you doing?',
can't you stop the heels from moving?'

Severe deformation. Finally, found!
'Hot iron, sister!' A fizzing sound.

You're lucky again this time, my son.
Perforation had nearly begun.
'Do you notice the little green bit? –
Three hours to fill the belly with shit.'

11

Bauch zu. Haut zu. »Heftpflaster her!
Guten Morgen, die Herrn.«

                        Der Saal wird leer.
Wütend klappert und knirscht mit den Backen
der Tod und schleicht in die Krebsbaracken.

Belly closed, skin closed. 'Plaster here!
Good morning, gentlemen.'
                              The theatre clear.
Death gnashing and grinding his teeth in fury
slinks in the cancer shed for another sortie.

Mann und Frau gehn durch die Krebsbaracke

Der Mann:
Hier diese Reihe sind zerfallene Schöße
und diese Reihe ist zerfallene Brust.
Bett stinkt bei Bett. Die Schwestern wechseln stündlich.

Komm, hebe ruhig diese Decke auf.
Sieh, dieser Klumpen Fett und faule Säfte,
das war einst irgendeinem Mann groß
und hieß auch Rausch und Heimat.

Komm, sieh auf diese Narbe an der Brust.
Fühlst du den Rosenkranz von weichen Knoten?
Fühl ruhig hin. Das Fleisch ist weich und schmerzt nicht.

Hier diese blutet wie aus dreißig Leibern.
Kein Mensch hat so viel Blut.
Hier dieser schnitt man
erst noch ein Kind aus dem verkrebsten Schoß.

Man läßt sie schlafen. Tag und Nacht. – Den Neuen
sagt man: Hier schläft man sich gesund. – Nur Sonntags
für den Besuch läßt man sie etwas wacher.

Nahrung wird wenig noch verzehrt. Die Rücken
sind wund. Du siehst die Fliegen. Manchmal
wäscht sie die Schwester. Wie man Bänke wäscht.

Hier schwillt der Acker schon um jedes Bett.
Fleisch ebnet sich zu Land. Glut gibt sich fort.
Saft schickt sich an zu rinnen. Erde ruft.

Man and woman walk through the cancer shed

1912

The man:
This row here is rotten womb
and this row rotten breasts.
Bed stinks by bed. The nurses change on the hour.

Go on, lift this sheet and look.
This lump of fat and putrid juices
meant everything to some man once –
he called it heaven and home.

Come and look at this scar on the breast.
Can you feel the rosary of soft lumps?
Go on, feel. The flesh is soft and without pain.

This one is bleeding enough for thirty.
No human has so much blood.
This one first had a baby
cut from her cancerous womb.

They're kept asleep. Day and night. The new ones
are told: You'll have a sleep cure here. Only on Sundays
for visiting are they let wake a bit.

They eat next to nothing. Their backs
are raw. You can see the flies. Sometimes
the nurses wash them. Like washing trestles.

Loam already churns about each bed.
Flesh flattens into land. Warmth dissipates.
Juice prepares to flow. Earth calls.

D-Zug

Braun wie Kognak. Braun wie Laub. Rotbraun. Malaiengelb.
D-Zug Berlin-Trelleborg und die Ostseebäder.

Fleisch, das nackt ging.
Bis in den Mund gebräunt vom Meer.
Reif gesenkt, zu griechischem Glück.
In Sichel-Sehnsucht: wie weit der Sommer ist!
Vorletzter Tag des neunten Monats schon!

Stoppel und letzte Mandel lechzt in uns.
Entfaltungen, das Blut, die Müdigkeiten,
die Georginennähe macht uns wirr.

Männerbraun stürzt sich auf Frauenbraun:

Eine Frau ist etwas für eine Nacht.
Und wenn es schön war, noch für die nächste!
Oh! Und dann wieder dies Bei-sich-selbst-sein!
Diese Stummheiten! Dies Getriebenwerden!

Eine Frau ist etwas mit Geruch.
Unsägliches! Stirb hin! Resede.
Darin ist Süden, Hirt und Meer.
An jedem Abhang lehnt ein Glück.

Frauenhellbraun taumelt an Männerdunkelbraun:

Halte mich! Du, ich falle!
Ich bin im Nacken so müde.
Oh, dieser fiebernde süße
letzte Geruch aus den Gärten.

Express

1912

Brown as cognac. Brown as leaves. Red-brown. Malayan yellow.
Berlin express from Trelleborg and the Baltic beaches.

Flesh that walked naked.
Tanned to the lips by the sea.
Drooping ripely, like Greek hedonists.
Missing sickles: how long since summer!
And tomorrow the final day of the ninth month!

Stubble and last almonds thirst in us.
Unfoldings, our blood and tirednesses,
the proximity of dahlias confuses us.

Male tan in collision with female tan:

A woman is good for one night.
And if it went well, for the next one too!
Oh! and then being alone again!
These silences! This sense of being driven!

A woman is something with fragrance.
Inexpressible! Pass away! Mignonette.
Enclosing the South, shepherds and sea.
On every slope a happiness leans.

Female light brown staggers against male dark brown:

Hold me, love! I'm falling!
My back is so exhausted.
Oh, this feverish final
sweet fragrance from the gardens.

17

Nachtcafé

824: Der Frauen Liebe und Leben.
Das Cello trinkt rasch mal. Die Flöte
rülpst tief drei Takte lang: das schöne Abendbrot.
Die Trommel liest den Kriminalroman zu Ende.

Grüne Zähne, Pickel im Gesicht
winkt einer Lidrandentzündung.

Fett im Haar
spricht zu offenem Mund mit Rachenmandel
Glaube Liebe Hoffnung um den Hals.

Junger Kropf ist Sattelnase gut.
Er bezahlt für sie drei Biere.

Bartflechte kauft Nelken.
Doppelkinn zu erweichen.

B-moll: de 35. Sonate.
Zwei Augen brüllen auf:
Spritzt nicht das Blut von Chopin in den Saal,
damit das Pack drauf rumlatscht!
Schluß! He, Gigi! –

Die Tür fließt hin: ein Weib.
Wüste ausgedörrt. Kanaanitisch braun.
Keusch. Höhlenreich. Ein Duft kommt mit. Kaum Duft.
Es ist nur eine süße Vorwölbung der Luft
gegen mein Gehirn.

Eine Fettleibigkeit trippelt hinterher.

Night café

824: Frauenliebe und -leben.
The cello has a quick swig. The flute
belches three bars away: supper was good.
The drum reads the end of his detective story.

Green teeth, acned face
waves to lids with styes.

Oily hair
is talking to open mouth with tonsils,
faith hope and charity round her neck.

Young goitre fancies saddle-nose.
He buys her three beers.

Barber's itch buys carnations.
To soften up double chin.

Opus 35: B flat minor sonata.
Two eyes roar up:
Don't squirt Chopin's blood down here
so the pack can scuff about on it!
Enough! Hey, Gigi! –

The door dissolves. A woman.
Utterly dried out. Canaanite brown.
Chaste. Full of caverns. A scent comes with her. Hardly scent.
Merely a gentle arching of air
against my brain.

An obesity trips after her.

Frauenliebe und -leben is Schumann's song-cycle to poems by Adalbert von Chamisso
(1781–1838), op. 42. '824' may be an inaccurate reference to the last, tragic song,
no. 8.

Gesänge

I

O daß wir unsere Ururahnen wären.
Ein Klümpchen Schleim in einem warmen Moor.
Leben und Tod, Befruchten und Gebären
glitte aus unseren stummen Säften vor.

Ein Algenblatt oder ein Dünenhügel,
vom Wind Geformtes und nach unter schwer.
Schon ein Libellenkopf, ein Möwenflügel
wäre zu weit und litte schon zu sehr.

II

Verächtlich sind die Liebenden, die Spötter,
alles Verzweifeln, Sehnsucht, und wer hofft.
Wir sind so schmerzliche durchseuchte Götter
und dennoch denken wir des Gottes oft.

Die weiche Bucht. Die dunklen Wälderträume.
Die Sterne, schneeballblütengroß und schwer.
Die Panther springen lautlos durch die Bäume.
Alles ist Ufer. Ewig ruft das Meer –

Songs

1913

I

O could we restart our primal mission
and be a speck of slime in a tepid fen.
Life, death, insemination, parturition
would slip out from our voiceless fluids then.

A leaf of algae or a sand-dune growing
under the wind and gravity's firm touch.
Even a dragonfly's head, a gull's wing blowing
would go too far and suffer much too much.

II

Despise the infatuated and the callous,
nostalgia, desperation, a hope of sorts.
We gods are rotten with disease and sadness,
and yet a god is often in our thoughts.

The bay is soft. Our dreams are dark with promise.
The stars hang big as snowball blossoms there.
Panthers are hunting soundless through the forest.
All is shore. The sea calls everywhere –

Da fiel uns Ikarus vor die Füße

Da fiel uns Ikarus vor die Füße,
schrie: treibt Gattung, Kinder!
Rein ins schlechtgelüftete Thermopylä! –
Warf uns einen seiner Unterschenkel hinterher,
schlug um, war alle.

Then Icarus

1913

Then Icarus crashed down at our feet
and screamed: Get fucking, kids!
Get in there, into that stale Thermopylae! –
Then threw us one of his shin-bones,
keeled over, snuffed it.

Untergrundbahn

Die weichen Schauer. Blütenfrühe. Wie
aus warmen Fellen kommt es aus den Wäldern.
Ein Rot schwärmt auf. Das große Blut steigt an.

Durch all den Frühling kommt die fremde Frau.
Der Strumpf am Spann ist da. Doch, wo er endet,
ist weit von mir. Ich schluchze auf der Schwelle:
laues Geblühe, fremde Feuchtigkeiten.

Oh, wie ihr Mund die laue Luft verpraßt!
Du Rosenhirn, Meer-Blut, du Götter-Zwielicht,
du Erdenbeet, wie strömen deine Hüften
so kühl den Gang hervor, in dem du gehst!

Dunkel: nun lebt es unter ihren Kleidern:
nur weißes Tier, gelöst und stummer Duft.

Ein armer Hirnhund, schwer mit Gott behangen.
Ich bin der Stirn so satt. Oh, ein Gerüste
von Blütenkolben löste sanft sie ab
und schwölle mit und schauerte und triefte.

So losgelöst. So müde. Ich will wandern.
Blutlos die Wege. Lieder aus den Gärten.
Schatten und Sintflut. Fernes Glück: ein Sterben
hin in des Meeres erlösend tiefes Blau.

Underground train

1913

The gentle showers. Flowering dawn. As if
from downy furs arriving from the forests.
A red swarms up. Blood's greatness starts to grow.

Through all this springtime comes an unknown woman.
The stocking on her instep. But where it ends
is far from me. I sob there at the threshold:
tepid florescence, unknown dampnesses.

Oh, how her mouth squanders the tepid air!
You rose-brain, sea-blood, twilight of the gods,
you bed of earth, oh how your hips stream forth
the cool precision of the way you walk!

Darkness: alive now under what she wears:
animal whiteness, relaxed, dumb fragrances.

Pathetic brain-dog, heavy laden with God.
I am so tired of thinking. Oh a lattice
of flower-heads could so softly fill its place,
could swell with me and burst in showers and droplets.

So disconnected. So tired. Let me wander.
Bloodless the pathways. Singing from the gardens.
Shadows, the Flood. A distant joy; to die
beneath the sea's redeeming deep, deep blue.

Englisches Café

Das ganz schmalschuhige Raubpack,
Russinnen, Jüdinnen, tote Völker, ferne Küsten,
schleicht durch die Frühjahrsnacht

Die Geigen grünen. Mai ist um die Harfe.
Die Palmen röten sich. Im Wüstenwind.

Rahel, die schmale Golduhr am Gelenk:
Geschlecht behütend und Gehirn bedrohend:
Feindin! Doch deine Hand ist eine Erde:
süßbraun, fast ewig, überweht vom Schoß.

Freundlicher Ohrring kommt. In Charme d'Orsay.
Die hellen Osterblumen sind so schön:
breitmäulig gelb, mit Wiese an den Füßen.

O Blond! O Sommer dieses Nackens! O
diese jasmindurchseuchte Ellenbeuge!
Oh, ich bin gut zu dir. Ich streichle
dir deine Schultern. Du, wir reisen:

Tyrrhenisches Meer. Ein frevelhaftes Blau.
Die Dorertempel. In Rosenschwangerschaft
die Ebenen. Felder
sterben den Asphodelentod.

Lippen, verschwärmt und tiefgefüllt wie Becher,
als zögerte das Blut des süßen Orts,
rauschen durch eines Mundes ersten Herbst

O wehe Stirn! Du Kranke, tief im Flor
der dunklen Brauen! Lächle, werde hell:
die Geigen schimmern einen Regenbogen.

English café

1913

The quite narrow-shoed pack of robbers,
Russian women, Jewesses, dead peoples, distant coasts,
slips through the spring night.

The violins turning green. May surrounds the harp.
The palm-trees redden. In the desert wind.

Rachel, a slim gold watch at her wrist:
forbidding sex and threatening my brain:
my enemy! and yet your hand is clay:
sweet brown, almost eternal, in your fragrant lap.

Friendly earring arrives. In Charme d'Orsay.
The bright beauty of your Easter lilies:
their wide mouths yellow, with meadow at their feet.

O blonde! O summer-ripened back! And Oh
how jasmine-infected is your elbow!
Oh, I adore you. Let me stroke
your shoulders. You and I should travel:

Tyrrhenian Sea. A blasphemous blue.
The Doric temples. Pregnant with roses
the plains. Fields dying
the death of asphodel.

Lips, intoxicated, deeply filled like chalices,
their sweet blood hesitating, it would seem,
rustling through a mouth's first autumn.

O aching brow: sickness deep in the mourning
of your dark eyebrows! Smile, be bright:
the violins are shimmering a rainbow.

27

Drohungen

Aber wisse:
Ich lebe Tiertage. Ich bin eine Wasserstunde.
Des Abends schläfert mein Lid wie Wald und Himmel.
Meine Liebe weiß nur wenig Worte:

Es ist so schön an deinem Blut. –

Mein königlicher Becher!
Meine schweifende Hyäne!
Komm in meine Höhle. Wir wollen helle Haut sein.
Bis der Zedernschatten über die kleine Eidechse lief:
Du – Glück –

Ich bin Affen-Adam. Rosen blühn in mein Haar.
Meine Vorderflossen sind schon lang und haarig.
Baumast-lüstern. An den starken Daumen
Kann man tagelang herunterhängen. –

Ich treibe Tierliebe.
In der ersten Nacht ist alles entschieden.
Man faßt mit den Zähnen, wonach man sich sehnt.
Hyänen, Tiger, Geier sind mein Wappen. –

Nun fährst du über Wasser. Selbst so segelhaft.
Blondhäutig. Kühles Spiel.
Doch bitterrot, das Blut darin ist tot,
Ein Spalt voll Schreie ist dein Mund.
Du, daß wir nicht an einem Ufer landen!
Du machst mir Liebe: blutigelhaft:
Ich will von dir. –

Du bist Ruth. Du hast Aehren an deinem Hut.
Dein Nacken ist braun von Makkabäerblut.
Deine Stirn ist fliehend: Du sahst so lange
Ueber die Mandeln nach Boas aus.

Threats

Know this:
I live the days of a beast. I am a water-hour.
At evening I am heavy-lidded like forest and sky.
My love knows but few words:

all is beautiful about your blood.

My royal chalice!
My roaming hyena!
Come into my cave. Let us be bright-skinned.
Until the cedar shadow ran across the little lizard:
you – happiness –

I am ape-Adam. Roses bloom in my hair.
My fore-flippers have grown long and hairy.
Tree-branch lustful. From my mighty thumb
you can hang down all day. –

I make love as a beast.
In the first night everything is decided.
We take in our teeth all we desire.
Hyenas, tigers, raptors are my escutcheon. –

Now you move over water. So like a sail yourself.
Fair-skinned. Cool in play
Yet bitter-red, the blood inside is dead,
a cleft of screams your mouth.
You, let us not land on a shore!
You make love to me: like a leech:
let me get away –

You are Ruth, cornstalks on your hat.
Your back is brown from your Maccabee blood.
Your brow is fleeing: you watched so long
for Boaz across the almonds.

Du trägst sie wie ein Meer, daß nichts Vergossenes
Im Spiel die Erde netzt.

Nun rüste einen Blick durch deine Lider:

Sieh: Abgrund über tausend Sternen naht.
Sieh: Schlund, in den du es ergießen sollst.
Sieh: Ich. –

You carry them like a sea, not to let anything
spilt in play wet the earth.

Now arm a look through your lids:

see: abyss nearing across a thousand stars,
see: gorge, into which you must pour it,
see: I. —

Schnellzug

Das Gleitende, das in den Fenstern steht!
Von meinen Schultern blättern die Gefilde,
die Lauben und die zugewachsenen Dörfer;
verschollene Mütter; das ganze Land
ein Grab voll Väter: – nun sind die Söhne groß
und prunken mit der roten Götterstirne,
nackt und im Taumel des entbundenen Bluts. –

Das Schwärende schickt kranke Stimmen hoch:
Wo grenzten wir ans Glück? Wir kleine Forst,
kein Adler und kein Wild! Armseliges
Geblühe färbt sich matt in unsere Flur. –

Aufschrei das Herz: O Haar! Du Dagmar-blond!
Du Nest! Du tröstende erblühte Hand!
Die weiten Felder der Verlassenheit!
Das Rot der Ebereschen hat schon Blut.
O sei bei mir. Es schweigt so aus den Gärten. –

Doch Gleitendes, das in dem Fenster steht:
Von meinen Schultern blättern die Gefilde,
Väter und Hügelgram und Hügelglück –:
Die Söhne wurden groß. Die Söhne gehn
nackt und im Grame des entbundenen Blutes,
die Stirn aufrötet fern ein Abgrund-glück.

Express-train

Gliding things that stand still in the windows!
Like leaves the fields are falling from my shoulders,
the little plots and growth-dead villages;
mothers gone missing; the entire country
a grave full of fathers: – now the sons are tall
and swagger with their reddened brows of gods,
naked, giddy with liberated blood.

The ulcerous sounds off with sickly voices:
where were we close to happiness? We little
forest, no eagles and no deer! Pathetic
plants, dull colours on our land.

The heart cries out: O hair! You Dagmar-blonde!
You nest! You comforting, you blossoming hand!
The outspread meadows of abandonment!
The rowanberries' red is ripe with blood.
O be with me. The gardens are so silent.

Yet gliding things that stand still in the windows:
like leaves the fields are falling from my shoulders,
fathers and hilly grief and hilly joy –:
the sons have grown so tall. The sons are walking
naked, grieving with liberated blood,
red brows reflect a far abyss of joy.

33

Räuber-Schiller

Ich bringe Pest. Ich bin Gestank.
Vom Rand der Erde komm ich her.
Mir läuft manchmal im Maule was zusammen,
wenn ich das speie, zischten noch die Sterne
und hier ersöffe das ganze feige
Pietzengeschlabber und Abelblut.

Weil meine Mutter weint? Weil meinem Vater
das Haar vergreist? Ich schreie:
Ihr grauer Schlaf! Ihr ausgeborenen Schluchten!
Bald sä'n euch ein paar Handvoll Erde zu.
Mir aber rauscht die Stirn wie Wolkenflug.

Das bißchen Seuche
aus Hurenschleim in mein Blut gesickert?
Ein Bröckel Tod stinkt immer aus der Ecke –
pfeif darauf! Wisch ihm eins! Pah!

Robbers-*Schiller*

1913

I bring plague. I am stench.
I come from the edge of the earth.
Sometimes in my mouth a confluence,
if I were to spit it out, the stars would still be sizzling
and here would drown all the cowardly
titty-slobberers and Abel's blood.

Because my mother weeps? Because my father's
hair is going white? I yell:
You grey sleep! You canyons done with birthing!
Soon a couple of handfuls of earth will cover you with seeds.
But my brow rustles alive like cloud-flights.

The dram of infection
from whore-slime trickled into my blood?
A crumb of death forever stinking from the corner –
throw it out! Smash it! Pah!

The Robbers (1781) was the first, revolutionary, play by the young Johann Christoph
Friedrich Schiller (1759–1805); its printed motto was *In tyrannos* (Against tyrants).

Hier ist kein Trost

Keiner wird mein Wegrand sein.
Laß deine Blüten nur verblühen.
Mein Weg flutet und geht allein.

Zwei Hände sind eine zu kleine Schale.
Ein Herz ist ein zu kleiner Hügel,
um dran zu ruhn.
Du, ich lebe immer am Strand
und unter dem Blütenfall des Meeres,
Ägypten liegt vor meinem Herzen,
Asien dämmert auf.

Mein einer Arm liegt immer im Feuer.
Mein Blut ist Asche. Ich schluchze immer
vorbei an Brüsten und Gebeinen
den tyrrhenischen Inseln zu:

Dämmert ein Tal mit weißen Pappeln
ein Ilyssos mit Wiesenufern
Eden und Adam und eine Erde
aus Nihilismus und Musik.

No comfort here

1913

No-one will be the border of my path.
Just let your blossoms fade.
My path floods and moves alone.

Two hands are much too small a basin.
One heart is a hill too small
to rest upon.
You, my life is always on the beach
and under the falling blossoms of the sea,
Egypt lies before my heart,
Asia dawns.

One of my arms lies always in the fire.
My blood is ash. I always sob
past breasts and skeletons
towards the Tyrrhenian islands:

dawning a valley with white poplars
an Ilyssos with meadow-banks
Eden and Adam and an earth
of nihilism and music.

This is a reply to the poem '*Höre!*' (Listen!) by Benn's lover at the time, Else Lasker-Schüler (1869–1945), which contains the lines 'Ich bin dein Wegrand./ Die dich streift,/ stürzt ab' (I am the border of your path. She who brushes against you plunges down).

Nachtcafé IV

Es lohnt kaum den Kakau. Dann schiebt man ein
und stürzt: ich bin an Gottes Saum hervor;
liebst du mich auch? Ich war so sehr allein.

Das Weserlied erregt die Sau gemütlich.
Die Lippen weinen mit. Den Strom herunter.
Das süße Tal! Da sitzt sie mit der Laute.

Der Ober rudert mit den Schlummerpünschen.
Er schwimmt sich frei. Fleischlaub und Hurenherbste,
ein welker Streif. Fett furcht sich. Gruben röhren:
das Fleisch ist flüssig; gieß es wie du willst,
um dich;
ein Spalt voll Schreie unser Mund.

Night café IV

1914

It's hardly worth the effort. Then you thrust
and fall: out from the hem of God;
love me too? I was so very alone.

The Weserlied has made the sow receptive.
Her lips are weeping along. And down the river
the happy valley! She sits there with her lute.

The waiter rows about with nightcap punch.
He swims to freedom. Flesh foliage and whorish autumn,
a shrivelled strip. Fat forks apart. Pits rumble:
flesh is fluid: pour it as you will,
around you;
a cleft of cries our mouth.

The '*Weserlied*' (Song of the River Weser): a popular nationalist drinking song whose first verse begins 'Wo die Weser einen grossen Bogen macht/ wo der Kaiser Wilhelm hält die treue Wacht ...' (Where the Weser makes a great curve, where Kaiser Wilhelm keeps faithful watch).

O Nacht

O Nacht! Ich nahm schon Kokain,
und Blutverteilung ist im Gange,
das Haar wird grau, die Jahre fliehn,
ich muß, ich muß im Überschwange
noch einmal vorm Vergängnis blühn.

O Nacht! Ich will ja nicht so viel,
ein kleines Stück Zusammenballung,
ein Abendnebel, eine Wallung
von Raumverdrang, von Ichgefühl.

Tastkörperchen, Rotzellensaum,
ein Hin und Her und mit Gerüchen,
zerfetzt von Worte-Wolkenbrüchen –:
zu tief im Hirn, zu schmal im Traum.

Die Steine flügeln an die Erde,
nach kleinen Schatten schnappt der Fisch,
nur tückisch durch das Ding-Gewerde
taumelt der Schädel-Flederwisch.

O Nacht! Ich mag dich kaum bemühn!
Ein kleines Stück nur, eine Spange
von Ichgefühl – im Überschwange
noch einmal vorm Vergängnis blühn!

O Nacht, o leih mir Stirn und Haar,
verfließ dich um das Tag-verblühte;
sei, die mich aus der Nervenmythe
zu Kelch und Krone heimgebar.

O still! Ich spüre kleines Rammeln,
Es sternt mich an – es ist kein Spott –:
Gesicht, ich: mich, einsamen Gott,
sich groß um einen Donner sammeln.

O night

1916

O night! I've taken a shot of cocaine
and blood-division is set in motion,
grey grows my hair, the years unconstrained,
I must, I must in a great explosion
before dissolution bloom again.

O night! That's not a lot to ask,
a little piece of concentration,
an evening mist, a counterblast
to space, of individuation.

Feeler threads, corpuscular rims,
a to and fro, with scents dispersed,
tattered by cumulus language-bursts –:
too deep in brain, too narrow in dreams.

Stones shoot to earth, and fishes muster
to snap at shadows, while with malice
through the mess of things evolving
tumbles the skull's own feather duster.

O night! Let me not cause you pain!
A tiny chip of selfhood awoken,
let me in a great explosion
before dissolution bloom again!

O night, reface my naked bone
and melt around what day has faded;
homeward deliver me unaided
from febrile myths to chalice and crown.

O hush! I sense a coming rut,
my stars shine out – no how or what –
a vision, I: me, lonely god,
collecting my self round a grand thunderbolt.

41

Karyatide

Entrücke dich dem Stein! Zerbirst
die Höhle, die dich knechtet! Rausche
doch in die Flur! Verhöhne die Gesimse –
sieh: durch den Bart des trunkenen Silen
aus einem ewig überrauschten
lauten einmaligen durchdröhnten Blut
träuft Wein in seine Scham!

Bespei die Säulensucht: toderschlagene
greisige Hände bebten sie
verhangenen Himmeln zu. Stürze
die Tempel vor die Sehnsucht deines Knies,
in dem der Tanz begehrt!

Breite dich hin, zerblühe dich, oh, blute
dein weiches Beet aus großen Wunden hin:
sieh, Venus mit den Tauben gürtet
sich Rosen um der Hüften Liebestor –
sieh dieses Sommers letzten blauen Hauch
auf Astermeeren an die fernen
baumbraunen Ufer treiben; tagen
sieh diese letzte Glück-Lügenstunde
unserer Südlichkeit
hochgewölbt.

Caryatid

1916

Abstract yourself from stone! Explode
the cavern that enslaves you! Rush
away into fields! Despise the entablature –
look, through the beard of the drunken Silenus
from his eternally over-addicted
loud, unmatched and roaring blood
wine drips into his crotch!

Spit on the mania for columns: death-slain
old men's hands quivered them
towards darkling skies. Smash down
temples from the longing in your knees
where dancing is urgent!

Spread out your limbs, shed blossoms, oh, bleed
away your gentle bed from splendid wounds:
look, dove-circled Venus is winding
roses around her hips' threshold of love –
look, this summer's last blue breath of love
floats across aster seas to distant
tree-brown shores; dawning
see this last lying hour of happiness,
our meridian,
arched on high.

Durchs Erlenholz kam sie entlang gestrichen

die Schnepfe nämlich – erzählte der Pfarrer –:
Da traten kahle Äste gegen die Luft: ehern.
Ein Himmel blaute: unbedenkbar. Die Schulter mit der Büchse,
des Pfarrers Spannung, der kleine Hund,
selbst Treiber, die dem Herrn die Freude gönnten:
Unerschütterlich.
Dann weltumgoldet: der Schuß:
Einbeziehung vieler Vorgänge,
Erwägen von Möglichkeiten,
Bedenkung physikalischer Verhältnisse,
einschließlich Parabel und Geschoßgarbe,
Luftdichte, Barometerstand, Isobaren – –
aber durch alles hindurch: die Sicherstellung,
die Ausschaltung des Fraglichen,
die Zusammenraffung,
eine Pranke in den Nacken der Erkenntnis,
blutüberströmt zuckt ihr Plunder
unter dem Begriff: Schnepfenjagd.
Da verschied Kopernikus. Kein Newton mehr.
                         Kein drittes Wärmegesetz –
eine kleine Stadt dämmert auf: Kellergeruch: Konditorjungen,
Bedürfnisanstalt mit Wartefrau,
das Handtuch über den Sitz wischend
zum Zweck der öffentlichen Gesundheitspflege;
ein Büro, ein junger Registrator
mit Ärmelschutz, mit Frühstücksbrötchen
den Brief der Patentante lesend.

Through the alder wood it was making its way

the snipe, I mean – recounted the parson –:
and naked branches stuck out against the air: brazen.
A sky was blue: indubitably. The shouldered shotgun,
the parson's tension, the little dog,
the beaters even, granting the master his pleasure:
unshakeable.
Then gilding the world: the shot:
taking into account many actions,
weighing up possibilities,
considering physical conditions,
including parabolas and the cone of fire,
air density, barometric pressure, isobars – –
but pervading everything: inevitability,
the exclusion of all questions,
everything pulled together,
a wild beast's claw at perception's neck,
its prey convulsed in streams of blood
under the concept: snipe-hunt.
Copernicus died there. No more Newton. No third law of
                                    thermodynamics –
a little town shades into view: cellar smells: bakers' boys,
conveniences with a woman guard,
wiping the seat with a hand-cloth
in the interest of public hygiene;
an office, a young registrar
with cuff protectors, with his morning snack,
reading a letter from his godmother aunt.

Reise

O dieses Lichts! Die Insel kränzt
sternblaues Wasser um sich her,
am Saum gestillt, zu Strand ergänzt,
und sättigt täglich sich am Meer.

Es muß nichts zueinander hin,
die Alke, das gelappte Laub
erfüllen sich; es liegt ihr Sinn
im Mittelpunkt, den nichts beraubt.

Auch ich zu: braun! Ich zu: besonnt!
Zu Flachem, das sich selbst benennt!
Das Auge lief am Horizont,
der keine Vertikale kennt.

Schon schwindet der Verknüpfungsdrang,
schon löst sich das Bezugssystem
und unter dunklem Hautgesang
erhebt sich Blut-Methusalem.

Journey

1916

O this light! The island wraps
itself in star-blue liquidly,
still at the edge, with sands perhaps,
and takes its daily fill of sea.

Nothing needs to seek a prize,
the auks, the dipping foliage
are self-fulfilled, their meaning lies
in a centred anchorage.

I join in: brown! I also: tanned!
Low-lying, that's self-quarantine!
Horizons take the eye in hand
and verticals remain unseen.

Compulsive contacts disappear,
relational systems compromise,
and song-dark under the skin's veneer
blood-Methuselah starts to rise.

Der Arzt

I

Mir klebt die süße Leiblichkeit
wie ein Belag am Gaumensaum.
Was je an Saft und mürbem Fleisch
um Kalkknochen schlotterte,
dunstet mit Milch und Schweiß in meine Nase.
Ich weiß, wie Huren und Madonnen riechen
nach einem Gang und morgens beim Erwachen
und zu Gezeiten ihres Bluts –
und Herren kommen in mein Sprechzimmer,
denen ist das Geschlecht zugewachsen:
die Frau denkt, sie wird befruchtet
und aufgeworfen zu einem Gotteshügel;
aber der Mann ist vernarbt,
sein Gehirn wildert über einer Nebelsteppe,
und lautlos fällt sein Samen ein.
Ich lebe vor dem Leib: und in der Mitte
klebt überall die Scham. Dahin wittert
der Schädel auch. Ich ahne: einst
werden die Spalte und der Stoß
zum Himmel klaffen von der Stirn.

II

Die Krone der Schöpfung, das Schwein, der Mensch –:
geht doch mit anderen Tieren um!
Mit siebzehn Jahren Filzläuse,
zwischen üblen Schnauzen hin und her,
Darmkrankheiten und Alimente,
Weiber und Infusorien,
mit vierzig fängt die Blase an zu laufen –:
meint ihr, um solch Geknolle wuchs die Erde
von Sonne bis zum Mond –? Was kläfft ihr denn?

48

The doctor

1917

I

Sweet carnality sticks like a film
to the edge of my palate.
All the juice and decaying flesh
that ever shook around calcified bones
in my nose a miasma with milk and sweat.
I know how whores and madonnas smell
after stool and when they wake in the morning
and at the tides of their blood –
and men come into my consulting-room
whose sexual organ has sealed itself:
the wife thinks she's being impregnated
and blown up into a sacred mound;
but the husband is scarred,
his brain roams wild over a misty steppe,
his seed falls in without a sound.
I live in the body's presence: and in the middle
the genitals sticking to everything. The skull
gets a whiff of it too. I sense
that one day cleft and ramrod
will gape to heaven from the brow.

II

The crown of creation, man, the swine –:
get lost, consort with other beasts!
At seventeen the crabs,
swapping one evil gob for another,
gut diseases and benefit,
women and infusoria,
at forty the bladder beginning to leak –
was it for such louts, do you think, that the earth
grew from sun to moon – ? Why do you curse?

49

Ihr sprecht von Seele – was ist eure Seele?
Verkackt die Greisin Nacht für Nacht ihr Bett –
schmiert sich der Greis die mürben Schenkel zu,
und ihr reicht Fraß, es in den Darm zu lümmeln,
meint ihr, die Sterne samten ab vor Glück…?
Äh! – Aus erkaltendem Gedärm
spie Erde wie aus anderen Löchern Feuer,
eine Schnauze Blut empor –:
das torkelt
den Abwärtsbogen
selbstgefällig in den Schatten.

III

Mit Pickeln in der Haut und faulen Zähnen
paart sich das in ein Bett und drängt zusammen
und säet Samen in des Fleisches Furchen
und fühlt sich Gott bei Göttin. Und die Frucht –:
das wird sehr häufig schon verquiemt geboren:
mit Beuteln auf dem Rücken, Rachenspalten,
schieläugig, hodenlos, in breite Brüche
entschlüpft die Därme –; aber selbst was heil
endlich ans Licht quillt, ist nicht eben viel,
und durch die Löcher tropft die Erde:
Spaziergang –: Föten, Gattungspack –:
ergangen wird sich. Hingesetzt. –
Finger wird berochen.
Rosine aus dem Zahn geholt
Die Goldfischchen –!!! –!
Erhebung! Aufstieg! Weserlied!
Das Allgemeine wird gestreift. Gott
als Käseglocke auf die Scham gestülpt –:
der gute Hirte –!! – – Allgemeingefühl! –
Und abends springt der Bock die Zibbe an.

You speak of soul – what is your soul?
The old woman shits her bed night after night –
the old man embalms his rotten thighs,
and you grab grub to cram it in your gut,
do you think the stars ejaculate with bliss ... ?
Eugh! – From cooling colons
spit earth and from other orifices fire,
a gobful of blood –:
it tumbles down
in an arc
complacently into the shadow.

III

With acned skin and rotten teeth
they couple in a bed and press together
and sow the seed in fleshy folds
and feel like god and goddess. And the fruit –:
that is often born deformed:
with cysts on the back, cleft palate,
a squint, anorchic, the intestine
escaping from wide ruptures –: but even what's whole,
bubbling to light, is not much good,
and through the holes drops earth:
a walk –: foetuses, breeding pack –:
taking the air. Sitting down.
Smell the finger.
Get the raisin out of that tooth.
The little goldfish – !!! – !
A lift! A rise! The Weserlied!
Generalities in passing. God
as cheese-cover stuck over the genitals –:
the Good Shepherd – !! – feelings of universality! –
and at evening the billy-goat goes at his nan.

Pappel

Verhalten,
ungeöffnet in Ast und Ranke,
um in das Blau des Himmels aufzuschrein –:
nur Stamm, Geschlossenheiten,
hoch und zitternd,
eine Kurve.

Die Mispel flüchtet,
Samentöter,
und wann der Blitze segnendes Zerbrechen
rauschte um meinen Schaft
enteinheitend,
weitverteilend
Baumgewesenes?
Und wer sah Pappelwälder?

Einzeln,
und an der Kronenstirn das Mal der Schreie,
das ruhelos die Nächte und den Tag
über der Gärten hinresedeten
süßen aufklaffenden Vergang,
was ihm die Wurzel saugt, die Rinde frißt,
in tote Räume bietet
hin und her.

Poplar

1917

Reserved,
unopened in branch and shoot
to shout up into heaven's blue –:
trunk only, closednesses,
tall and trembling,
a curve.

The medlar flees,
killer of seeds,
and when lightnings' shattering blessing
whistled round my shaft
disuniting,
far scattering
what once was tree?
Who ever saw forests of poplar?

Solitary,
and on the brow of the crown the scar of cries,
unceasing through nights and days
above old mignon-scented gardens'
sweet and gaping decomposition,
offering what roots and bark can absorb
into dead spaces aloft
to and fro.

Kokain

Den Ich-Zerfall, den süßen, tiefersehnten,
den gibst du mir: schon ist die Kehle rauh,
schon ist der fremde Klang an unerwähnten
Gebilden meines Ichs am Unterbau.

Nicht mehr am Schwerte, das der Mutter Scheide
entsprang, um da und dort ein Werk zu tun,
und stählern schlägt –: gesunken in die Heide,
wo Hügel kaum enthüllter Formen ruhn!

Ein laues Glatt, ein kleines Etwas, Eben –
und nun entsteigt für Hauche eines Wehns
das Ur, geballt, Nicht-seine beben
Hirnschauer mürbesten Vorübergehns.

Zersprengtes Ich – o aufgetrunkene Schwäre –
verwehte Fieber – süß zerborstene Wehr –:
verströme, o verströme du – gebäre
blutbäuchig das Entformte her.

Cocaine

1917

Decay of self, so sweet, longed for so deeply
is what you give me: already my throat is sore,
already the foreign sound's at work, so freely
dismantling structures of the self and more.

No further swords delivered from the mother's
sheath to instigate a work or two
and smash with steel –: but under heathland covers
where possibilities may lurk from view.

A tepid slide, a little something flatter –
and now emerges for a breath of a breeze
the Origin, compacted non-beings clatter
brain-shudders full of rotting disloyalties.

Exploded self – o swallowed suppuration –
fevers swept off – so sweet the burst defence –:
stream out, stream out and end the long gestation
with the bloody birth of formlessness.

Synthese

Schweigende Nacht. Schweigendes Haus.
Ich aber bin der stillsten Sterne,
ich treibe auch mein eignes Licht
noch in die eigne Nacht hinaus.

Ich bin gehirnlich heimgekehrt
aus Höhlen, Himmeln, Dreck und Vieh.
Auch was sich noch der Frau gewährt,
ist dunkle süße Onanie.

Ich wälze Welt. Ich röchle Raub.
Und nächtens nackte ich im Glück:
es ringt kein Tod, es stinkt kein Staub
mich, Ich-Begriff, zur Welt zurück.

Synthesis

1917

Silent house. A silent night.
I am among the stars immobile,
still driving into my own darkness
my very own created light.

My brain returns to its resting-place
from caverns, heavens, atavism.
The most a woman can embrace
is dark delicious onanism.

I roll in world. I rattle rape.
At night my naked triumph's hurled:
no death can force, no dust can scrape
me, concept-I, back to the world.

Das Instrument

O du Leugnung Berkeleys,
breitbäuchig wälzt der Raum sich dir entgegen!
Gepanzertstes Gehirn zum Zweck des Zweckes,
funkelnd vor Männerfaust, bekämpfter Kurzsichtigkeit und jener
                                              Achselhohle,
des Morgens nur ganz sachlich ausgewaschen! –

Der Mann im Sprung, sich bäumend vor Begattung,
Straußeier fressend, daß die Schwellung schwillt.
Harnröhrenplätterin, Mutterband nadelnd
ans Bauchfett für die Samen-Winkelriede! – –

O nimm mich in den Jubel deiner Kante:
Der Raum ist Raum! O, in das Blitzen
des Griffes: Fokus, virtuelles Bild,
gesetzlich abgespielt! O, in den Augen
der Spitze funkelt
bieder blutgeboren:
ZIEL.

The instrument

1917

O you denial of Berkeley,
space, broad-bellied, rolls towards you!
Most armoured brain for the aim of aims,
sparkling with male clout, combated myopia and that armpit
washed in the morning as objectively as possible! –

The man mounting, rearing to copulate,
eating ostrich eggs to swell the swelling.
Urethral ironing-woman, needling the womb-ligament
to belly-fat for the sperm-Winkelrieds! – –

O take me up into the jubilation of your bevel:
space is space! O in the flashing
of the handle: focus, virtual image,
enacted according to the law! O, in the eyes
of the point sparkles
trusty, blood-birthed
TARGET.

George Berkeley (1685–1753), Anglo-Irish philosopher, could be misinterpreted to have maintained that what is not perceived cannot exist. Arnold von Winkelried is the legendary hero of the Battle of Sempach (1386) between the Swiss Cantons and Austria, in which he is said to have created a way through the enemy ranks by gathering a large number of pikes into his body.

Marie

Du Vollweib!
Deine Maße sind normal,
jedes Kind kann durch dein Becken.
Breithingelagert
empfähest du bis in die Stirn
und gehst. –

Marie

1919

O fully female!
Your measurements are normal,
every child can pass through your pelvis.
Lying broadly spread
you conceive up to your brow
and go. –

Curettage

Nun liegt sie in derselben Pose,
wie sie empfing,
die Schenkel lose
im Eisenring.

Der Kopf verströmt und ohne Dauer,
als ob sie rief:
gib, gib, ich gurgle deine Schauer
bis in mein Tief.

Der Leib noch stark von wenig Äther
und wirft sich zu:
nach uns die Sintflut und das Später
nur du, nur du…

Die Wände fallen, Tische und Stühle
sind alle voll von Wesen, krank
nach Blutung, lechzendem Gewühle
und einem nahen Untergang.

Curettage

1922

She's lying in the same position
as when she took,
her thighs akimbo
in the iron hook.

Her head dissolved, without a rudder,
as if she cried:
give, give, I'll gurgle every shudder
deep inside.

Her body, still strong from little morphine,
is crashing through,
forget the Flood and later hygiene,
just you, just you ...

The walls collapsing. Chairs and table,
all are full of being, crave
blood-letting, thirsty grappling, fatal
highway to the grave.

Schutt

Spuk. Alle Skalen
toset die Seele bei Nacht,
Griff und Kuß und die fahlen
Fratzen, wenn man erwacht.
Bruch, und ach deine Züge
alle funkelnd von Flor,
Maréchal Niel der Lüge –
never –, o nevermore.

Schutt, alle Trümmer
liegen morgens so bloß,
wahr ist immer nur eines:
du und das Grenzenlos –
trinke und alle Schatten
hängen die Lippe ins Glas,
fütterst du dein Ermatten –
laß –!

Schamloses Schaumgeboren,
Akropolen und Gral,
Tempel, dämmernde Foren
katadyomenal;
fiebernde Galoppade,
Spuk, alle Skalen tief
schluchzend Hypermalade,
letztes Pronom jactif.

Komm, die Lettern verzogen,
hinter Gitter gebannt,
himmelleer, schütternde Wogen
alles, Züge und Hand.
Fall: verwehende Märe,
Wandel: lächelt euch zu –
alles: Sonne und Sphäre,
Pole und Astren: du.

Rubble

1922

Ghosts. The soul is roaring
its mighty gamut of fire.
Grope and kiss and the boring
grimaces of dawn-dead desire.
Breach, and ah your girlhood
sparkling at its death's door,
Maréchal Niel of falsehood –
never, oh nevermore.

Rubble, every fragment
in daylight dystrophy
leaves but this transparent:
you and infinity –
drink, and every shadow
hangs its lips in the glass,
stop feeding your tired da capos –
impasse – !

Immodesty born from sea-foam,
Acropolis, Grail decay,
fora, a twilit maelstrom
plunging the other way;
frenzied horsemen retreating,
ghosts, the soul roars its grief,
sobbing, self-defeating,
the final pronom jactif.

Come, the letters distorted
that bars of iron encase,
heavenless, finally thwarted
everything, hand and face.
Falling: fading stories,
change: a smile to renew –
everything: sunshine glories,
poles and asteroids: you.

Komm, und drängt sich mit Brüsten
Eutern zu Tête-à-tête
letztes Lebensgelüsten,
laß, es ist schon zu spät,
komm, alle Skalen tosen
Spuk, Entformungsgefühl –
komm, es fallen wie Rosen
Götter und Götter-Spiel.

Come, if it must be carnal,
udders for tête-à-tête,
a final stab at Nirvana,
wait, it's already too late,
come, the gamut closes,
ghosts, form dissolves and is gone,
come, like falling roses,
the gods and their games are done.

Palau

„Rot ist der Abend auf der Insel von Palau
und die Schatten sinken –"
singe, auch aus den Kelchen der Frau
läßt es sich trinken,
Totenvögel schrein
und die Totenuhren
pochen, bald wird es sein
Nacht und Lemuren.

Heiße Riffe. Aus Eukalypten geht
Tropik und Palmung,
was sich noch hält und steht,
will auch Zermalmung
bis in das Gliederlos,
bis in die Leere,
lief in den Schöpfungsschoß
dämmernder Meere.

Rot ist der Abend auf der Insel von Palau
und im Schattenschimmer
hebt sich steigend aus Dämmer und Tau:
„niemals und immer",
alle Tode der Welt
sind Fähren und Furten,
und von Fremdem umstellt
auch deine Geburten –

Einmal mit Opferfett
auf dem Piniengerüste
trägt sich dein Flammenbett
wie Wein zur Küste,
Megalithen zuhauf
und die Gräber und Hallen,
Hammer des Thor im Lauf
zu den Asen zerfallen –

Palau

1922

'Evening is red on the island of Palau
and shadows sinking – '
sing, women are vessels too,
would have you drinking,
the little owls call,
death-watch tick-tocking,
soon night will fall
with lemurs mocking.

Burning reefs. Eucalyptus conjures
palmtropic sensation,
all that still stands and endures
craves annihilation,
into paralysis,
impossibilities,
into the womb's abyss
of twilit seas.

Evening is red on the island of Palau
and in the shadowy haze
there rises from twilight and dew:
'never and always',
all the deaths of the world
are ferried to groundings,
and the new born uncurled
in alien surroundings –

Once anointed with oils
for your immolation,
your flaming bed rolls
to shore, a libation,
megaliths in might,
sepulchres, barrows,
Thor's hammer in flight
to the Norns' charnel-houses –

Wie die Götter vergehn
und die großen Cäsaren,
von der Wange des Zeus
emporgefahren –
singe, wandert die Welt
schon in fremdestem Schwunge,
schmeckt uns das Charonsgeld
längst unter der Zunge.

Paarung. Dein Meer belebt
Sepien, Korallen,
was sich noch hält und hebt,
will auch zerfallen,
rot ist der Abend auf der Insel von Palau,
Eukalyptenschimmer
hebt in Runen aus Dämmer und Tau:
niemals und immer.

As the gods pass away
and the greatest of Caesars
deified, they say,
by the favour of Zeus –
sing, the world runs at a pace
as alien as any,
the old familiar taste
of Charon's penny.

Coition. Your sea is decked
in sepia and coral,
all that still stands erect
craves utter downfall,
evening is red on the island of Palau,
eucalyptus haze
raises in runes of twilight and dew:
never and always.

Trunkene Flut

Trunkene Flut,
trance- und traumgefleckt,
o Absolut,
das meine Stirne deckt,
um das ich ringe,
aus dem der Preis
der tiefen Dinge,
die die Seele weiß.

In Sternenfieber,
das nie ein Auge maß,
Nächte, Lieber,
daß man des Tods vergaß,
im Zeiten-Einen,
im Schöpfungsschrei
kommt das Vereinen,
nimmt hin – vorbei.

Dann du alleine
nach großer Nacht,
Korn und Weine
dargebracht,
die Wälder nieder,
die Hörner leer,
zu Gräbern wieder
steigt Demeter,

dir noch im Rücken,
im Knochenbau,
dann ein Entzücken,
ein Golf aus Blau,
von Tränen alt,
aus Not und Gebrest
eine Schöpfergestalt,
die uns leben läßt,

Drunken flood

1922

Drunken flood
dappled with dream and trance,
o absolute,
my being's circumstance
which I fight to preserve,
ensuring the prize
of the deep things observed
by the soul's seeing eyes.

In astral fever
never yet recorded,
nights, unbeliever,
when death's memory was thwarted,
in synchrony
and creation's call
comes unity,
take it – or fall.

Alone returning
from a nocturnal glut,
harvest emergent
offered up,
the forests are dying,
the horns are drained,
Demeter climbing
to graves again,

she's still in your memory,
pervading you,
then comes a melody,
a gulf of blue,
old with tears,
from all that's negative
a creator appears,
and allows us to live,

73

die viel gelitten,
die vieles sah,
immer in Schritten
dem Ufer nah
der trunkenen Flut,
die die Seele deckt
groß wie der Fingerhut
sommers die Berge fleckt.

a figure of suffering
seeing much more,
forever striding
close to the shore
of the drunken flood,
my soul's circumstance,
like June's great foxglove
dappling the hills' expanse.

Das späte Ich

I

O du, sieh an: Levkoienwelle,
der schon das Auge übergeht,
Abgänger, Eigen-Immortelle,
es ist schon spät.

Bei Rosenletztem, da die Fabel
des Sommers längst die Flur verließ –
moi haïssable,
noch so mänadisch analys.

II

Im Anfang war die Flut. Ein Floß Lemuren
schiebt Elch, das Vieh, ihn schwängerte ein Stein.
Aus Totenreich, Erinnern, Tiertorturen
steigt Gott hinein.

Alle die großen Tiere: Adler der Kohorten,
Tauben aus Golgathal –
alle die großen Städte: Palm- und Purpurborden –
Blumen der Wüste, Traum des Baal.

Ost-Gerölle, Marmara-Fähre,
Rom, gib die Pferde des Lysippus her –
letztes Blut des weißen Stiers über die schweigenden Altäre
und der Amphitrite letztes Meer –

Schutt. Bacchanalien. Propheturen.
Barkarolen. Schweinerein.
Im Anfang war die Flut. Ein Floß Lemuren
schiebt in die letzten Meere ein.

The later I

1922

I

O love, look there, a wave of stocks,
flowers enough to make us weep,
playing immortelles, a paradox,
their time to sleep.

With roses' ruins, where the fable
of summer is an old hypothesis –
moi haïssable
still so drunk with analysis.

II

In the beginning was the Flood. A raft of lemurs,
cattle-drivers, elk fertilised by a stone.
From death's domain, memory, animal tortures
God has grown.

All the great animals: the cohorts' eagles,
doves from the valley of the skull –
all the great cities: borders of palm and purple –
flowers of the desert, dreams of Baal.

Marmara ferry, Eastern tears,
give us the horsemen of Lysippos, Rome –
on the silent altars the last blood of white steers
and Amphitrite's last sea foam –

Rubble. Bacchanals. Prophet dreamers.
Barcaroles. Swineries.
In the beginning was the Flood. A raft of lemurs
for the last time on the last seas.

III

O Seele, um und um verweste,
kaum lebst du noch und noch zuviel,
da doch kein Staub aus keinen Feldern,
da doch kein Laub aus keinen Wäldern
nicht schwer durch deine Schatten fiel.

Die Felsen glühn, der Tartarus ist blau,
der Hades steigt in Oleanderfarben
dem Schlaf ins Lid und brennt zu Garben
mythischen Glücks die Totenschau.

Der Gummibaum, der Bambusquoll,
der See verwäscht die Inkaplatten,
das Mondchâteau: Geröll und Schatten
uralte blaue Mauern voll.

Welch Bruderglück um Kain und Abel,
für die Gott durch die Wolken strich –
kausalgenetisch, haïssable:
das späte Ich.

III

O soul, decrepit through and through,
you scarcely live, and life's too shallow,
from any field there's not a speck,
from any wood there's not a fleck
which did not overload your shadow.

Tartarus is blue, the crag's aglow
and Hades' oleander colours creep
under sleep's lids and burn in a heap
of mythic joy the mortality show.

The rubber plantation, the bamboo source
washes away the Inca plateau,
rubble and shadows: the moon château,
blue ramparts full of ancient force.

Great brotherhood of Cain and Abel
for whom God chose through clouds to fly,
genetic causality, haïssable:
the later I.

Staatsbibliothek

Staatsbibliothek, Kaschemme,
Resultatverlies,
Satzbordell, Maremme,
Fieberparadies:
wenn die Katakomben
glühn im Wortvibrier,
und die Hetakomben
sind *ein* weißer Stier –

wenn Vergang der Zeiten,
wenn die Stunde stockt,
weil im Satz der Seiten
eine Silbe lockt,
die den Zweckgewalten,
reinem Lustgewinn
rauscht in Sturzgestalten
löwenhaft den Sinn –:

wenn das Säkulare,
tausendstimmig Blut
auferlebt im Aare
neuer Himmel ruht:
Opfer, Beil und Wunde,
Hades, Mutterhort
für der Schöpfungsstunde
traumbeladenes Wort.

State Library

1922

State Library, den of robbers,
dungeon of advice,
phrase brothel, peat deposits,
fever paradise:
when the catacombs are glowing
with one pulsing idea,
and the hecatombs bowing
to one albino steer –

when the decline of ages,
when the hour-hand sticks,
because in printed pages
a single morpheme clicks,
whose sense to vulgarians,
offering pure delight,
rustles in postlapsarians
as a lion roars in flight –:

when history's upheavals,
thousand-voiced in blood,
soar again as eagles
breasting new heavens would:
the victim axed and broken,
Hades, maternal hoard,
for the creative moment
a dream-encrusted word.

Nebel

Ach, du zerrinnender
und schon gestürzter Laut,
eben beginnender
Lust vom Munde getaut,
ach so zerrinnst du,
Stunde, und hast kein Sein,
ewig schon spinnst du
weit in die Nebel dich ein.

Ach, wir sagen es immer,
daß es nie enden kann,
und vergessen den Schimmer
Schnees des neige d'antan,
in das durchküßte, durchtränte
nächtedurchschluchzte Sein
strömt das Fließend-Entlehnte,
spinnen die Nebel sich ein.

Ach, wir rufen und leiden
ältesten Göttern zu:
ewig über uns beiden
»immer und alles: du«,
aber den Widdern, den Zweigen,
Altar und Opferstein,
hoch zu den Göttern, die schweigen,
spinnen die Nebel sich ein.

Mists

1924

Ah, disappearing
and misfortuned sound,
once pioneering,
bliss left the lips unfound,
ah, you too, hour,
disappear and never are,
spinning dead power
into the mists from afar.

Ah, we claim together
to outwit the ferryman
and to forget forever
shimmering neige d'antan,
into the kissing, obsession,
and sobs that kept us awake
streamed the shift to pretension,
the mists are growing opaque.

Ah, we cry out, importune
yesterday's gods to be true:
willing our mutual fortune
'always and everything: you',
but into the stars and the trident,
altar and slaughter-stone,
and on high to the gods who are silent
the mists come into their own.

Die Dänin

I

Charon oder die Hermen
oder der Daimlerflug,
was aus den Weltenschwärmen
tief dich im Atem trug,
war deine Mutter im Haine
südlich, Thalassa, o lau –
trug deine Mutter alleine
dich, den nördlichen Tau –

meerisch lagernde Stunde,
Bläue, mythischer Flor,
eine Muschel am Munde,
goldene Conca d'or –
die dich im Atem getragen:
da bist du: und alles ist gut,
was in Kismet und Haimarmene
und Knien der Götter ruht.

Stehst du, ist die Magnolie
stumm und weniger rein,
aber die große Folie
ist dein Zerlassensein:
Stäubende: – tiefe Szene,
wo sich die Seele tränkt,
während der Schizophrene
trostlos die Stirne senkt.

Rings nur Rundung und Reigen,
Trift und lohnende Odds –
ach, wer kennte das Schweigen
schlummerlosen Gotts –
noch um die Golgathascheite
schlingt sich das goldene Vließ:

The Danish girl

I 1924, II 1925

I

Herms or Charon's ferry
or maybe a Daimler in flight,
what from the stars' assembly
breathed you in deep delight,
a grove was your mother's playground,
with the South, thalassa, she grew
and alone bore you spellbound,
you, the Nordic dew –

languorous hour on the sea-shore,
blueness, mythical haze,
a seashell whispers: explore,
Conca d'or, golden days –
these breathed you out at sunset:
you are here; all is well
which rests in lares and kismet
under the gods and their spell.

When you stand, the magnolia
is silent and less pure,
but when you melt, ambrosia,
intoxicating cure:
nectar: – a well majestic
where the soul can finally drink,
while the comfortless schizophrenic
allows his head to sink.

Cradled in curves, in a round-dance,
cogency, favourable odds –
ah, if you knew the silence
of a never-sleeping god –
still about Golgotha's sorrow
winds the golden fleece:

»morgen an meiner Seite
bist du im Paradies.«

Auch Prometheus in Schmieden
ist nicht der einsame Mann,
Io, die Okeaniden
ruft er als Zeugen an –
Philosophia perennis,
Hegels schauender Akt –:
Biologie und Tennis
über Verrat geflaggt.

Monde fallen, die Blüte
fällt im Schauer des Spät,
Nebel am Haupt die Mythe
siegenden Manns vergeht,
tief mit Rosengefälle
wird nur Verwehtes beschenkt,
während die ewige Stelle
trostlos die Stirne senkt.

II

Es ist kaum zu denken:
du in dem Garten am Meer,
die Wasser heben und senken
das Ewig-Sinnlose her,
vermischte – Didos Karthagen
und vom Saharaportal –
vermischte Wasser tragen
dahin Notturn final.

Die Fjorde blau, die Tore,
der Donner und das Licht,
durch die das Oratore
der großen Erde bricht,
davon bist du die Dolde

'thou shalt be tomorrow
with me in Paradise'.

Prometheus even in fetters
is never a man alone,
Io, the daughters of Tethys
speak on his telephone –
philosophia perennis,
Hegel's visionary act –:
biology and tennis,
treacherous compact.

Moons decline, the flowerhead
falls shudderingly late,
fabled in fog the sickbed
of man's unworthy fate,
cascading roses' splendour
on vanished figments shrinks,
while the eternal centre
its head disconsolate sinks.

II

You are difficult to imagine
in the garden by the sea,
the high and low tides happen
never meaningfully,
mixtures – Dido's Carthage,
oasis, grand canal,
tidal admixed messages,
perdendosi, nocturne final.

The fjords are blue, the gateway
of thunder and of light
through which the choral high-day
of the earth resounds in might,
you are its inflorescence

und blühst den Himmeln zu,
und doch des Nichts Isolde,
Vergänglichkeit auch du.

Um deinen Bau, Terrasse,
zerfällt das Nelkenhaus,
der Gärtner fegt die blasse
verblühte Stunde aus,
auch du, woher geschritten,
auch du, wohin verweht,
und was um dich gelitten,
wird auch schon kühl und spät.

Wo Räume uns umziehen,
durch die schon mancher ging,
und Wolke, die im Fliehen
um andre Häupter hing,
und Land sich an Gestalten
mit tausend Trieben gibt,
den sterblichen Gewalten,
die so wie du geliebt.

In Mythen tief, in Sagen
liegt schon der Garten am Meer;
Zerfall, in wieviel Tagen
sind Gärten und Meere leer,
vermischte – Didos Zeiten
und vom Saharaportal –
tragen die Einsamkeiten
weiter – Notturn final.

and bloom to the skies anew,
Isolde of evanescence
and doomed oblivion too.

Around your villa, terrace,
the beds of carnations fade,
the gardener sweeps the helpless
withered hour away,
you also, your trajectory,
you also, your sheltering-place,
and what you put in jeopardy,
all growing cool and late.

Where spaces shift around us
which echoed to other treads,
and clouds, those manic prowlers,
have shadowed other heads,
and landscapes opened portals
to thousandfold desires
for countless other mortals
who also loved like you.

In legend deep, in saga
is the garden by the sea,
decay, as their days grow darker
and both reclaim privacy,
mixtures – Dido's losses,
sand in the grand canal,
far out stretch lonelinesses,
perduto – nocturne final.

Der Sänger

Keime, Begriffsgenesen,
Broadways, Azimut,
Turf- und Nebelwesen
mischt der Sänger im Blut,
immer in Gestaltung,
immer dem Worte zu
nach Vergessen der Spaltung
zwischen ich und du.

Neurogene Leier,
fahle Hyperämien,
Blutdruckschleier
mittels Koffein,
keiner kann ermessen
dies: dem einen zu,
ewig dem Vergessen
zwischen ich und du.

Wenn es einst der Sänger
dualistisch trieb,
heute ist er Zersprenger
mittels Gehirnprinzips,
stündlich webt er im Ganzen
drängend zum Traum des Gedichts
seine schweren Substanzen
selten und langsam ins Nichts.

The singer

1925

Buds, the birth of concepts,
Broadways, azimuth,
cloudy and turf-adepts
the singer blends in his blood,
always his disposition,
back to the words anew,
forgotten the division
between the I and you.

Neurogenic lyre,
pallid hyperaemias,
arterial misfire
with caffeine asthenias,
no calculating bridges,
eternally pursue
the unforgotten abysses
between the I and you.

Once perhaps the singer
served duality,
now explosion-bringer
intellectually,
weaving a dream, he forces
against their stubbornness,
all his heavy sources
into nothingness.

Banane

Banane, yes, Banane!
vie méditerranée,
Bartwichse, Lappentrane:
vie Pol, Sargassosee:
Dreck, Hündinnen, Schakale
Geschlechtstrieb im Gesicht
und aasblau das Finale –
der Bagno läßt uns nicht.

Die großen Götter Panne,
defekt der Mythenflor,
die Machmeds und Johanne
speicheln aus Eignem vor,
der alten Samenbarden
Begattungsclownerie,
das Sago der Milliarden,
der Nil von Hedonie.

Nachts wahllos zwischen Horden
verschluckt der Zeugungsakt,
Gestirne? wo? geworden!
gewuchert! fleischlich Fakt!
Gestirne? wo? im Schweigen
eines Wechsels von Fernher –
Zyklen, Kreisen der Reigen,
Bedürfniswiederkehr.

Sinnlose Existenzen:
dreißig Millionen die Pest,
und die andern Pestilenzen
lecken am Rest,
Hochdruck! unter die Brause!
in Pferdemist und Spelt
beerdige zu Hause –
das ist das Antlitz der Welt!

Banana

1925

Banana, ja, banana:
vie méditerranée,
brilliantine, Lappish blubber,
vie polaire, Sargasso Sea:
dirt, bitches, jackals, bosses,
sex-drive in glances on show,
a finale the colour of corpses –
that bordello won't let us go.

Pans, great gods in the plural,
opaque, defective myths,
Mohammeds and John the rural
spit out their own little bits,
the clownish sexual stories
of ancient Sami bards,
Cleopatra's glories
the sago of milliards.

The hordes' regressive nightmare,
random sexual acts,
what constellations? nowhere!
too many! carnal facts!
What constellations? in the silence
of change from far away –
cycles, the dances of science,
obsessional replay.

All beings irrelevancies:
thirty million in one plague
and the other pestilences
lick at the masquerade.
High pressure! take a shower!
straw and manure are hurled
in the home burial hour –
that is the face of the world.

Hauch von Schaufeln und Feuer
ist die Blume des Weins,
Hungerratten und Geier
sind die Lilien des Seins,
Erde birst sich zu Kreuzen,
Flußbett und Meere fällt,
sinnlose Phallen schneuzen
sich ins Antlitz der Welt.

Ewig endlose Züge
vor dem sinkenden Blick,
weite Wogen, Flüge –
wohin – zurück
in die dämmernden Rufe,
an den Schierling: Vollbracht,
umflorte Stufe
zur Urne der Nacht –

A whiff of shovels and burning
in the bouquet of wine,
black rats, raptors circling
lilies of life divine,
earth explodes into crosses,
river-beds, oceans fall,
senseless phallic blotches
in the face of the world, no recall.

Eternally endless processions
before the sinking eye,
distant waves, evanescence –
where do they lead us? – why,
back to the cries' decrescendo,
to the hemlock, the end of light,
but a step lamentando
to the urn of the night.

Schädelstätten

Schwer von Vergessen
und ach so hangend schon,
aus Unermessen
Ton um Ton,
und Schattenmale
des letzten Lichts,
o Finale,
Nächte des Nichts.

Die Welten halten,
Aeonen-Bann.
Schwer das Erkalten
fühlt nur der Mann,
Wälder zu schweigen
und Waidmannsruh –
wenn wir uns neigen,
wer warst du,
Du?

Punisch in Jochen,
Heredität,
kranke Knochen
von Philoktet,
Fratze der Glaube,
Fratze das Glück,
leer kommt die Taube
Noahs zurück.

Schädelstätten,
Begriffsmanie,
kein Zeitwort zu retten
noch Historie –
allem Vergessen,
allem Verschmähn,
dem Unermessen
Panathenaen –

Golgothas

1925

Heavy forgetting
and ah! to hang alone,
from loss descending
tone by tone,
and traces darkly,
mark of dying lights,
o finale
nothingness nights.

Worlds surviving
the magic of time,
only man dying
of cold in his prime,
no reference to forests
or the huntsman's halloo –
what were we promised,
where were you,
you?

Punic in shackles,
heredities,
sick bones that rankle
Philoctetes,
belief in mind-numbing
and joy makes no mark,
the dove carries nothing
back to the Ark.

Golgothas scare us,
for concepts we crave
without verbs to reassure us
or history to save –
for every forgetting
and every disdain,
from loss descending
hold Athenian games –

in Heiligtumen
tyrrhenischer See
Stier unter Blumen
an Danaë,
in Leuenzügen
Mänadenklang,
und Götter fügen
den Untergang.

in a precinct unfastened
by the Tyrrhenian sea
a bull in garlands
for Danaë,
in lion processions
the maenads call,
and gods' intentions:
decline and fall.

Theogonien

Theogonien –
von den Dingen der Welt
ziehn Melancholien
an der Sterne Zelt,
weben Götter und Drachen,
singen Brände und Baal,
sinnvoll zu machen
Knechtschaft und Qual.

Fährt Er mit leuchtender Barke
über das Himmelsmeer,
ist Er der Widder, der Starke,
von Sonnen und Monden schwer,
naht Er sich in Gewittern,
als der die Felsen verschiebt
und von den Bösen, den Bittern
die Kühe den Priestern gibt.

Ach, um Fluten, um Elche
rankt sich die Traurigkeit:
sie fahren; Stürme; welche
tauchen, das Land ist weit,
da: ihrem Möwentume
stäubt sich ein Körnchen schwer,
und Er macht aus der Krume
eine Insel auf dem Meer.

Wie mußten sie alle leiden,
um so zum Traum zu fliehn,
und sein des Kummers Weiden
wie hier die Algonkin!
Auch anderen Tieren, Steinen
vertrauten sie ihren Tod
und gingen hin zu weinen
die Völker, weiß und rot.

Theogonies

1925

Theogonies –
from the world's lament
stream melancholies
to the firmament,
weave gods, magic beings,
sing Baal and beltane,
to give some meaning
to serfdom and pain.

If He sails dazzling ferries
across waves in the sky,
if He is the strongman, is Aries,
with suns and moons as they fly,
if He visits us in thunder
as the one who makes cliffs retreat
and from the wicked, the hunter
gives cattle to the priest.

Ah, round elks, round the torrents,
sadness assembles its blight:
they go, suffer storms abhorrent,
some dive, no land is in sight,
and there, like a crumb for a seabird
a speck of dust is sent
and He creates from the keyword
an island before life is spent.

What suffering they all were reaping
to take refuge in such dreams,
how they grieved, like willows weeping,
like Algonquin tribes, it seems!
Some entrusted themselves to totems,
to stones when they were dead
and went to mourn the bowmen,
the peoples, white and red.

Wer bist du

Wer bist du – alle Mythen
zerrinnen. Was geschah,
Chimären, Leda-iten
sind einen Kniefall da,

gemalt mit Blut der Beeren
der Trunkenen Schläfe rot,
und die – des Manns Erwehren –
die nun als Lorbeer loht,

mit Schlangenhaar die Lende
an Zweig und Thyrsenstab,
in Trunkenheit und Ende
und um ein Göttergrab –

was ist, sind hohle Leichen,
die Wand aus Tang und Stein,
was scheint, ist ewiges Zeichen
und spielt die Tiefe rein –

in Schattenflur, in Malen,
das sich der Form entwand –:
Ulyss, der nach den Qualen
schlafend die Heimat fand.

Who are you

1925

Who are you – disappearance
of the mythic. What took place,
Leda stories, chimeras
only a moment's grace,

painted with blood of berries
the drunkards' temples red,
and she – for man unready –
burns as laurel instead,

in loins with hair like serpents,
on twigs and thyrsus tip,
in cups, in dark observance
a dead god's fellowship –

what is, are hollow corpses,
a wall of kelp and stone,
what seems, eternal sources
and signs of death unknown –

in shadowfields, in paintings
dispensing with form as a goal –
Ulysses, who after sea-ranging
sleeping returned to his home.

Schleierkraut

Schleierkraut, Schleierkraut rauschen,
rausche die Stunde an,
Himmel, die Himmel lauschen,
wer noch leben kann,
jeder weiß von den Tagen,
wo wir die Ferne sehn:
leben ist Brückenschlagen
über Ströme, die vergehn.

Schleierkraut, Schleierkraut rauschen,
es ist die Ewigkeit,
wo Herbst und Rosen tauschen
den Blick vom Sterben weit,
da klingt auch von den Meeren
das Ruhelose ein,
von fahlen Stränden, von Schären
der Woge Schein.

Schleierkraut, Schleierkraut neigen
zu tief Musik,
Sterbendes will schweigen:
silence panique,
erst die Brücken geschlagen,
das Blutplateau,
dann, wenn die Brücken tragen,
die Ströme – wo?

Gypsophila

1925

Gypsophila, soapwort rustling,
rustle down the day,
heaven, the sky is listening,
who can live this way,
everyone knows the experience
of distance seeming near:
life is building bridges
over rivers that disappear.

Gypsophila, soapwort rustling,
it is eternity,
with autumn and roses belying
the world's mortality,
then the sound of waves has freshened
a sense of restlessness,
leached sands reflect, and headlands
the breakers' regress.

Gypsophila, soapwort bending
to music deep,
dying things' voices ending:
silence panique,
firstly build your bridges,
the blood laid bare,
then when sure of their pillars,
the rivers go where?

Osterinsel

Eine so kleine Insel,
wie ein Vogel über dem Meer,
kaum ein Aschengerinnsel
und doch von Kräften nicht leer,
mit Steingebilden, losen,
die Ebene besät
von einer fast monstrosen
Irrealität.

Die großen alten Worte
– sagt Ure Vaeiko –
haben die Felsen zu Horte,
die kleinen leben so;
er schwelt auf seiner Matte
bei etwas kaltem Fisch,
hühnerfeindliche Ratte
kommt nicht auf seinen Tisch.

Vom Pazifik erschlagen,
von Ozeanen bedroht,
nie ward an Land getragen
ein Polynesierboot,
doch große Schwalbenfeiern
einem transzendenten Du,
Göttern von Vogeleiern
singen die Tänzer zu.

Tierhafte Alphabete
für Sonne, Mond und Stier
mit einer Haifischgräte
– Bustrophedonmanier –:
ein Zeichen für zwölf Laute,
ein Ruf für das, was schlief
und sich im Innern baute
aus wahrem Konstruktiv.

Easter Island

1927

Such a little island,
like a bird above the sea,
hardly ashes surviving
and yet some potency,
the plain is sown with statues,
isolated, stone,
nearly monstrous their virtues:
spare, unreal, alone.

The great old words are hidden
– says Ure Vaieko –
and buried in cliffs unwritten,
these small ones are on show;
he smoulders on his matting
chewing his cooling fish,
the rats go chicken-catching
and never grace his dish.

Battered by the Pacific,
threatened by lesser seas,
no landing-place logistic
for a Polynesian breeze,
but swallow-rituals
for a transcendent you,
sacred egg-syllables
for dancers to construe.

Animist alphabetising
for sun and moon and steer
drawn with a shark-bone stylus
– boustrophedon, that's clear –:
one sign for a dozen phonemes,
one cry for the dream-born prism
building itself in the bloodstream
of pure constructivism.

Woher die Seelenschichten,
da das Idol entsprang
zu diesen Steingesichten
und Riesenformungszwang –
die großen alten Worte
sind ewig unverwandt,
haben die Felsen zu Horte
und alles Unbekannt.

In the soul, what strata
produced these effigies
compelled by a master
of ordered immensities –
the great old words are hidden,
still indivisible,
buried in cliffs unwritten
and inexplicable.

Several ethnographic details and the personal name here appeared first in the account of an expedition to Easter Island in the *Smithsonian Institution Report 1889*.

Orphische Zellen

Es schlummern orphische Zellen
in Hirnen des Okzident,
Fisch und Wein und Stellen,
an denen das Opfer brennt,
die Esse aus Haschisch und Meten
und Kraut und das delphische Lied
vom Zuge der Auleten,
wenn er am Gott verschied.

Wer nie das Haupt verhüllte
und niederstieg, ein Stier,
ein rieselnd Blut erfüllte
das Grab und Sargrevier,
wen nie Vermischungslüste
mit Todesschweiß bedrohn,
der ist auch nicht der Myste
aus der phrygischen Kommunion.

Um Feuerstein, um Herde
hat sich der Sieg gerankt,
Er aber haßt das Werde,
das sich dem Sieg verdankt,
Er drängt nach andern Brüsten
nach andern Meeren ein,
schon nähern sich die Küsten,
die Brandungsvögel schrein.

Nun mag den Sansibaren
der Himmel hoch und still,
eine Insel voll Nelkenwaren
und der Blüte der Bougainville,
wo sie in Höfen drehen
die Mühlen für Zuckerrohr,
nun mag das still vergehen –:
Er tritt als Opfer vor.

Orphic cells

Orphic cells are sleeping
in occidental brains,
fish and wine concealing
the latent holy flames,
the hearth of mead and hashish,
the poppy, the Delphic lay
the flute-players sang in anguish
as god departed, and they.

Whose head was never covered
to climb down to a grave,
as flowing steer's blood smothered
the coffin and the cave,
whom never cold sweats threaten
in lust for union
is not of the mystic brethren
in the Phrygian communion.

By firestone and by hearthside
the victory has grown,
but this man hates the high tide
the victory has blown,
he longs for different lovers
to sail on different seas,
new coasts greet the newcomer,
surf-seagulls greet the breeze.

Now Zanzibars' insignia,
their heavens high and still,
islands of bougainvillea,
carnations on the hill,
where grinding-mills are turning
cane-sugar paradise,
yet none of that concerns him –:
he wills his sacrifice.

111

Und wo Vergang: in Gittern,
an denen der Mörder weint,
wo sonst Vergang, ach Zittern
löst schon die Stunde, die eint –:
ihm beben Schmerz und Schaden
im Haupt, das niemand kennt,
die Brandungsvögel baden,
das Opfer brennt.

And where decay is: in prison
where a murderer weeps at night,
and other decays, where division
cuts short the hours that unite –:
pain and damage contending
in the head for which no-one turns,
surf-seagulls dipping, ascending,
the sacrifice burns.

Qui sait

Aber der Mensch wird trauern –
solange Gott, falls es das gibt,
immer neue Schauern
von Gehirnen schiebt
von den Hellesponten
zum Hobokenquai,
immer neue Fronten –
wozu, qui sait?

Spurii: die Gesäten
war einst der Männer Los,
Frauen streiften und mähten
den Samen in ihren Schoß;
dann eine Insel voll Tauben
und Werften: Schiffe fürs Meer,
und so begann der Glauben
an Handel und Verkehr.

Aber der Mensch wird trauern –
Masse, muskelstark,
Cowboy und Zentauern,
Nurmi als Jeanne d'Arc –:
Stadionsakrale
mit Khasanaspray,
Züchtungspastorale,
wozu, qui sait?

Aber der Mensch wird trauern –
kosmopoler Chic
neue Tempelmauern
Kraftwerk Pazifik:
die Meere ausgeweidet,
Kalorien-Avalun:
Meer, das wärmt, Meer, das kleidet –
neue Mythe des Neptun.

114

Qui sait

But man will always sorrow –
as long as God, if such there be,
sends shuddering pain to follow
thinking, at his decree,
from Leander's Hellespontos
to Hobokenquai,
always some new locus –
but why, qui sait?

Spurii: the he-man's business
once, to sow the seed,
stripping, mowing for the mistress,
conception guaranteed;
next came a dove-filled island
and wharves: the clipper style,
establishing our thriving
progress mercantile.

But man will always sorrow –
masses, razor-sharp,
cowboy, centaurs follow,
Nurmi as Jeanne d'Arc –:
stadium religion
with cosmetic spray,
eugenic malnutrition,
but why, qui sait?

But man will always sorrow –
cosmopolitan chic
a new temple for tomorrow,
power-station pacifique:
harvest the seas to extinction,
calory Avalon:
the sea the latest wonder prescription –
Neptune, sine qua non.

115

Bis nach tausend Jahren
einbricht in das Wrack
Geißlerscharen,
zementiertes Pack
mit Orang-Utanhauern
oder Kaiser Henry Clay –
wer wird das überdauern,
welch Pack – qui sait?

After the thousand-year cycle
this wreck will suffer defeat,
flagellant disciples
a rabble hard as concrete
with orang-utan incisors
or with Emperor Henry Clay –
who will then survive it,
what rabble – qui sait?

Paavo Nurmi (1897–1973), Finnish middle- and long-distance runner, medal-winner at three Olympic Games, 1920–28. Henry Clay (1777–1852), American politician, proponent of the 'American system' of economics.

Sieh die Sterne, die Fänge

Sieh die Sterne, die Fänge
Lichts und Himmel und Meer,
welche Hirtengesänge,
dämmernde, treiben sie her,
du auch, die Stimmen gerufen
und deinen Kreis durchdacht,
folge die schweigenden Stufen
abwärts dem Boten der Nacht.

Wenn du die Mythen und Worte
entleert hast, sollst du gehn,
eine neue Götterkohorte
wirst du nicht mehr sehn,
nicht ihre Euphratthrone,
nicht ihre Schrift und Wand –
gieße, Myrmidone,
den dunklen Wein ins Land.

Wie dann die Stunden auch hießen,
Qual und Tränen des Seins,
alles blüht im Verfließen
dieses nächtigen Weins,
schweigend strömt die Aeone,
kaum noch von Ufern ein Stück –
gib nun dem Boten die Krone,
Traum und Götter zurück.

Behold the stars

1927

Behold the stars, ensnaring
light and heaven and sea,
what eclogues are they preparing
for their darkening decree?
You too, after bearing witness
with your mind's completed sphere,
follow night's envoy wishless,
descend the silent stair.

When you have cleared words and legends
of meaning, you must go,
new cohorts of gods in the heavens
you will never know,
not their thrones on Euphrates,
not the writing on the wall –
libate, soldier of Achilles
dark wine before your fall.

Whatever names they were given,
those hours of torture and tears,
everything blooms in the elision
of the wine's nocturnal lees,
the Aeon is silently streaming,
hardly a span from the shore –
to the moment lost your dreaming,
the crown and the gods restore.

119

Was singst du denn

Was singst du denn, die Sunde
sind hell von Dorerschnee,
es ist eine alte Stunde,
eine alte Sage der See:
Meerwiddern und Delphinen
die leichtbewegte Last –
gilt es den Göttern, ihnen,
was du gesungen hast?

Singst du des Blickes Sage,
des Menschenauges Schein,
über Werden und Frage,
tief von Ferne und Sein,
eingewoben der Kummer
und der Verluste Zug,
nur manchmal ein Glanz, ein stummer,
des, was man litt und trug?

Singst du der Liebe Leben,
des Mannes Qualenlied,
dem doch ein Gott gegeben,
dass er die Glücke flieht,
der immer neu sich kettet
und immer neu vorbei
sich zu sich selber rettet –,
den Fluch- und Felsenschrei?

Ja singe nur das Eine,
das Eine ist so tief:
die Rettung sie alleine
des Hirn ins Regressiv:
die Fjorde und die Sunde
im taumelnden Vergeh' –
singe die alte Stunde,
die alte Sage der See.

What are you singing?

1927

What are you singing, the straits
are bright with Dorian snow,
perhaps of much earlier dates
and a sea-saga ancients know;
sea-rams and dolphins have shaken
a wilder dithyramb,
or did you address the great ones,
the gods, in the song you sang?

Do you sing the ballad of vision,
the light in the human eye,
question and answer, decision,
being and distance, the sky,
woven together with sorrow
and the nature of loss,
quiet reflections that follow
the rare complaining gloss?

Do you sing the life of loving,
the song of a man's dismay
finding a god begrudging
him happiness one day,
the man who chooses fetters
each time he passes by,
and battles his own errors,
the curse and rock-fall cry?

Sing of one thing only,
the only deep thing, yes:
deliverance invoking
in cerebral regress:
fjords and straits together
drunkenly ceasing to be –
sing the ancient endeavour,
the ancient saga of the sea.

Aus Fernen, aus Reichen

Was dann nach jener Stunde
sein wird, wenn dies geschah,
weiß niemand, keine Kunde
kam je von da,
von den erstickten Schlünden
von dem gebrochnen Licht,
wird es sich neu entzünden,
ich meine nicht.

Doch sehe ich ein Zeichen:
über das Schattenland
aus Fernen, aus Reichen
eine große, schöne Hand,
die wird mich nicht berühren,
das läßt der Raum nicht zu:
doch werde ich sie spüren,
und das bist du.

Und du wirst niedergleiten
am Strand, am Meer,
aus Fernen, aus Weiten:
» – erlöst auch er;«
ich kannte deine Blicke
und in des tiefsten Schoß
sammelst du unsere Glücke,
den Traum, das Los.

Ein Tag ist zu Ende,
die Reifen fortgebracht,
dann spielen noch zwei Hände
das Lied der Nacht,
vom Zimmer, wo die Tasten
den dunklen Laut verwehn,
sieht man das Meer und die Masten
hoch nach Norden gehn.

From distances, from kingdoms

1927

What follows from that moment,
what comes when you've had your day,
no man knows, no exponent
returns to say,
from stifled lamentation,
out of the broken look
comes new illumination,
not in my book.

But I can see a symptom:
across the shadowland
from distances, from kingdoms
a great, a lovely hand,
it will not ever touch me,
in space that is taboo,
but I will sense its beauty,
and that is you.

And you will glide down singing
by the beach and by the sea,
from distances, from kingdoms:
' – redeemed is he';
I knew your secret glances
and in heart's deepest state
you will in our calmest
dreams, our fate.

The day is completed,
gathered fruit not overripe,
two hands at last repeated
the song of the night,
from the music-room piano
when the dark sounds come forth,
you can still see the narrow
sails raised for the North.

Wenn die Nacht wird weichen,
wenn der Tag begann,
trägst du Zeichen,
die niemand deuten kann,
geheime Male
von fernen Stunden krank
und leerst die Schale,
aus der ich vor dir trank.

When the night is ended,
when the day began,
you bore the signs intended,
unreadable by man,
the sad sick comet
you recollect no more,
you drain the goblet
from which I drank before.

Immer schweigender

Du in die letzten Reiche,
du in das letzte Licht,
ist es kein Licht ins bleiche
starrende Angesicht,
da sind die Tränen deine,
da bist du dir entblößt
da ist der Gott, der eine,
der alle Qualen löst.

Aus unnennbaren Zeiten
eine hat dich zerstört,
Rufe, Lieder begleiten
dich, am Wasser gehört,
Trümmer tropischer Bäume,
Wälder vom Grunde des Meer,
grauendurchrauschte Räume
treiben sie her.

Uralt war dein Verlangen,
uralt Sonne und Nacht,
alles: Träume und Bangen
in die Irre gedacht,
immer endender, reiner
du in Fernen gestuft,
immer schweigender, keiner
wartet und keiner ruft.

Ever more silently

1929

Into the final empires
step out, the final light,
for your livid face no torchfire
staring into the night,
there you strip yourself naked,
there the tears are yours,
there is God the old stager
who the suffering soul restores.

Of the immemorial ages,
one chose you to undo,
whom shouts and song had elated
by waters echoing through,
fragmentary jungle spaces,
trees from the bed of the sea,
horror-resounding places
set it free.

Age-old was your yearning,
age-old sun and night,
everything: dream and recurring
fears that thought sets alight,
ever more finally, purely,
distance ordains your falls,
ever more silently, surely,
no-one waits, no-one calls.

Primäre Tage

Primäre Tage, Herbst, auf welchen Sonnen,
von welchem Meer durchblaut, vom Meer gekühlt,
hat dies unwandelbare Licht begonnen,
das rückwärts reicht und *alte* Dinge fühlt,
die Fernen mischen sich, die Völkerheere,
es klingt ein Horn, es klingt das Schilfrohr an:
es ist das Lied vom Busch der Alderbeere,
aus dem die Menschheit weich und sterblich rann.

Primäre Tage, Herbst, die Ebenen träumen,
wie hat das Kind die Tage so geliebt,
die Tage Ruths, die Ährensammler säumen
nach letzten Früchten, die die Stoppel gibt –
ach, da berührt mich was mit vagen Zeichen,
ach, da verführt mich was mit tiefern Zwang:
schon eine blaue Jalousie kann reichen
zu Asterhaftem, das aus Gärten drang.

Vielleicht ein Übergang, vielleicht das Ende,
vielleicht die Götter und vielleicht das Meer,
Rosen und Trauben trägt es auf der Lende:
uralter Wandel, Schattenwiederkehr.
Primäre Tage, Herbst, die Ebenen schweigen
in einem Licht, das *alte* Dinge liebt,
das Ernten fallen läßt und Schatten steigen
und alles nimmt und leise weitergibt.

Primal days

1930

Primal days, in autumn, in what sunshine,
from what cool sea with saturated blue
could such a changeless light the world refine
and touch and feel its *ancient* history too,
distances are mingled, battle-ranks of nations,
a horn-call sounds, the pan-pipes cut from reed:
that is the song in berry-laden places
from which soft humankind emerged to bleed.

Primal days, in autumn, the plains are dreaming,
how much the little child adored those days,
the days of Ruth, when gleaning followed reaping
and found the fruits, the last the stubble gave –
ah, there I feel the touch of a covert finger,
ah, there I am seduced with deep constraint,
even blue sun-blinds can around me trigger
the aster magic which from gardens raged.

Perhaps it is transition, perhaps finale,
perhaps the gods, perhaps the restless main,
its loins are girded with grapes and roses, starry,
of venerable age, and shadows come again.
Primal days, in autumn, the plains are quiet
under a light that loves the *ancient* things,
so harvest can fall and shadows ring defiant,
it hands on gently all its garnerings.

129

Zwei Auszüge aus dem Oratorium 'Das Unaufhörliche'. Musik von Paul Hindemith.

I Lied

Lebe wohl den frühen Tagen,
die mit Sommer, stillem Land
angefüllt und glücklich lagen
in des Kindes Träumerhand.
Lebe wohl, du großes Werde,
über Feldern, See und Haus,
in Gewittern brach die Erde
zu gerechtem Walten aus.
Lebe wohl, was je an Ahnen
mich aus solchem Sein gezeugt,
das sich noch den Sonnenbahnen,
das sich noch der Nacht gebeugt.
Von dem Frühen zu dem Späten,
und die Bilder sinken ab –
lebe wohl, aus großen Städten
ohne Traum und ohne Grab.

II Knabenchor

So sprach das Fleisch zu allen Zeiten:
nichts gibt es als das Satt- und Glücklichsein!
Uns aber soll ein andres Wort begleiten:
das Ringende geht in die Schöpfung ein.

Das Ringende, von dem die Glücke sinken,
das Schmerzliche, um das die Schatten wehn,

Two extracts from *The unceasing.* Oratorio in three parts for soloists, mixed choir, boys' choir and orchestra. Music by Paul Hindemith

1931

I Song

Say farewell to early childhood
bright with summer, a quiet land,
wondering, fulfilled and graceful,
happy in a dreamer's hand.
Say farewell, you growing pilgrim,
over fields and sea and town,
thunderstorms can help to kindle
justice in a world cast down.
Say farewell to family fathers
teaching me to take this road,
acknowledging the planet's charter
and night's oppressive, chilling load.
From the morning to the evening
pictures slipping in the haze,
say farewell, cities receding
without a dream, without a grave.

II Choirs of men and boys

Men.

Then flesh proclaimed at every season:
nothing exists but greed and affirmation!

Boys:

Let us choose to take a different lesson:
struggle joins the ladder of creation.
Struggle, annihilating dreams of freedom
and pain, around which shadows congregate,

131

die Lechzenden, die aus zwei Bechern trinken,
und beide Becher sind voll Untergehn.

Des Menschen Gieriges, das Fraß und Paarung
als letzte Schreie durch die Welten ruft,
verwest an Fetten, Falten und Bejahrung,
und seine Fäulnis stößt es in die Gruft.

Das Leidende wird es erstreiten,
das Einsame, das Stille, das allein
die alten Mächte fühlt, die uns begleiten –:
und dieser Mensch wird unaufhörlich sein.

the thirsty ones who drink from pairs of beakers,
in both the beakers brims destructive fate.

Men:

Man's animal voracity for coupling
and fodder, final cries of the universe,
decays with age, obesity, joints rusting,
putrescence filling coffins in the hearse.

Boys:

Suffering will be consolidation's mainstay,
solitariness, and only peace
can feel the ancient powers about our pathway –:
and then the human being will not cease.

This translation restores Benn's original allocation of lines to the choirs of men and
boys alternately, as present in Hindemith's score also.

Dennoch die Schwerter halten

Der soziologische Nenner,
der hinter Jahrtausenden schlief,
heißt: ein paar große Männer
und die litten lief.

Heißt: ein paar schweigende Stunden
in Sils-Maria Wind,
Erfüllung ist schwer von Wunden,
wenn es Erfüllungen sind.

Heißt: ein paar sterbende Krieger
gequält und schattenblaß,
sie heute und morgen der Sieger –:
warum erschufst du das?

Heißt: Schlangen schlagen die Hauer,
das Gift, den Biß, den Zahn,
die Ecce-homo-Schauer
dem Mann in Blut und Bahn –

heißt: so viel Trümmer winken:
die Rassen wollen Ruh,
lasse dich doch versinken
dem nie Endenden zu –

und heißt dann: schweigen und walten,
wissend, daß sie zerfällt,
dennoch die Schwerter halten
vor die Stunde der Welt.

Hold the swords in defiance

1933

The sociological denominator,
from millennial sleep,
is: a few men were greater
and their suffering was deep.

Is: a few silent noons
in the Sils-Maria wind,
fulfilment is heavy with wounds,
if anything can be fulfilled.

Is: a few dying warriors,
tortured and shadow-pale,
as victors they are loftier –:
could you create them to fail?

Is: miners obliterate serpents,
their poison, bite and tooth,
but Ecce-homo burdens
for that man on his bloody path.

Is: so many ruins beckon:
the races yearn for rest,
sink down in the direction
of never-endingness –

and then is: manage in silence,
knowing that it will decay,
hold the swords in defiance
against the world's own day.

Nietzsche had a house in Sils-Maria, in the mountains in Engadine, Switzerland.

Am Brückenwehr

I

»Ich habe weit gedacht,
nun lasse ich die Dinge
und löse ihre Ringe
der neuen Macht.

Gelehnt am Brückenwehr –
die hellen Wasser rauschen,
die Elemente tauschen
sich hin und her.

Der Lauf ist schiefergrau,
der Ton der Urgesteine,
als noch das Land alleine
im Schichtenbau.

Des Sommers Agonie
gibt auch ein Rebgehänge,
Kelter- und Weingesänge
durchstreifen sie.

Wessen ist das und wer?
Dessen, der alles machte,
dessen, der es dann dachte
vom Ende her?

Ich habe weit gedacht,
ich lebte in Gedanken,
bis ihre Häupter sanken
vor welcher Macht?«

On the bridge

1934

I

My thoughts toiled hour on hour,
but now let things resurgent
release their native circles
to the new power.

I lean on the parapet –
brightly rushing water,
the elements out of order
are passionate.

The current grey as slate,
these the primal strata
as the land alone grew harder
building its fate.

Summer's agony
hangs vines on hillsides,
winepress singing sometimes
sounds magically.

Who owns it, who is he?
The one who made it happen
or the one who saw a pattern
finally?

My thoughts toiled hour on hour,
I lived as their creature
until their allegiance yielded
to what new power?

II

»»Vor keiner Macht zu sinken,
vor keinem Rausch zur Ruh,
du selbst bist Trank und Trinken,
der Denker, du.

Du bist ja nicht der Hirte
und ziehst nicht mit Schalmein,
wenn der, wie du, sich irrte,
ist nie Verzeihn.

Du bist ja nicht der Jäger
aus Megalith und Ur,
du bist der Formenpräger
der weißen Spur.

So viele sind vergangen
im Bach- und Brückenschein,
wer kennt nicht das Verlangen
zum Urgestein –:

Doch dir bestimmt: kein Werden,
du bleibst gebannt und bist
der Himmel und der Erden
Formalist.

Du kannst es keinem zeigen
und keinem du entfliehn,
du trägst durch Nacht und Schweigen
den Denker – ihn.‹«

II

'To no power bow and whimper,
let no draught put you to sleep,
you are drink and drinker,
the thinker, deep.

For you are not the shepherd
and eclogues are unused,
if he like you has erred,
he's not excused.

For you are not the hunter
of megalithic space,
you are the form-cutter
of the white race.

So many before you thronging
in the light of bridge and stream,
who does not know the longing
for the primal seam –:

Your fate: no transformations,
forever you're dismissed,
in heaven and earth your station's
a formalist.

You cannot ask for guidance,
not seek an interim,
you bear through night and silence
the thinker – him.'

III

»Doch wenn dann Stunden sind,
wo ohne Rang und Reue
das Alte und das Neue
zusammenrinnt,

wo ohne Unterschied
das Wasser und die Welle,
das Dunkle und das Helle
das eine Lied,

ein Lied, des Stimme rief
gegen Geschichtsgewalten
das in sich selbst Gestalten,
asiatisch tief –

ach, wenn die Stunden dann kommen
und dichter werden und mehr
Sommer und Jahre verglommen,
singt man am Brückenwehr:

laß mich noch einmal reich sein,
wie es die Jugend gedacht,
laß mich noch einmal weich sein
im Blumengeruch der Nacht,

nimm mir die Hölle, die Hülle,
die Form, den Formungstrieb,
gib mir die Tiefe, die Fülle,
die Schöpfung – gib!«

III

Yet if those hours arrive
when, random and unrepentant,
the historic and the present
coincide,

when undividedly
water and wave regardless,
sunlight, deepest darkness
in one song agree,

a song whose insistent breath
was against historic junctures
and for building internal structures
of Asiatic depth –

ah, if these hours are persistent,
grow denser and denser yet,
summers and years are more distant,
you sing at the parapet:

let me regain the riches
my youth had promised me,
let me hear softer whispers
in night's blossom filigree,

take my hell, my armour,
form and its urge to live,
give me depth, a harbour,
creation – give!

IV

»›Bist du auf Grate gestiegen,
sahst du die Gipfel klar:
Adler, die wirklichen, fliegen
schweigend und unfruchtbar.

Kürzer steht es in Früchten,
früher, daß es verblich,
nahe am Schöpfer züchten
wenige Arten sich.

Ewig schweigend das Blaue,
wer noch an Stimmen denkt,
hat schon den Blick, die Braue
wieder in Sehnsucht gesenkt.

Du aber dienst Gestalten
über dem Brückenwehr,
über den stumpfen Gewalten
Völker und Schnee und Meer:

formen, das ist deine Fülle,
der Rasse auferlegt,
formen, bis in die Hülle
die ganze Tiefe trägt,

die Hülle wird dann zeigen,
und keiner kann entfliehn,
daß Form und Tiefe Reigen,
durch den die Adler ziehn.‹«

IV

'From ascents death-defying
you've seen peaks in clarity,
eagles, real ones, flying
silently, barrenly.

The shorter the fruiting season,
the less a tree will succeed,
close to the creator
few new species breed.

The blue is eternally silent,
he who misses a voice
has dipped his gaze, his eyelid,
longing for the absent choice.

What you serve are structures
over the parapet,
over the dull conjunctures
of peoples, snow, sea and regret:

form-making is your harbour,
enjoined upon the race,
form-making, into armour
bearing depth with grace,

the armour will bear witness
which no-one can ignore
that form and depth are figures
through which the eagles soar.'

Valse triste

Verfeinerung, Abstieg, Trauer –
dem Wüten der Natur,
der Völker, der Siegesschauer
folgt eine andere Spur:
Verwerfen von Siegen und Thronen,
die große Szene am Nil,
wo der Feldherr der Pharaonen
den Liedern der Sklavin verfiel.

Durch den Isthmus, griechisch, die Wachen
Schleuder, Schilde und Stein
treibt im Zephyr ein Nachen
tieferen Meeren ein:
die Parthenongötter, die weißen,
ihre Zeiten, ihr Entstehn,
die schon Verfall geheißen
und den Hermenfrevel gesehn.

Verfeinerte Rinden, Blöße.
Rauschnah und todverfärbt
das Fremde, das Steile, die Größe,
die das Jahrhundert erbt,
getanzt aus Tempeln und Toren
schweigenden Einsamseins,
Erben und Ahnen verloren:
Niemandes –: Deins!

Getanzt vor den finnischen Schären –
Valse triste, der Träume Schoß,
Valse triste, nur Klinge gewähren
dies eine menschliche Los:
Rosen, die blühten und hatten,
und die Farben fließen ins Meer,
blau, tiefblau atmen die Schatten
und die Nacht verzögert so sehr.

Valse triste

1936

Refinement, absence, mourning –
after nature's rages
and man's triumphal warning
there follow different pages:
repudiate triumphs and rank;
the champion of Egypt's kings
seduced on the Nile's dark bank
by the song the slave-girl sings.

Past Greek cliffs rising sheer,
catapults, shields and sentries,
a skiff is blown by a zephyr
into far deeper seas:
what the Parthenon's white gods brought,
achieving even on their terms
but a falling-off, it was thought,
with the desecration of herms.

The cortex refined, they are naked.
Half-drunk, the colour of death,
the other, the steep, their fated
greatness the century's breath,
from silent cultic solitude
dancing through open doors,
no kinship bonds are renewed:
nobody's –: yours!

Danced under cliffs in Finland –
Valse triste, the womb of dreams,
Valse triste, only music granting
one favour for man, it seems:
the bloom and decay of the rose
as the colours flow into the sea,
as blue, deep blue breathe shadows
and night is still longing to be.

Getanzt vor dem einen, dem selten
blutenden Zaubergerät,
das sich am Saume der Welten
öffnet: Identität –:
einmal in Versen beschworen,
einmal im Marmor des Steins,
einmal zu Klängen erkoren:
Niemandes –: Seins!

Niemandes –: beuge, beuge
dein Haupt in Dorn und Schlehn,
in Blut und Wunden zeuge
die Form, das Auferstehn,
gehüllt in Tücher, als Labe
den Schwamm mit Essig am Rohr,
so tritt aus den Steinen, dem Grabe
Auferstehung hervor.

The machine that can bleed to your dancing,
that magical entity
at the hem of the cosmos advancing
alone: identity –:
once it was summoned in cantos,
once it was chiselled by Phidias,
once it sang in corantos:
nobody's – his!

Nobody's – bow, surrounded
by blackthorn's sharp rejection,
o head in blood sore wounded,
make form and resurrection,
a vinegar sponge libation,
in linen shrouds of pain,
thus from annihilation
you can rise again.

Tag, der den Sommer endet

Tag, der den Sommer endet,
Herz, dem das Zeichen fiel:
die Flammen sind versendet,
die Fluten und das Spiel.

Die Bilder werden blasser,
entrücken sich der Zeit,
wohl spiegelt sie noch ein Wasser,
doch auch dies Wasser ist weit.

Du hast eine Schlacht erfahren,
trägst noch ihr Stürmen, ihr Fliehn,
indessen die Schwärme, die Scharen,
die Heere weiterziehn.

Rosen und Waffenspanner,
Pfeile und Flammen weit –:
die Zeichen sinken, die Banner –:
Unwiederbringlichkeit.

Day, when summer ended

Day, when summer ended,
heart, whose omen came:
the flames are all expended,
the high tides, the bright game.

The images grow dimmer,
their leave from time they take,
their reflection may still glimmer
in someone's distant lake.

You've been through a violent battle,
still feel its attacks and retreats,
while the swarms of human cattle
sweep on to further defeats.

Far off are roses, bowmen,
arrows and flames all fall;
the banners sink, the omen –
time beyond recall.

Auf deine Lider senk ich Schlummer

Auf deine Lider senk ich Schlummer,
auf deine Lippen send ich Kuß,
indessen ich die Nacht, den Kummer,
den Traum alleine tragen muß.

Um deine Züge leg ich Trauer,
um deine Züge leg ich Lust,
indes die Nacht, die Todesschauer
weben allein durch meine Brust.

Du, die zu schwach, um tief zu geben,
du, die nicht trüge, wie ich bin –
drum muß ich abends mich erheben
und sende Kuß und Schlummer hin.

I give your lids the gift of slumber

1936

I give your lids the gift of slumber
and on your lips a kiss send down,
while only me night's griefs encumber,
and I must bear the dream alone.

About your features I lay mourning,
to all your features bliss impart,
while I alone must bear till dawning
death's shudders weaving round my heart.

You, too weak to give profoundly,
would never bear me being like this –
and so I rise and leave you soundly
slumbering, and send a kiss.

Das Ganze

Im Taumel war ein Teil, ein Teil in Tränen,
in manchen Stunden war ein Schein und mehr,
in diesen Jahren war das Herz, in jenen
waren die Stürme – wessen Stürme – wer?

Niemals im Glücke, selten mit Begleiter,
meistens verschleiert, da es tief geschah,
und alle Ströme liefen wachsend weiter
und alles Außen ward nur innen nah.

Der sah dich hart, der andre sah dich milder,
der wie es ordnet, der wie es zerstört,
doch was sie sahn, das waren halbe Bilder,
da dir das Ganze nur allein gehört.

Im Anfang war es heller, was du wolltest
und zielte vor und war dem Glauben nah,
doch als du dann erblicktest, was du solltest,
was auf das Ganze steinern niedersah,

da war es kaum ein Glanz und kaum ein Feuer,
in dem dein Blick, der letzte, sich verfing:
ein nacktes Haupt, in Blut, ein Ungeheuer,
an dessen Wimper eine Träne hing.

The whole

1936

One part intoxication, tears the other,
with promise in several hours and more in few,
in certain years the heart was master, thunder
raged at other times – whose thunder – who?

Never happy, rarely with companions,
camouflaged mostly, things happening at depth,
and all the rivers flowed with growing passions,
inside only approaching outer breadth.

One frowned at you, another's look was gentler,
one found order, one destruction shown,
yet what they saw was always half the picture
because the whole belongs to you alone.

At first, you had intended something brighter,
close to belief, you set yourself that goal,
yet when you saw you had to be a fighter,
and what stony eye stared down upon the whole,

hardly a glint was left for fire to ponder
whether to look before you disappear:
a naked head, covered in blood, a monster,
from whose lashes at last there hung a tear.

Turin

»Ich Laufe auf zerrissenen Sohlen«,
schrieb dieses große Weltgenie
in seinem letzten Brief – dann holen
sie ihn nach Jena – Psychiatrie.

Ich kann mir keine Bücher kaufen,
ich sitze in den Librairien:
Notizen – dann nach Aufschnitt laufen: –
das sind die Tage von Turin.

Indes Europas Edelfäule
an Pan, Bayreuth und Epsom sog,
umarmte er zwei Droschkengäule,
bis ihn sein Wirt nach Hause zog.

Turin (I)

1936

'The soles of my shoes are torn to pieces'
wrote this world genius finally,
no more letters, then his keepers
take him to Jena – psychiatry.

Buying books is quite beyond me,
I sit around in a librairie,
make notes – and grab charcuterie: –
his Turin days, reportedly.

While Europe's rotten ruling classes
sucked Pau and Epsom and Bayreuth's foam,
he hugged two wretched cabman's horses
until his landlord took him home.

Nietzsche suffered a mental breakdown in Turin in 1889.

Am Saum des nordischen Meers

Melancholie der Seele –
ein Haus, eine Stimme singt,
es ist ein Haus ohne Fehle,
wo englisch money klingt,
ein Heim von heiteren Losen
geselligen Verkehrs,
vier Wände aus Silber und Rosen
am Saum des nordischen Meers.

Sie singt – und die hohe Klasse
der Nord- und English-Mann,
die gierige weiße Rasse
hält den Atem an,
auch die Ladies, die erlauchten,
geschmückt mit Pelz und Stein
und den Perlen, den ertauchten
um die Inseln von Bahrein.

Die Stimme singt – ohne Fehle,
fremde Worte sind im Raum:
»ruhe in Frieden, Seele,
die vollendet süßen Traum –«
vollendet –! und alle trinken
die Schubertsche Litanei
und die Räuberwelten versinken
von Capetown bis Shanghai.

Geschmuggelt, gebrannt, geschunden
in Jurten und Bambuszelt,
die Peitsche durch Niggerwunden,
die Dollars durchs Opiumfeld –:
die hohe Rasse aus Norden,
die abendländische Pracht
im Raum ist still geworden –
aus die Mythe der Macht!

On the edge of the Baltic Sea

1936

The soul's melancholia –
a house, a Schubert Lied,
a house beyond well-chosen,
English cash guaranteed,
gambling den for posers
and high society,
partitions of silver and roses
on the edge of the Baltic Sea.

She sings – and in its majesty
the Nordic and English elite,
with all the white race's voracity
holds its collective breath,
the ladies too, the insiders,
with sables and a diamond chain
and pearls retrieved by divers
from the islands near Bahrain.

The voice – beyond well-chosen,
singing in a foreign tongue:
'Peace to the soul in token
when its suffering way is done – '
done – and all are drinking
Schubert's Litanei,
and the venal worlds are sinking
from Capetown to Shanghai.

Smuggled, branded and broken
in yourts and bamboo shacks,
niggers' backs whipped open,
dollars grow opium stacks –:
the Nordic race defiant,
the West's triumphant hour:
the room has fallen silent –
ended the myth of power.

Fern, fern aus Silber und Rosen
das Haus und die Stimme singt
die Lieder, die grenzenlosen,
die ein anderes Volk ihr bringt,
die machen die Macht zur Beute
einer anderen Mächtigkeit:
der Mensch ist ewig und heute
fernen Himmeln geweiht.

Englische – finnische Wände –:
Häuser – die Stimme singt:
Germany ohne Ende,
wenn german song erklingt,
dann ist es ohne Fehle
und gibt seinen Söhnen Ruh –
Melancholie der Seele
der weißen Rasse, du.

Far, far from roses and silver
the house with the singing voice,
what limitless Lieder deliver
a different people's choice,
they make of power the plunder
of a different potency:
man is eternal and under
distant heavens today.

English – Finnish partitions –:
houses – hear the voice sing:
Deutschland's endless mission
when a German Lied takes wing,
then it's beyond well-chosen
and gives to its sons their due –
the soul's melancholia
and the white race's, you.

Einsamer nie

Einsamer nie als im August:
Erfüllungsstunde – im Gelände
die roten und die goldenen Brände
doch wo ist deiner Gärten Lust?

Die Seen hell, die Himmel weich,
die Äcker rein und glänzen leise,
doch wo sind Sieg und Siegsbeweise
aus dem von dir vertretenen Reich?

Wo alles sich durch Glück beweist
und tauscht den Blick und tauscht die Ringe
im Weingeruch, im Rausch der Dinge –:
dienst du dem Gegenglück, dem Geist.

The loneliest time

1936

August is the loneliest time,
hour of fulfilment – in country havens
red and golden conflagrations,
your gardens, though, are anodyne.

The lakes are bright, the skies are pale,
the fields are pure and softly glitter,
but why do the deeds and proofs of a victor
in the kingdom that you stood for fail?

While joy for achievement is unconfined
in exchange of glances and rings,
in wine's bouquet, delirious things –:
you serve the counter-joy, the mind.

Wer allein ist

Wer allein ist, ist auch im Geheimnis,
immer steht er in der Bilder Flut,
ihrer Zeugung, ihrer Keimnis,
selbst die Schatten tragen ihre Glut.

Trächtig ist er jeder Schichtung
denkerisch erfüllt und aufgespart,
mächtig ist er der Vernichtung
allem Menschlichen, das nährt und paart.

Ohne Rührung sieht er, wie die Erde
eine andere ward, als ihm begann,
nicht mehr Stirb und nicht mehr Werde:
formstill sieht ihn die Vollendung an.

He who's alone

1936

He who's alone is party to the secret,
always surrounded by images in flow,
their conception, their growing seed-head,
even shadows reflect their glow.

He is pregnant with the chain of creation,
fulfilled in mind and saved by luck,
he has the power of annihilation
over humanity that couples and gives suck.

Without emotion, he sees the world as something
grown different in the interim,
no more Die, no more Becoming:
perfection, form-immutable, looks at him.

The penultimate line is a reference to Goethe's poem '*Selige Sehnsucht*' (1814), which
ends with the lines: 'Und so lang du das nicht hast,/ dieses: Stirb und werde!/ bist
du nur ein trüber Gast/ auf der dunklen Erde' (And as long as you do not have that:
Die and become! you are only a gloomy guest on the dark earth).

Die Gefährten

Bis du dich selbst vergißt,
so treiben es die Mächte,
im Labyrinth der Schächte
verwandelt bist.

Ein wechselndes Gefühl,
spärliche Fackelbrände,
du tastest und die Wände
sind fremd und kühl.

Einsamer Gang wie nie,
die letzten, die Bewährten
der Jahre, die Gefährten
du ließest sie,

Für wen und welche Macht?
Du siehst der Ufer keines
und nur das Leid ist deines,
das sie entfacht,

Und was sie sagen will,
fühlst du vielleicht nach Jahren,
doch eh du es erfahren,
ist der Gefährte still.

The companions

1937

Until you your self forget,
the powers amended their deadline,
in shafts labyrinthine
on change you're set.

A feeling malleable,
sporadic flaming torches,
you grope, the walls and corners
are strange and cool.

Never so lonely a track,
your old friends you abandon,
your trusted companions,
you turned your back,

for whom and what new power?
No shore on your horizon,
the bands of suffering tighten
in the given hour,

and what it may intend
you may learn in a decade,
long before then your comrade
has reached the silent end.

Du trägst

Du trägst die Züge der Heloten
und lebst von Griffen mancher Art,
ein Außensein ist dem verboten,
der das Gedicht im Keim bewahrt.

Du kannst dein Wesen keinem nennen,
verschlossen jedem Bund und Brauch,
du kannst dich nur im Wort erkennen
und geben dich und trauern auch.

Gefragt nach deinem Tun und Meinen,
nach deinen Ernten, deiner Saat,
kannst du die Frage nur verneinen
und deuten auf geheime Tat.

You bear

1937

You bear the features of the helots
and live by tricks of various kinds,
an outward life in the worldly desert's
forbidden to poets with a seed inside.

You cannot bare your soul to others,
closed off from juncture everywhere,
the word alone reveals your colours,
you live in it and know despair.

Questions about your life and opinions,
about good harvests, grain and weeds,
a disconcerting answer's given,
hinting there may be secret deeds.

So still –

Es würden Vögel, wanderweit,
sich ruhig und in breiten Massen
in ihren Ästen niederlassen:
so still ist die Unendlichkeit.

Auch unerbittlich ist das nicht!
sie spinnen und die Spindeln rauschen
und Lachesis und Klotho tauschen
den Rocken und die Wolleschicht.

Auch ob es wachte, ob es schlief,
ob es Gestaltung zeigt und Weiten –:
in Schöpfungen, in Dunkelheiten
sind es die Götter, fremd und tief.

So tranquil

Migrating birds from far away,
huge flocks as one to order wheeling
would settle in its boughs at evening:
so tranquil is infinity.

And not inexorable, you ask?
they spin, and rearrange the spindles,
and Lachesis and Klotho mingle
distaff and wheel in a single task.

Whether in waking or in sleep,
whether construction, breadth of vision –:
in creation, in dark fruition
gods are working, strange and deep.

Wenn dir am Ende der Reise

»Wenn dir am Ende der Reise
Erde und Wolke verrinnt,
sie nur noch Laute, leise,
vom Himmel gefallene sind,

und nur noch Farben, getönte
aus einem wechselnden Reich,
nicht bittere, nicht versöhnte,
Austausch alles und gleich,

wenn dir die Blicke nach oben
und dir die Blicke zu Tal
schweigend das Nämliche loben,
schweigend die nämliche Qual,

schliessen sich die Gesichte
über der lastenden Flut:
ach, die vielen Gewichte,
doch die Waage, sie ruht.«

If at your journey's limit

1939

'If at your journey's limit
earth and clouds ally,
are nothing more than a whisper
fallen from the sky,

colours deep, transparent,
from a different palette compiled,
give and take in balance,
neither bitter nor reconciled,

when your upward glances
and the other kind
silently praise the same answers,
identical sufferings find,

visions will found a conclusion
after the flood obsessed,
ah, what weights in confusion,
but the scales will be at rest.'

Dann gliederten sich die Laute

»Dann gliederten sich die Laute,
erst war nur Chaos und Schrei,
fremde Sprachen, uralte,
vergangene Stimmen dabei.

Die eine sagte: gelitten,
die zweite sagte: geweint,
die dritte: keine Bitten
nützen, der Gott verneint.

eine gellende: in Räuschen
aus Kraut, aus Säften, aus Wein –:
vergessen, vergessen, täuschen
dich selbst und jeden, der dein.

eine andere: keine Zeichen,
keine Weisung und kein Sinn –,
im Wechsel Blüten und Leichen
und Geier drüber hin.

eine andere: Müdigkeiten,
eine Schwäche ohne Mass –
und nur laute Hunde, die streiten,
erhalten Knochen und Frass.

Doch dann in zögernder Wende
und die Stimmen hielten sich an –,
sprach eine: ich sehe am Ende
einen grossen schweigenden Mann.

Der weiss, dass keinen Bitten
jemals ein Gott erscheint,
er hat es ausgelitten,
er weiss, der Gott verneint.

Then the sounds created a structure

1939

'Then the sounds created a structure
after pure chaos and cries,
foreign tongues, now rusting,
vanished voices and sighs.

One said: ah, I have suffered,
the second: I have shed tears,
the third: let no prayers be offered,
God has been deaf for years.

One very noisily, drunken
with weed, with juice, with wine:
forgotten, forgotten, corruption
for everyone, yours and mine.

Another: no clear, no Morses,
no instruction, no good sense –
alternately blossoms and corpses
and vultures in flocks on the fence.

Another: pure exhaustion,
the weakness of the have-nots,
and only dogs by extortion
win their bones and slops.

But then with faltering diction
the voices stopped as they began,
one said: I can see in the distance
a tall and silent man.

He knows that it's no use praying
for God to appear below,
from experience heartbreaking
he knows that God says no.

173

Er sieht den Menschen vergehen
im Raub- und Rassenraum,
er lässt die Welt geschehen
und bildet seinen Traum.«

He sees how people lose value,
only theft and race grab esteem,
he lets the world continue
and shapes his private dream.'

Wer Wiederkehr in Träumen weiss

»Wer Wiederkehr in Träumen weiss,
den dämmt kein sterbliches Gefüge,
dem aufersteht der alte Kreis,
die Sphinxallee, die Sagenzüge.

Starben die Götter? Nein, sie leben her!
Sie haben noch ihr Tier und ihre Reben
und nehmen Opfer über und vergeben,
wohnen im Hain und wandeln auf dem Meer.

Das Auge stirbt nur, das sich über sah,
das seinen Blick ins Unbegrenzte rollte,
das sich vor dem nicht senkte, was geschah
und still in jedem wirkt und wirken sollte.

Wer sich begrenzt, vollendet seine Spur,
wer trägt, damit es nicht das Sein verletze,
verzögernd sich, den sammelt die Natur,
den Schweigenden erhalten die Gesetze.«

He who dreams the dead recur

1940

'He who dreams the dead recur
cannot be caged by mortal limits,
rising again: the old milieu,
cultic processions, the road of sphinxes.

Did the gods perish? No, here they relive!
Each has his totem and his vineyard,
they favour sacrifices and forgive,
live in their groves and maybe visit Scylla.

The eye that dies will once have seen too much,
turning its gaze towards the infinite,
not looking away before the silent judge
of history, what is and is not fit.

Who limits himself can thus fulfil his due,
who holds himself aloof from what may occur,
nature renews him in her retinue,
because the silent man the laws preserve.'

Monolog

Den Darm mit Rotz genährt, das Hirn mit Lügen –
erwählte Völker Narren eines Clowns,
in Späße, Sternelesen, Vogelzug
den eigenen Unrat deutend! Sklaven –
aus kalten Ländern und aus glühenden,
immer mehr Sklaven, ungezieferschwere,
hungernde, peitschenüberschwungene Haufen:
dann schwillt das Eigene an, der eigene Flaum,
der grindige, zum Barte des Propheten!

Ach, Alexander und Olympias Sproß
das wenigste! Sie zwinkern Hellesponte
und schäumen Asien! Aufgetriebenes, Blasen
mit Vorhut, Günstlingen, verdeckten Staffeln,
daß keiner sticht! Günstlinge: – gute Plätze
für Ring- und Rechtsgeschehn! Wenn keiner sticht!
Günstlinge, Lustvolk, Binden, breite Bänder –
mit breiten Bändern flattert Traum und Welt:
Klumpfüße sehn die Stadien zerstört,
Stinktiere treten die Lupinenfelder,
weil sie der Duft am eigenen irre macht:
nur Stoff vom After! – Fette
verfolgen die Gazelle,
die windeseilige, das schöne Tier!
Hier kehrt das Maß sich um:
die Pfütze prüft den Quell, der Wurm die Elle,
die Kröte spritzt dem Veilchen in den Mund
– Halleluja! – und wetzt den Bauch im Kies:
die Paddentrift als Mahnmal der Geschichte!
Die Ptolemäerspur als Gaunerzinke,
die Ratte kommt als Labsal gegen Pest.
Meuchel besingt den Mord. Spitzel locken
aus Psalmen Unzucht.

Monologue

1941

The gut fed with snot, the brain with lies –
the chosen peoples fooled by a clown,
from jokes, astrology, the flight of birds
interpreting one's own excrement!
Slaves, from freezing and from burning lands,
slaves upon slaves, heaps heavy with vermin,
starving, cowering under cracking whips:
and then one's scabby trichome starts to sprout,
one's very own. By the Prophet's Beard!

Ah, Olympia and Alexander's offspring
the least of it! They twinkle Hellesponts
and remove the froth from Asia! Distensions, blisters
with privileges, favourites, hidden squadrons,
no stabs in the back! Favourites – good seats
for wrestling and legal struggles! No stabs, please!
Favourites, entertainers, sashes, banners –
broad banners fluttering in dream and fact:
club-feet see the stadia destroyed,
skunks trample down the fields of lupins
because the scent confuses them about their own:
the arse the only provider! – Fatties
hunt gazelles,
the beautiful animal that runs like the wind!
All measure turns in reverse:
the puddle checks the source, the worm the ell,
the toad squirts in the violet's mouth –
Hallelujah! – and whets its belly in gravel:
the trail of slime as time's memorial!
The Ptolemies' track a chalk-mark left for thieves,
the rat arrives as easement in the plague.
The plotter praises murder. Secret agents
entice unchastity from psalms.

Und diese Erde lispelt mit dem Mond,
dann schürzt sie sich ein Maifest um die Hüfte,
dann läßt sie Rosen durch, dann schmort sie Korn,
läßt den Vesuv nicht spein, läßt nicht die Wolke
zu Lauge werden, die der Tiere Abart,
die dies erlistet, sticht und niederbrennt –
ach, dieser Erde Frucht- und Rosenspiel
ist heimgestellt der Wucherung des Bösen,
der Hirne Schwamm, der Kehle Lügensprenkeln
der obgenannten Art – die maßverkehrte!

Sterben heißt, dies alles ungelöst verlassen,
die Bilder ungesichert, die Träume
im Riß der Welten stehn und hungern lassen –
doch Handeln heißt, die Niedrigkeit bedienen,
der Schande Hilfe leihn, die Einsamkeit,
die große Lösung der Gesichte,
das Traumverlangen hinterhältig fällen
für Vorteil, Schmuck, Beförderungen, Nachruf,
indes das Ende, taumelnd wie ein Falter,
gleichgültig wie ein Sprengstück nahe ist
und anderen Sinn verkündet –

– Ein Klang, ein Bogen, fast ein Sprung aus Bläue
stieß eines Abends durch den Park hervor,
darin ich stand –: ein Lied,
ein Abriß nur, drei hingeworfene Noten
und füllte so den Raum und lud so sehr
die Nacht, den Garten mit Erscheinungen voll
und schuf die Welt und bettete den Nacken
mir in das Strömende, die trauervolle
erhabene Schwäche der Geburt des Seins –:
ein Klang, ein Bogen nur –: Geburt des Seins –
ein Bogen nur und trug das Maß zurück,
und alles schloß es ein: die Tat, die Träume …

Aus einem Kranz scharlachener Gehirne,
des Blüten der verstreuten Fiebersaat

And this earth lisps about the moon,
then girds a Mayday round its hips,
then lets roses through, and then brews Korn,
stops incendiaries spitting, stops the cloud
becoming caustic, stinging, burning down
to the degenerate beasts who plotted this,
ah, this earth's play of fruit and roses
delivered up to evil's rampant growth,
mental wipeouts, voices sprinkling lies
of the kind described – inverted measure!

Dying means abandoning all this
unsolved, the pictures unsecured, the dreams
left to starve, standing in the cleft of worlds –
but acting means to service infamy,
aiding disgrace, suffering loneliness,
the great solution to your visions,
longing to dream stifled in secret
for profit, decoration, promotion, fame,
meanwhile the end, reeling like a butterfly,
indifferently approaches like a bomb,
announces meaning of a different kind –

A sound, a bow, almost a leap from blueness
one evening startled me, spreading through the park
I stood in – a song,
a sketch at most, three scribbled notes,
still it filled all space, still charged the night,
the garden to the brim with apparitions,
created the world and made a pillow for me
in the stream of things, the grief-stricken,
sublime weakness of the birth of being –:
only a sound, a bow –: the birth of being –
only a bow, and yet it brought back measure,
everything enfolding: the act, the dreams …

Out of a ring of scarlet brains, alone,
holding themselves aloof from the blossoming

sich einzeln halten, nur einander:
»unbeugsam in der Farbe« und »ausgezähnt
am Saum das letzte Haar«, »gefeilt in Kälte«
zurufen, gesalzene Laken des Urstoffs:
hier geht Verwandlung aus: der Tiere Abart
wird faulen, daß für sie das Wort Verwesung
zu sehr nach Himmeln riecht – schon streichen
die Geier an, die Falken hungern schon –!

of the scattered fever-seed, to one another
calling: 'stubbornly true to colour', 'the last
hair tweezered from the hem', 'polished in coldness',
salted strips woven from primal matter:
here transformation starts. Degenerate beasts
will rot away, for them the word decay
has too much scent of heaven in it – already
vultures congregate, the hawks are circling – !

Gedichte

Im Namen dessen, der die Stunden spendet,
im Schicksal des Geschlechts, dem du gehört,
hast du fraglosen Aug's den Blick gewendet
in eine Stunde, die den Blick zerstört,
die Dinge dringen kalt in die Gesichte
und reißen sich der alten Bindung fort,
es gibt nur ein Begegnen: im Gedichte
die Dinge mystisch bannen durch das Wort.

Am Steingeröll der großen Weltruine,
dem Ölberg, wo die tiefste Seele litt,
vorbei am Posilipp der Anjouine,
dem Stauferblut und ihrem Racheschritt:
ein neues Kreuz, ein neues Hochgerichte,
doch eine Stätte ohne Blut und Strang,
sie schwört in Strophen, urteilt im Gedichte,
die Spindeln drehen still: die Parze sang.

Im Namen dessen, der die Stunden spendet,
erahnbar nur, wenn er vorüberzieht
an einem Schatten, der das Jahr vollendet,
doch unausdeutbar bleibt das Stundenlied –
ein Jahr am Steingeröll der Weltgeschichte,
Geröll der Himmel und Geröll der Macht,
und nun die Stunde, deine: im Gedichte
das Selbstgespräch des Leides und der Nacht.

Poems

1941

In the name of him by whom the hours are given,
following your blood-line's destined ways,
you chose to turn your eye, unbidden,
into a time which shatters every gaze,
where things press coldly in for you to see them
and tear the bonds tradition had preferred,
there is one meeting only: in the poem
mystic conjuration with the word.

Past rubble from the world disasters, go
where the deepest soul suffered in Olivet,
past the maid of Anjou's Posilipo
and where the Hohenstaufens spread their net,
to a new cross and execution time,
but a bloodless scaffold with no torturers' gang,
with oaths in stanzas, sentences in rhyme,
the spindles turn in silence, the Parca sang.

In the name of him by whom the hours are given,
sensed faintly only when he passes by
because a shadow ends the year half-hidden,
though hours still sing their song inscrutably –
a year beside the rubble of conflicts growing,
rubble of heavens, rubble of human might,
and now the hour, your hour: in the poem
the monologue of suffering and of night.

185

Verse

Wenn je die Gottheit, tief und unerkenntlich
in einem Wesen auferstand und sprach,
so sind es Verse, da unendlich
in ihnen sich die Qual der Herzen brach;
die Herzen treiben längst im Strom der Weite,
die Strophe aber streift von Mund zu Mund,
sie übersteht die Völkerstreite
und überdauert Macht und Mörderbund.

Auch Lieder, die ein kleiner Stamm gesungen,
Indianer, Yakis mit Aztekenwort,
längst von der Gier des weißen Manns bezwungen,
leben als stille Ackerstrophen fort:
»komm, Kindlein, komm im Schmuck der Siebenähren,
komm, Kindlein, komm in Kett' und Jadestein,
der Maisgott stellt ins Feld, uns zu ernähren,
den Rasselstab und du sollst Opfer sein –«

Das große Murmeln dem, der seine Fahrten
versenkt und angejocht dem Geiste lieh,
Einhauche, Aushauch, Weghauch – Atemarten
indischer Büßungen und Fakirie –
das große Selbst, der Alltraum, einem jeden
ins Herz gegeben, der sich schweigend weiht
hält sich in Psalmen und in Veden
und spottet alles Tuns und trotzt der Zeit.

Zwei Welten stehn in Spiel und Widerstreben,
allein der Mensch ist nieder, wenn er schwankt,
er kann vom Augenblick nicht leben,
obwohl er sich dem Augenblicke dankt;
die Macht vergeht im Abschaum ihrer Tücken,
indes ein Vers der Völker Träume baut,
die sie der Niedrigkeit entrücken,
Unsterblichkeit im Worte und im Laut.

Verses

If ever the godhead, deep, of unknown meaning,
in a single being lived again and spoke,
then verses were the vessel, reaching
the bounds of anguish in the heart that broke;
men's hearts have long been tossed on widening waters,
from mouth to mouth a strophe may migrate,
it sees past international forces
and outlives power and the league of hate.

Songs even, from voices of a vanished nation,
Indians, Yakis in an Aztec tongue,
enslaved and yoked long since by white predation,
live on, in quiet farmers' spells restrung:
'come, my child, come in cornstalks seven,
come, my child, in jade from paradise,
the maize god brings the rattle-staffs together
to feed us, you shall be the sacrifice – '

The murmured prayers to him whose journey deepened,
lending them to others to set the spirit free,
inhale, exhale, blow sharply – kinds of breathing
for Hindu penitents and devotees –
the greater self, the dream of cosmic union
in reach of every pious, silent heart,
in psalms and vedas in profusion,
mocks action, sings as time-defying art.

In play are two worlds set in opposition,
and man alone is lost in faltering ranks,
he cannot live in the moment's prison,
however much it earns his fleeting thanks;
night dissolves in the scum its deceits engender,
a verse can build the dreams of polity
which give a glimpse of something better:
in words and sounds is immortality.

Ein Wort

Ein Wort, ein Satz –: aus Chiffern steigen
erkanntes Leben, jäher Sinn,
die Sonne steht, die Sphären schweigen
und alles ballt sich zu ihm hin.

Ein Wort – ein Glanz, ein Flug, ein Feuer,
ein Flammenwurf, ein Sternenstrich –
und wieder Dunkel, ungeheuer,
im leeren Raum um Welt und Ich.

A word

A word, a sentence – out of ciphers
climb life untangled, sudden sense,
the sun stands still, the spheres quieten,
all things about that point condense.

A word – a flash, a fire, flamethrower,
flight, a shooting star of pain –
then dark inexorably taking over
in the space round world and self again.

Abschied

Du füllst mich an wie Blut die frische Wunde
und rinnst hernieder seine dunkle Spur,
du dehnst dich aus wie Nacht in jener Stunde,
da sich die Matte färbt zur Schattenflur,
du blühst wie Rosen schwer in Gärten allen,
du Einsamkeit aus Alter und Verlust,
du Überleben, wenn die Träume fallen,
zuviel gelitten und zuviel gewußt.

Entfremdet früh dem Wahn der Wirklichkeiten,
versagend sich der schnell gegebenen Welt,
ermüdet von dem Trug der Einzelheiten,
da keine sich dem tiefen Ich gesellt;
nun aus der Tiefe selbst, durch nichts zu rühren,
und die kein Wort und Zeichen je verrät,
mußt du dein Schweigen nehmen, Abwärtsführen
zu Nacht und Trauer und den Rosen spät.

Manchmal noch denkst du dich –: die eigene Sage –:
das warst du doch – ? ach, wie du dich vergaßt!
war das dein Bild? war das nicht deine Frage,
dein Wort, dein Himmelslicht, das du besaßt?
Mein Wort, mein Himmelslicht, dereinst besessen,
mein Wort, mein Himmelslicht, zerstört, vertan –
wem das geschah, der muß sich wohl vergessen
und rührt nicht mehr die alten Stunden an.

Ein letzter Tag –: spätglühend, weite Räume,
ein Wasser führt dich zu entrücktem Ziel,
ein hohes Licht umströmt die alten Bäume
und schafft im Schatten sich ein Widerspiel,
von Früchten nichts, aus Ähren keine Krone
und auch nach Ernten hat er nicht gefragt –
er spielt sein Spiel, und fühlt sein Licht und ohne
Erinnern nieder – alles ist gesagt.

Departure

1941

You fill me up as blood the laceration
and run down the track its darkness leaves,
like night you spread in tardy variation
where the fading hillside colours shadow sheaves,
you flower like heavy roses in every garden,
you, solitude from bearing loss and age,
you, still surviving when our dreams dishearten,
suffering and knowledge too often on your page.

Early estranged from reality's illusion,
denying yourself the quickly proffered world,
exhausted by the details in confusion
of which not one around the deep self uncurled;
now from that depth itself that none can fathom,
forever yet to word or sign unknown,
you needs must take your silence, in the cavern
of night and grief and roses overblown.

Sometimes you reflect –: your self-expression –:
and was that really you – ? a memory lapse!
was that your image? was that not your question,
your word, your light of heaven, your own perhaps?
My word, my light of heaven, once my possession,
my word, my light of heaven, squandered, destroyed –
whoever had such a fate must learn his lesson:
forget yourself, old hours are to avoid.

A final day –: late-glowing, open spaces,
flowing water leads you to a distant shore,
exalted light streams through the tree-filled places,
in counterplay with shadows making more,
nowhere are fruits, no coronet of seed-heads,
no harvest-home for him, of questions not a shred –
he plays his game, he feels his light, to reed-beds
he sinks without remembering – all is said.

Verlorenes Ich

Verlorenes Ich, zersprengt von Stratosphären,
Opfer des Ion –: Gamma-Strahlen-Lamm –
Teilchen und Feld –: Unendlichkeitschimären
auf deinem grauen Stein von Notre-Dame.

Die Tage gehn dir ohne Nacht und Morgen,
die Jahre halten ohne Schnee und Frucht
bedrohend das Unendliche verborgen –
die Welt als Flucht.

Wo endest du, wo lagerst du, wo breiten
sich deine Sphären an – Verlust, Gewinn –:
ein Spiel von Bestien: Ewigkeiten,
an ihren Gittern fliehst du hin.

Der Bestienblick: die Sterne als Kaldaunen,
der Dschungeltod als Seins- und Schöpfungsgrund,
Mensch, Völkerschlachten, Katalaunen
hinab den Bestienschlund.

Die Welt zerdacht. Und Raum und Zeiten
und was die Menschheit wob und wog,
Funktion nur von Unendlichkeiten –
die Mythe log.

Woher, wohin – nicht Nacht, nicht Morgen,
kein Evoë, kein Requiem,
du möchtest dir ein Stichwort borgen –
allein bei wem?

Ach, als sich alle einer Mitte neigten
und auch die Denker nur den Gott gedacht,
sie sich den Hirten und dem Lamm verzweigten,
wenn aus dem Kelch das Blut sie rein gemacht,

Lost I

Lost I, whom stratospheres have blown to pieces,
I ionised – I radiation's lamb –
particle, field –: eternal gargoyle faces
across your darkened stone of Notre Dame.

The years pass by you, harvestless, snowless,
the days that have no morning and no night;
their constant threat hides only endlessness –
the world as flight.

Where is your end, your bivouac, where skies
to let your spheres unfurl – losses, gains –
a game for beasts: eternities,
and you fly past their sealed domains.

What the beasts see: stars as dripping entrails,
life and creation red in tooth and claw;
man, empires, Catalaunian fields
crammed down the bestial maw.

Thought self-destroyed. And space, and time
and all that man achieved and why
a function of infinities, no more –
the myth a lie.

Whither, whence – not night, not morning,
no evoe, no requiem,
no proverbs worthy of recalling –
no help from them.

Alas, when all was uniformly centred
and even thinkers only thought of God,
their hardest option between lamb and shepherd,
once the chalice had given them the nod,

und alle rannen aus der einen Wunde,
brechen das Brot, das jeglicher genoß –
o ferne zwingende erfüllte Stunde,
die einst auch das verlorne Ich umschloß.

then from one wound their common blood was falling
and they broke bread together, firm and true,
o distant sweetly fulfilled, compelling dawning
that once embraced all men, the lost I too.

Nachzeichnung

I

O jene Jahre! Der Morgen grünes Licht,
auch die noch nicht gefegten Lusttrottoire –
der Sommer schrie von Ebenen in der Stadt
und sog an einem Horn,
das sich von oben füllte.

Lautlose Stunde. Wässrige Farben
eines hellgrünen Aug's verdünnten Strahls,
Bilder aus diesem Zaubergrün, gläserne Reigen:
Hirten und Weiher, eine Kuppel, Tauben –
gewoben und gesandt, erglänzt, erklungen –,
verwandelbare Wolken eines Glücks!

So standest du vor Tag: die Spring-
brunnen noch ohne Perlen, tatenlos
Gebautes und die Steige; die Häuser
verschlossen, du *erschufst*
den Morgen, jasminene Frühe,
sein Jauchzen, uranfänglich
sein Strahl – noch ohne Ende – o jene Jahre!

Ein Unauslöschliches im Herzen,
Ergänzungen vom Himmel und der Erde;
Zuströmendes aus Schilf und Gärten,
Gewitter abends
tränkten die Dolden ehern,
die barsten dunkel, gespannt von ihren Seimen;
und Meer und Strände,
bewimpelte mit Zelten,
glühenden Sandes trächtig,
bräunende Wochen, gerbend alles
zu Fell für Küsse, die niedergingen
achtlos und schnell verflogen
wie Wolkenbrüche!

A drawing after

1943

I

O those years! Green light in the morning,
and the promenades not yet swept –
summer shouted from open spaces in town
and sucked at a horn
filling itself from the top.

Soundless hour. Watery colours
of a bright green eye's thinned ray,
pictures in this magic green, glassy round-dances,
shepherds and lakes, a dome, and doves –
woven and sent, shone, sounded –
changeable clouds of happiness!

You stood so before dawn: no pearls
as yet from the fountains, no movement
from buildings and steps: the houses
shut up, you *created*
the morning, jasmine's early hours,
morning's exultation, in the first beginning,
its ray – unending still – o those years!

Ineradicable heartsease,
supplements from sky and earth;
streamings-in from sedge and gardens,
thunderstorms at evening
watering umbels with brass,
darkly they burst, tense with their juices;
and sea and beaches,
tents fluttering,
pregnant with glowing sand,
weeks growing brown, tanning everything
into skin for kisses that fell
negligently and fled fast away
like cloudbursts!

197

Darüber hing die Schwere
auch jetzt – doch Trauben
aus ihr,

die Zweige niederziehend und wieder hochlassend,
nur einige Beeren,
wenn du mochtest,
erst –

noch nicht so drängend und überhangen
von kolbengroßen Fruchtfladen,
altem schwerem Traubenfleisch –

o jene Jahre!

II

Dunkle Tage des Frühlings,
nicht weichender Dämmer um Laub;
Fliederblüte gebeugt, kaum hochblickend
narzissenfarben und starken Todesgeruchs,
Glückausfälle,
sieglose Trauer des Unerfüllten.

Und in den Regen hinein,
der auf das Laub fällt,
höre ich ein altes Wälderlied,
von Wäldern, die ich einst durchfuhr
und wiedersah, doch ich ging nicht
in die Halle, wo das Lied erklungen war,
die Tasten schwiegen längst,
die Hände ruhten irgendwo,
gelöst von jenen Armen, die mich hielten,
zu Tränen rührten,
Hände aus den Oststeppen,
blutig zertretenen längst –
nur noch ihr Wälderlied

Above hung heaviness,
today as well – but it yielded
grapes,

pulling down the twigs and letting them spring back,
only a few berries,
if you wanted,
firstly –

not yet so urgent and overhung
with club-sized bundles of fruit,
heavy old grape-flesh –

o those years!

II

Dark days of spring,
twilight not letting foliage go;
elder-blossom dipping, scarcely looking up,
narcissus-coloured, smelling strongly of death,
happiness deficits,
victoryless mourning of unfulfilment.

And into the rain
falling on foliage,
I hear an old forest song,
from forests I once drove through
and saw again, but I did not go
into the hall where the song had sounded,
the keys fell silent long ago,
the hands at rest somewhere,
separated from the arms that held me,
moved me to tears,
hands from the Eastern steppes,
long trampled bloodily –
only their forest song

in den Regen hinein
an dunklen Tagen des Frühlings
den ewigen Steppen zu.

into the rain
on dark days of spring
towards the eternal steppes.

Welle der Nacht

Welle der Nacht – Meerwidder und Delphine
mit Hyakinthos leichtbewegter Last,
die Lorbeerrosen und die Travertine
wehn um den leeren istrischen Palast,

Welle der Nacht – zwei Muscheln miterkoren,
die Fluten strömen sie, die Felsen her,
dann Diadem und Purpur mitverloren,
die weiße Perle rollt zurück ins Meer.

Wave of the night

1943

Wave of the night – sea-rams and graceful dolphins
with Hyakinthos' gently-shifting weight,
crystal travertine and laurel-roses
float round the empty Istrian estate,

wave of the night – two sea-shells in the circle,
the tides empower it, cause the cliffs to be,
lost alike then diadem and purple,
the pure white pearl rolls back into the sea.

V. Jahrhundert

I

»Und Einer stellt die attische Lekythe,
auf der die Überfahrt von Schlaf und Staub
in weißen Grund gemalt als Hadesmythe,
zwischen die Myrte und das Pappellaub.

Und Einer steckt Zypresse an die Pfosten
der lieben Tür, mit Rosen oft behängt,
nun weißer Thymian, Tarant und Dosten
den letztesmal Gekränzten unterfängt.

Das Mahl. Der Weiheguß. Die Räucherschwaden.
Dann wird ein Hain gepflanzt das Grab umziehn
und eine Flöte singt von den Cykladen,
doch keiner folgt mir in die Plutonien.«

II

Das Tal stand silbern in Olivenzweigen,
dazwischen war es von Magnolien weiß,
doch alles trug sich schwer, in Schicksalsschweigen,
sie blühten marmorn, doch es fror sie leis.

Die Felder rauh, die Herden ungesegnet,
Kore geraubt und Demeter verirrt,
bis sich die beiden Göttinnen begegnet
am Schwarzen Felsen und Eleusis wird.

Nun glüht sich in das Land die ferne Küste,
du gehst im Zuge, jedes Schicksal ruht,
glühst und zerreißest dich, du bist der Myste
und alte Dinge öffnen dir dein Blut

Fifth century

1945

I

'And one man places the Attic lekythos
on which the frontier of sleep and dust
is painted on white ground as a Hades-mythos,
between the poplar and the myrtle brush.

And one man ties some cypress to the door-post
of the beloved door, where roses often climb,
but now white thyme and marjoram are foremost
as in Taranto, to crown him one last time.

The feast. Libation. Incense smoke ascending.
The burial procession, a grave is planned,
a flute sings of the Cyclades unending,
but no-one follows me to Pluto's land.'

II

The valley silver under olive branches,
magnolias between them standing white,
but blossoms were a burden, fateful marches
silent, marble lightly touched with ice.

The fields unkempt, the flocks unconsecrated,
Kore raped, with grief Demeter wild
until these goddesses were reunited
at the Black Cliff, in Eleusis reconciled.

The distant coastline glows, the land idyllic,
you walk in the procession, no fate is new,
glow and tear yourself, you are the mystic
and ancient things reveal your blood to you.

205

III

Leukée – die weiße Insel des Achill!
Bisweilen hört man ihn den Päan singen,
Vögel mit den vom Meer benetzten Schwingen
streifen die Tempelwand, sonst ist es still.

Anlandende versinken oft im Traum.
Dann sehn sie ihn, er hat wohl viel vergessen,
er gibt ein Zeichen, zwischen den Zypressen,
weiße Zypresse ist der Hadesbaum.

Wer landet, muß vor Nacht zurück aufs Meer.
Nur Helena bleibt manchmal mit den Tauben,
dann spielen sie, an Schatten *nicht* zu glauben:
»– Paris gab dem den Pfeil, den Apfel der –«

III

Leuké – Achilles' island of the blessed!
His voice is heard at times singing paeans,
apart from birds with their salt-sea-splashed pinions
skimming the precinct wall, all is at rest.

The newly disembarked may sink in stages
of a dream, and then they see him, who little recalls,
he gives a sign between the cypress walls –
the white cypress is the tree of Hades.

Embark again by dusk, who landed here.
Helen alone may stay with doves in the meadows,
they pretend not to believe in shadows:
' – Paris gave him an arrow, the apple to her – '

207

September

I

Du, über den Zaun gebeugt mit Phlox
(vom Regenguß zerspalten,
seltsamen Wildgeruchs),
der gern auf Stoppeln geht,
zu alten Leuten tritt,
die Balsaminen pflücken,
Rauch auf Feldern
mit Lust und Trauer atmet –

aufsteigenden Gemäuers,
das noch sein Dach vor Schnee und Winter will,
kalklöschenden Gesellen
ein: »ach, vergebens« zuzurufen
nur zögernd sich verhält –

gedrungen eher als hochgebaut,
auch unflätigen Kürbis nackt am Schuh,
fett und gesichtslos, dies Krötengewächs –

Ebenen-entstiegener,
Endmond aller Flammen,
aus Frucht- und Fieberschwellungen
abfallend, schon verdunkelten Gesichts –
Narr oder Täufer,
des Sommers Narr, Nachplapperer, Nachruf
oder der Gletscher Vorlied,
jedenfalls Nußknacker,
Schilfmäher,
Beschäftigter mit Binsenwahrheiten –

vor dir der Schnee,
Hochschweigen, unfruchtbar
die Unbesambarkeit der Weite:

September

1945

I

You, leaning over the fence with phlox
(furrowed by cloudbursts,
with a strange wild smell),
who love walking on stubble,
visiting old people,
picking balsamine,
breathing smoke on the fields
with delight and regret –

as walls are rising,
wanting their roof before snow and winter,
only hesitantly refraining
from calling out 'a waste of time, alas'
to lime-slaking apprentices –

stocky rather than tall,
nasty squashed pumpkin on your shoe,
fatty and faceless, this stunted growth –

down from the plains,
last moon for all fires,
from fear- and fever-swellings
falling away, your face already darkened –
fool or baptist,
summer's fool, repeater of gossip, obituary
or the prelude sung before glaciers,
in any case nutcracker,
common sedge-cutter,
commonplace-dealer –

ahead lies snow,
high silence, unfruitful
the unsowability of distances:

209

da langt dein Arm hin,
doch über den Zaun gebeugt
die Kraut- und Käferdränge,
das Lebenwollende,
Spinnen und Feldmäuse –

II

Du, ebereschenverhangen
von Frühherbst,
Stoppelgespinst,
Kohlweißlinge im Atem,
laß viele Zeiger laufen,
Kuckucksuhren schlagen,
lärme mit Vespergeläut,
gonge
die Stunde, die so golden feststeht,
so bestimmt dahinbräunt,
in ein zitternd Herz!

Du: – Anderes!
So ruhn nur Götter
oder Gewänder
unstürzbarer Titanen
langgeschaffener,
so tief eingestickt
Falter und Blumen
in die Bahnen!

Oder ein Schlummer früher Art,
als kein Erwachen war,
nur goldene Wärme und Purpurbeeren,
benagt von Schwalben, ewigen,
die nie von dannen ziehn –
Dies schlage, gonge,
diese Stunde,
denn

your arm can reach them,
but leaning over the fence
the press of plants and beetles,
wanting to live,
spiders and fieldmice –

II

You, overhung with rowan
in early autumn,
stubble webs,
cabbage-whites in your breath,
make many hands tick,
cuckoo-clocks strike,
ring noisy vespers,
gong
the hour that stands firm and golden
and turns brown so decidedly,
entering a trembling heart!

You – an other!
Only gods rest this way
or the robes
of unoverthrowable Titans
long-created,
so deeply insewn
butterflies and flowers
into the paths!

Or a slumber of an early kind,
when there was no waking,
just golden warmth and purple berries,
gnawed by swallows, everlasting,
that never fly away –
Strike it, gong
this hour,
for

wenn du schweigst,
drängen die Säume herab
pappelbestanden und schon kühler.

if you are silent,
the hems push down
lined with poplars and already cooler.

Ach, das ferne Land

Ach, das ferne Land,
wo das Herzzerreißende
auf runden Kiesel
oder Schilffläche libellenflüchtig
anmurmelt,
auch der Mond
verschlagenen Lichts
– halb Reif; halb Ährenweiß –
den Doppelgrund der Nacht
so tröstlich anhebt –

ach, das ferne Land,
wo vom Schimmer der Seen
die Hügel warm sind,
zum Beispiel Asolo, wo die Duse ruht,
von Pittsburg trug sie der »Duilio« heim,
alle Kriegsschiffe, auch die englischen, flaggten halbmast,
als er Gibraltar passierte –

dort Selbstgespräche
ohne Beziehungen auf Nahes,
Selbstgefühle,
frühe Mechanismen,
Totemfragmente
in die weiche Luft
etwas Rosinenbrot im Rock –
so fallen die Tage,
bis der Ast am Himmel steht,
auf dem die Vögel einruhn
nach langem Flug.

Ah, the distant land

1945

Ah, the distant land
where what tears the heart
laps murmuringly
at rounded pebbles
or darts like a dragonfly at banks of sedge,
the moon too
with light cast down –
half white as frost, half wheatear –
so comfortingly inaugurates
the double ground of night –

ah, the distant land
where from the shimmer of lakes
the hills are warm,
for instance Asolo where Duse lies at rest,
from Pittsburgh the *Duilio* carried her home,
all the warships, even the English ones, dipped their flags to half-mast
as it steamed past Gibraltar –

monologues there
unrelated to the contingent,
feeling of selfhood,
early mechanisms,
totem fragments
into soft air –
some fruit loaf in my pocket –
the days fall like that
until the branch stands against the sky
on which the birds come to rest
after a long flight.

The body of Eleonora Duse (1858–1924), the Italian actress of international renown
who died in Pittsburgh, was returned to Italy by steamer.

215

Chopin

Nicht sehr ergiebig im Gespräch,
Ansichten waren nicht seine Stärke,
Ansichten reden drum herum,
wenn Delacroix Theorien entwickelte,
wurde er unruhig, er seinerseits konnte
die Notturnos nicht begründen.

Schwacher Liebhaber;
Schatten in Nohant,
wo George Sands Kinder
keine erzieherischen Ratschläge
von ihm annahmen.

Brustkrank in jener Form
mit Blutungen und Narbenbildung,
die sich lange hinzieht;
stiller Tod
im Gegensatz zu einem
mit Schmerzparoxysmen
oder durch Gewehrsalven:
man rückte den Flügel (Erard) an die Tür
und Delphine Potocka
sang ihm in der letzten Stunde
ein Veilchenlied.

Nach England reiste er mit drei Flügeln:
Pleyel, Erard, Broadwood,
spielte für 20 Guineen abends
eine Viertelstunde
bei Rothschilds, Wellingtons, im Strafford House
und vor zahllosen Hosenbändern;
verdunkelt von Müdigkeit und Todesnähe
kehrte er heim
auf den Square d'Orléans.

Chopin

1945

Not very forthcoming in conversation,
opinions were not his strong point,
opinions only circle around,
when Delacroix developed his theories
he became restless, he could never
explain his own Nocturnes.

A poor lover;
shadows in Nohant
where George Sand's children
would not accept
his educational advice.

Lung-disease of the kind
with haemorrhages and scarring
that takes its time;
a quiet death,
the opposite of one
with paroxysms of pain
or from a hail of bullets:
they moved the piano (Erard) up to his door
and Delphine Potocka
in his last hour
sang him the song about a violet.

He travelled to England with three pianos:
Pleyel, Erard, Broadwood,
at 20 guineas an evening
played a quarter of an hour
for the Rothschilds, Wellingtons, in Stafford House,
and for any number of Garter knights;
darkened by tiredness and the approach of death
he went home
to the Square d'Orléans.

217

Dann verbrennt er seine Skizzen
und Manuskripte,
nur keine Restbestände, Fragmente, Notizen,
diese verräterischen Einblicke –
sagte zum Schluß:
»meine Versuche sind nach Maßgabe dessen vollendet,
was mir zu erreichen möglich war.«

Spielen sollte jeder Finger
mit der seinem Bau entsprechenden Kraft,
der vierte ist der schwächste
(nur siamesisch zum Mittelfinger).
Wenn er begann, lagen sie
auf e, fis, gis, h, c.

Wer je bestimmte Präludien
von ihm hörte,
sei es in Landhäusern oder
in einem Höhengelände
oder aus offenen Terrassentüren
beispielsweise aus einem Sanatorium,
wird es schwer vergessen.

Nie eine Oper komponiert,
keine Symphonie,
nur diese tragischen Progressionen
aus artistischer Überzeugung
und mit einer kleinen Hand.

Then he burns his sketches
and manuscripts,
leave no remains, fragments, notes,
those tell-tale insights –
said finally:
'my essays are fulfilled to the extent
of what it was possible for me to achieve'.

Each finger had to play
with the strength appropriate to its structure,
the fourth is the weakest
(like a Siamese twin of the middle finger).
When he began, they lay
on e, f sharp, g sharp, b, c.

Anyone who listened to
certain of his Preludes
in country houses or
in a highland landscape
or through open doors on a terrace,
for example from a sanatorium,
will find it hard to forget.

Never composed an opera
or a symphony,
only these tragic progressions
from artistic conviction
and with a small hand.

Chopin played before Queen Victoria and Prince Albert at Stafford (now Lancaster)
House, on 15 May 1848. The natural lie of his right hand on the piano keys would
have included B flat rather than B.

Überblickt man die Jahre

Überblickt man die Jahre
von Ur bis El Alamein,
wo lag denn nun das Wahre,
Kabbala, der Schwarze Stein –,
Perser, Hunnen, Lascaren,
Pfeile, Fahnen und Schwert –
über die Meere gefahren,
von den Meeren versehrt?

Wasser- und Sonnenuhren –
welche Stunde gemeint?
Welche Gestirne fuhren
häuptlings – Alles vereint?
Welche Wassercascade
bis in die Träume erscheint –:
jene Uhr als Dryade,
aus der es tränt und weint.

Waffen mit Lorbeer gereinigt
brachten den Sieg ins Haus,
Stirn und Lorbeer vereinigt
ruhten die Helden dann aus,
Lorbeer, Marmor, Pylone,
Gordon und Prinz Eugen,
goldene Städte, Zione –:
thanatogen –.

Palmen bei Christen, bei Heiden,
frühester Schöpfungsrest,
Palmen bei Myrten und Weiden
beim Laubhüttenfest,
Palmen an Syrten, an Küsten
königlich hoch und rein –,
doch dann wandern die Wüsten
in Palmyra ein.

If you survey tradition

1945

If you survey tradition
from Ur to El Alamein,
where did truth lie hidden,
Cabbala, the great black stone –
Persians, Huns and Lascars,
arrows, flags and the sword –
crossing the world under canvas,
treacherous seas aboard?

Water-clocks and sundials –
which the hour they intend?
Which constellation's triumphant
or do all in chaos contend?
Cascades whose fall is violent
that even appear in dreams –:
the clock in the shape of a Dryad
with tears that fall in streams.

Weapons crowned with laurels
brought victory into the house,
heroes were held immortals
and their fame allowed no doubts,
laurels, marble, pylons,
Gordon and Prince Eugene,
cities of gold and iron –
thanatogène –

Palm-leaves for Christians and heathen,
Sunday the day of rest,
palm, myrtle, willow Judaean
for the tabernacle feast,
palms by quicksand and headland,
royally tall and pure –
but then the deserts of legend
sealed Palmyra's sepulture.

Überblickt man die Jahre,
ewig wühlende Flut
und die dunkle Barke, die Bahre
mit Helden, Heeren und Blut,
und die Sonnen- und Wasseruhren
schatten und rinnen es ein:
alles deine Figuren,
Kabbala, Schwarzer Stein.

If you survey tradition,
eternally gnawing flood
and the bier, the barque to extinction
with heroes, armies and blood,
water-clocks and sundials
darkening, bringing it home:
your figures that brook no denials,
Cabbala, great black stone.

Statische Gedichte

Entwicklungsfremdheit
ist die Tiefe des Weisen,
Kinder und Kindeskinder
beunruhigen ihn nicht,
dringen nicht in ihn ein.

Richtungen vertreten,
Handeln,
Zu- und Abreisen
ist das Zeichen einer Welt,
die nicht klar sieht.
Vor meinem Fenster
– sagt der Weise –
liegt ein Tal,
darin sammeln sich die Schatten,
zwei Pappeln säumen einen Weg,
du weißt – wohin.

Perspektivismus
ist ein anderes Wort für seine Statik:
Linien anlegen,
sie weiterführen
nach Rankengesetz –
Ranken sprühen –,
auch Schwärme, Krähen,
auswerfen in Winterrot von Frühhimmeln,

dann sinken lassen –

du weißt – für wen.

Static poems

1945

Development aversion
is a wise man's depth.
Children and children's children
do not disturb him,
do not penetrate him.

Directions represented,
action,
arriving, leaving
is the mark of a world
which does not see clearly.
Outside my window –
says the wise man –
lies a valley,
shadows gather in it,
two poplars stand by a path,
you know – where it leads.

Perspectivism
is another word for his statics:
disposing lines,
continuing them
according to the law of tendrils –
tendrils spray out –
swarms too, crows,
cast them about in winter-red of early skies,

then let them sink –

you know   for whom.

Orpheus' Tod

Wie du mich zurückläßt, Liebste –
von Erebos gestoßen,
dem unwirtlichen Rhodope
Wald herziehend,
zweifarbige Beeren,
rotglühendes Obst –
Belaubung schaffend,
die Leier schlagend
den Daumen an der Saite!

Drei Jahre schon im Nordsturm!
An Totes zu denken, ist süß,
so Entfernte,
man hört die Stimme reiner,
fühlt die Küsse,
die flüchtigen und die tiefen –
doch du irrend bei den Schatten!

Wie du mich zurückläßt –
anstürmen die Flußnymphen,
anwinken die Felsenschönen,
gurren: »im öden Wald
nur Faune und Schratte, doch du,
Sänger, Aufwölber
von Bronzelicht, Schwalbenhimmeln –
fort die Töne –
Vergessen –!«

– drohen –!

Und eine starrt so seltsam.
Und eine Große, Gefleckte,
bunthäutig (»gelber Mohn«)
lockt unter Demut, Keuschheitsandeutungen
bei hemmungsloser Lust – (Purpur
im Kelch der Liebe –!) vergeblich!

The death of Orpheus

1946

How you leave me behind, dearest –
pushed out of Erebos,
dragging forest around me
from inhospitable Rhodope,
bicoloured berries,
fruit glowing red –
foliating,
striking the lyre,
my thumb on the string!

Three years gone in the North storm!
Thinking of dead things is sweet,
my thus separated one,
the voice is heard more purely,
the kisses felt,
the fleeting kisses and the deep –
but you wandering amongst the shades!

How you leave me behind –
besieged by river-nymphs,
beckoned by beauties of the cliff,
cooing: 'in the barren wood
nothing but fauns and satyrs, but you,
singer, raising domes
of bronze light, swallow skies –
the sounds are gone –
forgetting – !'

– threaten – !

And one stares so strangely.
And a tall one, dappled,
bright-skinned ('yellow poppy')
tempts demurely, hinting at chastity,
boundless pleasure – (purple
in love's chalice – !) in vain!

227

drohen –!

Nein, du sollst nicht verrinnen,
du sollst nicht übergehn in
Iole, Dryope, Prokne,
die Züge nicht vermischen mit Atalanta,
daß ich womöglich Eurydike
stammle bei Lais –

doch: drohen –!

und nun die Steine
nicht mehr der Stimme folgend,
dem Sänger,
mit Moos sich hüllend,
die Äste laubbeschwichtigt,
die Hacken ährenbesänftigt –:
nackte Haune –!

nun wehrlos dem Wurf der Hündinnen,
der wüsten –
nun schon die Wimper naß,
der Gaumen blutet –
und nun die Leier –
hinab den Fluß –

die Ufer tönen –

– threaten – !

No, you must not flow away,
you must not pass over into
Iole, Dryope, Procne,
not mix up your features with Atalanta,
so that I maybe stammer Eurydike
with Lais –

yet – threaten – !

and now the stones
no longer following the voice,
the singer,
enveloped in moss,
the boughs appeased in foliage,
heels soothed in ears of corn –:
naked axes – !

now defenceless under the bitches' missiles,
the wild ones –
eyelashes already wet,
the palate bleeds –
and now the lyre –
down the river –

the shores resound –

Gewisse Lebensabende

I

Du brauchst nicht immer die Kacheln zu scheuern, Hendrickje,
mein Auge trinkt sich selbst,
trinkt sich zu Ende –
aber an anderen Getränken mangelt es –
dort die Buddhastatue,
chinesischen Haingott,
gegen eine Kelle Hulstkamp,
bitte!

Nie etwas gemalt
in Frostweiß oder Schlittschuhläuferblau
oder dem irischen Grün,
aus dem der Purpur schimmert –
immer nur meine Eintönigkeit,
mein Schattenzwang –
nicht angenehm,
diesen Weg so deutlich zu verfolgen.

Größe – wo?
Ich nehme den Griffel
und gewisse Dinge stehn dann da
auf Papier, Leinwand
oder ähnlichem Zunder –
Resultat: Buddhabronze gegen Sprit –
aber Huldigungen unter Blattpflanzen,
Bankett der Pinselgilde –:
was fürs Genre –!

… Knarren,
Schäfchen, die quietschen,
Abziehbilder
flämisch, rubenisch
für die Enkelchen –!
(ebensolche Idioten –!)

Certain evenings of life

1946

I

You need not keep scrubbing the tiles, Hendrickje,
my eye drinks itself,
drinks its fill –
but there is a lack of other drinks –
the Buddha statue there,
the Chinese tutelary,
against a ladle of Hulstkamp,
please!

Never painted anything
in frost-white or skaters' blue
or in Irish green
with purple shining through –
only my monotones always,
my compulsive shadows –
not much fun,
following this path so distinctly.

Greatness – where?
I take my stylus
and certain things appear
on paper, canvas
or similar kindling –
result: bronze Buddha against spirits –
but homages under pot plants,
banquet of the brushmen's guild –:
a genre-piece – !

… Rattles,
lambs bleating,
transfer pictures
Flemish, Rubenic
for little grandchildren – !
(just as idiotic – !)

231

Ah – Hulstkamp –
Wärmezentrum,
Farbenmittelpunkt,
mein Schattenbraun –
Bartstoppelfluidum um Herz und Auge –

II

Der Kamin raucht
– schneuzt sich der Schwan vom Avon –,
die Stubben sind naß,
klamme Nacht, Leere vermählt mit Zugluft –
Schluß mit den Gestalten,
übervölkert die Erde
reichlicher Pfirsichfall, vier Rosenblüten
pro anno –
ausgestreut,
auf die Bretter geschoben
von dieser Hand,
faltig geworden
und mit erschlafften Adern!

Alle die Ophelias, Julias,
bekränzt, silbern, auch mörderisch –
alle die weichen Münder, die Seufzer,
die ich aus ihnen herausmanipulierte –
die ersten Aktricen längst Qualm,
Rost, ausgelaugt, Rattenpudding –
auch Herzens-Ariel bei den Elementen.

Die Epoche zieht sich den Bratenrock aus.
Diese Lord- und Läuseschädel,
ihre Gedankengänge,
die ich ins Extrem trieb –
meine Herren Geschichtsproduzenten
alles Kronen- und Szepteranalphabeten,
Großmächte des Weltraums
wie Fledermaus oder Papierdrachen!

Ah, Hulstkamp –
centre of warmth,
mid point of colour,
my shadow brown –
trichomic fluid around heart and eye –

II

The chimney smokes –
the Swan of Avon sneezes –
the logs are damp,
freezing night, emptiness wedded to draughts –
no more characters,
the earth over-populated
many ripe peaches, four roses bloom
pro anno –
disseminated,
shoved on the boards
by this hand,
wrinkled now
and with slack arteries!

All the Ophelias, Juliets,
garlanded, silver, murderous too –
all the soft mouths, the sighs
I manipulated from them –
their first embodiers long since ash,
rust, washed in lye, rat-pudding –
even Ariel my heart with the elements.

The age is taking off its dress-coat.
These lordly, lousy skulls,
the ways they think,
pushed to extremes by me –
my masters history-producers
all illiterates with crown and sceptre,
the big players of the universe
like bats or paper kites!

Sir Goon schrieb neulich an mich:
»der Rest ist Schweigen«: –
ich glaube, das ist von mir,
kann nur von mir sein,
Dante tot – eine große Leere
zwischen den Jahrhunderten
bis zu meinen Wortschatzzitaten –

aber wenn sie fehlten,
der Plunder nie aufgeschlagen,
die Buden, die Schafotte, die Schellen
nie geklungen hätten –:
Lücken –?? Vielleicht Zahnlücken,
aber das große Affengebiß
mahlte weiter
seine Leere, vermählt mit Zugluft –
die Stubben sind naß
und der Butler schnarcht in Porterträumen.

Sir Goon wrote to me recently:
'the rest is silence': –
I think I wrote that,
it has to be mine,
Dante dead – a great emptiness
between the centuries
down to quotes from my vocabulary –

but if they had not existed,
if the rubbish had never been opened,
the booths, the scaffolds, the little bells
had never sounded –:
gaps – ?? Maybe gaps in teeth,
but the great ape's jaw
went on grinding
its emptiness wedded to draughts –
the logs are damp
and the porter snores in beery dreams.

Kleines süßes Gesicht

Kleines süßes Gesicht,
eingesunken schon vor Vergängnis,
schneeblass und tödlich,
Ausschütter grossen Leids,
wenn du hingegangen
bald –

ach, wie wir spielten
entwicklungsvergessen,
Rück- und Weitblicke
abgefallen von unseren Rändern,
nichts lebend
ausser dem Umkreis
unserer Laute!

Beschränkt! Doch dann
einmal der astverborgenen Männer
Oliven Niederschlagen,
die Haufen gären.
Einmal Weine vom Löwengolf
in Rauchkammern, mit Seewasser beschönigt.
Oder Eukalyptus, Riesen, 156 Meter hoch
und das zitternde Zwielicht in ihren Wäldern.
Einmal Cotroceni –
nicht mehr!

Kleines Gesicht
Schneeflocke
immer so weiss
und dann die Ader an der Schläfe
vom Blau der Traubenhyazinthe,
die ligurische,
die bisamartig duftet.

Sweet little face

1946

Sweet little face,
already sunken with mortality,
snow-white and fatal,
spiller of great sorrow,
when you've departed
soon –

ah, how we played
forgetting development,
backward looks and distant
fallen from our limits,
nothing alive
beyond the circle
of our sounds!

Confined! But then
for once the branch-hidden men
olives raining down
in piles fermenting.
And once vintages from the Lion Gulf
in smoke-chambers, palliated with seawater.
Or eucalyptus, giants, one hundred and fifty-six metres tall
and the shivering twilight in the forest.
Once Cotroceni –
no more!

Little face
snowflake
always so white
and then the vein at your temple
the blue of grape-hyacinths
in Liguria
that have the scent of musk.

Cotroceni is a district in Bucharest.

Du liegst und schweigst und träumst der Stunde nach

Du liegst und schweigst und träumst der Stunde nach,
der Süssigkeit, dem sanften Sein des Andern,
keiner ist übermächtig oder schwach,
du giebst und nimmst und giebst – die Kräfte wandern.

Gewisses Fühlen und gewisses Sehn,
gewisse Worte aus gewisser Stunde –,
und keiner löst sich je aus diesem Bunde
der Veilchen, Nesseln und der Orchideen.

Und dennoch musst du es den Parzen lassen,
dem Fädenspinnen und dem Flockenstreun –,
du kannst nur diese Hand, die schmale, fassen
und diesmal noch das tiefe Wort erneu'n.

You lie in silence

1947

You lie in silence, dream this hour again
of sweetness, gentleness towards the partner,
neither the stronger nor the weaker feign,
you give, you take, the meandering vox humana.

Particular ways of feeling, a way to see,
particular words for this particular union,
neither ever seeking a conclusion,
violets, nettles, orchids in harmony.

And yet you must abandon all that lingers
– the Fates are spinning, dropping fields of snow –
you can only grasp these narrow fingers
and renew the recondite word, for now.

Acheron

Ein Traum: – von dir! Du Tote schrittest kühl
im Durcheinander streifender Gestalten,
die ich nie sah – ein wogendes Gewühl,
mein Blick, der suchte, konnte dich nicht halten.

Und alles starrte wie aus fremder Macht,
denn alles trank sich Rausch aus weißen Drogen,
selbst Kindern ward ein Lid herabgezogen
und in die Falte Salbe eingebracht.

Zwei Knaben führtest du – von mir doch nicht,
von dir und mir – nein, ich erhielt doch keine,
auch ließest du mich dann nicht so alleine
und zeigtest mir nur flüchtig dein Gesicht,

nein, du – Diana einst und alabastern,
ganz unvermischbar jedem Fall und Raum –
schwandest in diesem Zug aus Schmach und Lastern
und littest – sah ich so – in diesem Traum.

Acheron

1948

A dream: – of you! Your dead self walking cool,
with figures passing one another
whom I had never seen – a turbulent pool,
but you my seeking eye could not recover.

Everyone staring, under some power in control,
for everyone was drunk on little tablets,
even the children had to lift their lashes
to have a substance smeared within the fold.

You led two little boys – surely not mine,
not yours and mine – for there were none you gave me,
you'd not have left me then so solitary,
and showed but fleetingly your face so fine,

no, you – of alabaster, once Diana,
unmixable with any space and set –
you vanished in this shame and vice syntagma
and, dreaming, so it seemed to me – you wept.

Berlin

Wenn die Brücken, wenn die Bogen
von der Steppe aufgesogen
und die Burg im Sand verrinnt,
wenn die Häuser leer geworden,
wenn die Heere und die Horden
über unseren Gräbern sind,

Eines kann man nicht vertreiben:
dieser Steine Male bleiben
Löwen noch im Wüstensand,
wenn die Mauern niederbrechen,
werden noch die Trümmer sprechen
von dem grossen Abendland.

Berlin

1948

When the bridges, when the arches
are swallowed by the steppe, are marches,
the citadel dissolved in sand,
when the houses all stand empty,
when armies and vast hordes already
pass across our grave-filled land,

not to be erased forever,
stones will mark vestigial treasure:
lions from a monument,
though the noble walls are falling,
fragments eloquently calling:
behold the mighty Occident.

Radar

Ein Nebel wie auf See –
und meine Belle-Etage
fährt ohne Takelage
von Quai zu Quai.

Sie findet keinen Ort,
daran das Tau zu schlingen,
denn neue Wellen bringen
sie wieder fort.

Wie weit sind Sund und Belt
und schwer die Hafenfrage,
wenn – ohne Takelage –
noch Nebel fällt!

Radar

1949?

A mist like mist at sea –
and my belle-étage
sails without equipage
from quay to quay.

She finds no firm terrain,
no windlass and no painter,
because new waves misplace her,
adrift again.

How far are Baltic and Sound
and hard to pick a harbour
when – without equipage –
more mist falls around!

245

Notturno

Im Nebenzimmer die Würfel auf den Holztisch,
benachbart ein Paar im Ansaugestadium,
mit einem Kastanienast auf dem Klavier tritt die Natur hinzu –
ein Milieu, das mich anspricht.

Da versinken die Denkprozesse,
die Seekrankheit, die einem tagsüber
die Brechzentren bearbeitet,
gehn unter in Alkohol und Nebulosem –
endlich Daseinsschwund und Seelenausglanz!

Auf Wogen liegen –
natürlich kann man untergehn,
aber das ist eine Zeitfrage –
doch Zeit – vor Ozeanen –?
Die waren vorher,
vor Bewußtsein und Empfängnis,
keiner fischte ihre Ungeheuer,
keiner litt tiefer als drei Meter
und das ist wenig.

Notturno

1950

In the next room the sound of dice on a wooden table,
next door a couple reach the suction stage,
with a sprig of chestnut on the piano, a touch of nature –
my kind of milieu.

Then my thought-processes sink,
the sea-sickness that all day
busies my emetic responses,
descent into alcohol and nebulosity –
finally vanishing identity and the soul's last flicker!

Lying on waves –
of course one can sink,
but that's a question of time –
time, you say – before the open seas –?
They came previously,
before consciousness and conception,
no-one fished for their monsters,
no-one suffered more than six feet deep
and that's not much.

Der Dunkle

I

Ach, gäb er mir zurück die alte Trauer,
die einst mein Herz so zauberschwer umfing,
da gab es Jahre, wo von jeder Mauer
ein Tränenflor aus Tristanblicken hing.

Da littest du, doch es war Auferstehung,
da starbst du hin, doch es war Liebestod,
doch jetzt bei jedem Schritt und jeder Drehung
liegen die Fluren leer und ausgeloht.

Die Leere ist wohl auch von jenen Gaben,
in denen sich der Dunkle offenbart,
er gibt sie dir, du mußt sie trauernd haben,
doch diese Trauer ist von anderer Art.

II

Auch laß die Einsamkeiten größer werden,
nimm dich zurück aus allem, was begann,
reihe dich ein in jene Weideherden,
die dämmert schon die schwarze Erde an.

Licht ist von großen Sonnen, Licht ist Handeln,
in seiner Fülle nicht zu überstehn,
ich liebe auch den Flieder und die Mandeln
mehr in Verschleierung zur Blüte gehn.

Hier spricht der Dunkle, dem wir nie begegnen,
erst hebt er uns, indem er uns verführt,
doch ob es Träume sind, ob Fluch, ob Segnen,
das läßt er alles menschlich unberührt.

The dark one

1950

I

Ah, could he give me back the ancient sorrow
in which my heart with magic weight was strung,
from every wall once, apt for me to borrow,
a mourning veil of Tristan glances hung.

You suffered then, and then were resurrected,
you died away, your longed-for Liebestod,
but now each step and gesture is affected
as hearths lie empty where a fire once glowed.

Emptiness could be amongst the offerings
in which the dark one manifests his power,
he gives it you, your task is suffering,
a different sorrow in a different hour.

II

Wider solitudes lie beyond the battle,
withdraw yourself from everything begun,
take up a place with consecrated cattle
for which the earth moves further from the sun.

Light comes from greater stars and light is action,
too multitudinous to comprehend,
the elder-tree, the almond are my passion
when almost under veils their blooms ascend.

Here speaks the dark one, the unencountered being,
he lifts us up before he plays his game,
yet whether with curses, blessings, or in dreaming
in human terms to him is all the same.

249

III

Gemeinsamkeit von Geistern und von Weisen,
vielleicht, vielleicht auch nicht, in einem Raum,
bestimmt von Ozean und Wendekreisen
das ist für viele ein erhabner Traum.

Mythen bei Inkas und bei Sansibaren,
die Sintflutsage rings und völkerstet –
doch keiner hat noch etwas je erfahren,
das vor dem Dunklen nicht vorübergeht.

IV

Grau sind die Hügel und die Flüsse grau,
sie fragen schon Urahnen aller Jahre,
und nun am Ufer eine neue Frau
gewundene Hüften, aufgedrehte Haare.

Und auf der Wiese springen Stiere an,
gefährdend jedes, mit dem Horn zerklüften,
bis in die Koppel tritt geklärt ein Mann,
der bändigt alles, Hörner, Haare, Hüften.

Und nun beginnt der enggezogene Kreis,
der trächtige, der tragische, der schnelle,
der von der großen Wiederholung weiß –
und nur der Dunkle harrt auf seiner Stelle.

III

A commonwealth of spirits and of thinkers –
maybe, and maybe not, in a single plane,
by tide and tropic perfectly configured,
dreamed sublimity but dreamed in vain.

Inca myths and Zanzibari legends,
the universal story of the Flood,
yet never evidence for any question
that anything against the dark one stood.

IV

Grey are the hills, the rivers too are grey,
they've borne the endless dynasties of time,
on the bank an unknown woman's on her way
with hair upwound and graceful hips sublime.

The season in the meadow is for bulls to mate,
threatening to gore each careless interloper,
defiantly a man strides through the gate,
he tames the horns, the hair, the hips in total.

And now begin the narrow-drawing rings
of pregnancy, of fate and transience,
the eternal repetition of all things –
while the dark one waits within his battlements.

Restaurant

Der Herr drüben bestellt sich noch ein Bier,
das ist mir angenehm, dann brauche ich mir keinen Vorwurf
zu machen

daß ich auch gelegentlich einen zische.
Man denkt immer gleich, man ist süchtig,
in einer amerikanischen Zeitschrift las ich sogar,
jede Zigarette verkürze das Leben um sechsunddreißig Minuten,
das glaube ich nicht, vermutlich steht die Coca-Cola-Industrie
oder eine Kaugummifabrik hinter dem Artikel.
Ein normales Leben, ein normaler Tod
das ist auch nichts. Auch ein normales Leben
führt zu einem kranken Tod. Überhaupt hat der Tod
mit Gesundheit und Krankheit nichts zu tun,
er bedient sich ihrer zu seinem Zwecke.

Wie meinen Sie das: der Tod hat mit Krankheit nichts zu tun?
Ich meine das so: viele erkranken, ohne zu sterben,
also liegt hier noch etwas anderes vor,
ein Fragwürdigkeitsfragment,
ein Unsicherheitsfaktor,
er ist nicht so klar umrissen,
hat auch keine Hippe,
beobachtet, sieht um die Ecke, hält sich sogar zurück
und ist musikalisch in einer anderen Melodie.

Restaurant

1950

The gentleman over there orders another beer,
I like that, then I needn't feel guilty
because I occasionally down one myself.
You always think you're an addict,
I even read in an American magazine
that every cigarette shortens your life by thirty-six minutes,
I don't believe it, probably the Coca-Cola industry's behind the article
or some chewing-gum factory.

A normal life, a normal death,
don't you believe it. Even a normal life
leads to a sick death. Death has absolutely
nothing to do with health and sickness,
he just uses them for his own purpose.

What do you mean: death has nothing to do with sickness?
I mean this: many get sick without dying,
so something else is going on here too,
a questionable fragment,
the uncertainty factor,
his shape is unclear,
he doesn't have a scythe,
he watches, peeps round the corner, keeps well back
and his music has a different tune.

Was meinte Luther mit dem Apfelbaum?

Was meinte Luther mit dem Apfelbaum?
Mir ist es gleich – auch Untergang ist Traum –
ich stehe hier in meinem Apfelgarten
und kann den Untergang getrost erwarten –
ich bin in Gott, der ausserhalb der Welt
noch manchen Trumpf in seinem Skatblatt hält –
wenn morgen früh die Welt zu Brache geht,
ich bleibe ewig sein und sternestet –

meinte er das, der alte Biedermann
u. blickt noch einmal seine Käte an?
und trinkt noch einmal einen Humpen Bier
u. schläft, bis es beginnt – frühmorgens vier?
Dann war er wirklich ein sehr grosser Mann,
den man auch heute nur bewundern kann.

What did Luther mean by the apple tree?

1950

What did Luther mean by the apple tree?
The end is a dream as well, so it's all one to me –
from where I'm standing in my apple orchard
I can await the end of things undaunted –
I am in God, who is outside the world,
whose trumps at skat are one by one unfurled –
if in the morning the world should go to pot
I shall survive forever in a starry spot –

is that what he meant, the old and worthy man,
looking at his Katy as husbands can?
and drinking yet another quart of Helles
and sleeping till it starts – say 4 a.m.-ish?
Then he was truly one of the greatest of men,
deserving admiration now or then.

A saying attributed to Luther translates as follows: 'Even if I knew the world would
end tomorrow, I would still plant an apple tree today'.

Künstlermoral

Nur in Worten darfst du dich zeigen,
die klar in Formen stehn,
sein Menschliches muß verschweigen,
wer so mit Qualen versehn.

Du musst dich selber verzehren –
gib acht, dass es niemand sieht,
und lass es keinen beschweren,
was dir so dunkel geschieht.

Du trägst deine eigenen Sünden,
du trägst dein eigenes Blut,
du darfst nur dir selber verkünden,
auf wem dein Sterbliches ruht.

Artistic ethics

1950

Only in words may your self be written
that clearly stand in forms,
the human side he must keep hidden
whose torments come in swarms.

Consume your own exertion –
take care that no-one sees,
and do not share the burden
of dark infelicities.

You are your sins' own censor,
only your blood bears your cries,
tell only yourself as confessor
on whom your story relies.

257

Reisen

Meinen Sie Zürich zum Beispiel
sei eine tiefere Stadt,
wo man Wunder und Weihen
immer als Inhalt hat?

Meinen Sie, aus Habana,
weiß und hibiskusrot,
bräche ein ewiges Manna
für Ihre Wüstennot?

Bahnhofstraßen und Rueen,
Boulevards, Lidos, Laan –
selbst auf den Fifth Avenueen
fällt Sie die Leere an –

ach, vergeblich das Fahren!
Spät erst erfahren Sie sich:
bleiben und stille bewahren
das sich umgrenzende Ich.

Journeys

1950

Do you think Zürich, for example,
is a profounder place,
where miracle and marvel
are constant signs of grace?

Do you think, from Havana,
white and hibiscus red,
some kind of eternal manna
could soothe your desert head?

Bahnhof Streets, Piccadillies,
boulevards, lidos, Laan –
still for Fifth Avenue lilies
emptiness plays its pavane –

Ah, travel is nothing to relish!
you discover yourself by and by:
remain and quietly cherish
the self-circumscribing I.

Spät

I

Die alten schweren Bäume
in großen Parks
und die Blumengärten,
die feucht verwirrten –

herbstliche Süße,
Polster von Erika
die Autobahn entlang,
alles ist Lüneburger
Heide, lila und unfruchtbar,
Versonnenheiten, die zu Nichts führen,
in sich gekehrtes Kraut,
das bald hinabbräunt
– Frage eines Monats –
ins Nieerblühte.

Dies die Natur.
Und durch die City
in freundlichem Licht
fahren die Bierwagen
Ausklangssänfte, auch Unbesorgnis
vor Reizzuständen, Durst und Ungestilltem –
was stillt sich nicht? Nur kleine Kreise!
Die großen schwelgen
in Übermaßen.

II

So enden die Blicke, die Blicke zurück:
Felder und Seen eingewachsen in deine Tage
und die ersten Lieder
aus einem alten Klavier.

Late

1951

I

The heavy old trees
in big parks
and flower-gardens,
damply confused –

autumnal sweetness,
banks of heather
along the autobahn,
Lüneburg Heath everywhere,
pale violet, infertile,
reveries, aimless,
imbricated weeds
close to turning brown –
give them a month –
without having flowered.

This is nature.
And through the city
in friendly light
beer-lorries drive
end-of-season litters, no care
for stimulation, thirst and assuaging –
what cannot be assuaged? Only in small circles!
The big ones luxuriate
in excesses.

II

So end the glances, the looking back:
fields and lakes that grew into your days
and the first songs
from an old piano.

261

Begegnungen der Seele! Jugend!
Dann selbst gestaltet
Treubruch, Verfehlen, Verfall –
die Hintergründe der Glücke.

Und Liebe!
»Ich glaube dir, daß du gerne bei mir geblieben wärest,
aber es nicht konntest,
ich spreche dich frei von jeder Schuld« –
ja, Liebe
schwer und vielgestalt,
jahrelang verborgen
werden wir einander zurufen: »nicht vergessen«,
bis einer tot ist – –
so enden die Rosen,
Blatt um Blatt.

III

Noch einmal so sein wie früher:
unverantwortlich und nicht das Ende wissen,
das Fleisch fühlen: Durst, Zärtlichkeit, Erobern, Verlieren,
hinüberlangen in jenes Andere – in was?

Abends dasitzen, in den Schlund der Nacht sehn,
er verengert sich, aber am Grund sind Blumen,
es duftet herauf, kurz und zitternd,
dahinter natürlich die Verwesung,
dann ist es ganz dunkel und du weißt wieder dein Teil,
wirfst dein Geld hin und gehst –

soviel Lügen geliebt,
soviel Worten geglaubt,
die nur aus der Wölbung der Lippen kamen,
und dein eigenes Herz
so wandelbar, bodenlos und augenblicklich –

Meeting soul-mates! Youth!
Then your own doing,
breach of trust, not turning up, decay –
the backgrounds of joys.

And love!
'I do believe you wanted to stay with me
but couldn't,
I absolve you of any guilt' –
yes, love
heavy, multifarious,
hidden for years
we will call to one another: 'don't forget',
until one dies – –
that's how roses end,
petal by petal.

III

To be again as we once were:
irresponsible, not knowing the end,
aware of the flesh: thirst, gentleness, conquering, losing,
reaching out into that other – what?

Sitting in the evenings, looking into the gulf of night,
it narrows, but flowers cover the ground,
a scent rises, brief and fragile,
behind it of course is putrefaction,
then it is completely dark and you know your part again,
throw down your money and go –

so many lies loved,
so many words believed,
that merely emerged from the curve of your lips,
and your own heart
so changeable, bottomless and momentary –

263

soviel Lügen geliebt,
soviel Lippen gesucht
(»nimm das Rouge von deinem Munde,
gib ihn mir blaß«)

und der Fragen immer mehr –

IV

Little old lady
in a big red room
little old lady –
summt Marion Davies,
während Hearst, ihr Freund seit 30 Jahren,
in schwerem Kupfersarg unter dem Schutz einer starken Eskorte
und gefolgt von 22 Limousinen
vor dem Marmormausoleum eintrifft,
leise surren die Fernkameras.

Little old lady, großer roter Raum,
hennarot, sanft gladiolenrot, kaiserrot (Purpurschnecke),
Schlafzimmer in Santa Monica Schloß
à la Pompadour –

Louella, ruft sie, Radio!
Die Blues, Jitterbug – Zickzack!
Das Bürgertum im atlantischen Raum:
heiratsfähige Töchter und obliterierter Sexus,
Palazzos an den Bays, Daunendecken auf den Pfühlen,
die Welt teilen sie ein in Monde und Demimonde –
ich war immer letzteres –

Louella, meine Mischung – hochprozentig!
Was soll das alles –
gedemütigt, hochgekämpft, hündisch gelitten –
die Züge, häßliche Züge, mit denen jetzt der Kupfersarg Schluß mach
überrann ein Licht, wenn er mich sah,
auch Reiche lieben, zittern, kennen die Verdammnis.

so many lies loved,
so many lips sought
('wipe the lipstick from your mouth,
give it me pale')

and always more questions –

IV

Little old lady
in a big red room
little old lady –
hums Marion Davies,
while Hearst, her friend for thirty years,
in a heavy copper casket protected by a strong escort
and followed by twenty-two limousines,
arrives at the marble mausoleum,
the television cameras whirr gently.

Little old lady, big red room,
henna red, gladiolus red, imperial red (the purple snail).
Bedroom in Santa Monica Castle
à la Pompadour –

Louella, she calls, the radio!
The blues, jitterbug – zigzag!
The bourgeoisie in the Atlantic sphere:
marriageable daughter and no more sex,
palazzos on bay shores, daybeds by pools,
they divide the world into monde and demimonde –
I was always the latter –

Louella, my mixture – high percentage!
What's it all for –
humiliated, struggling up, suffering like a dog –
the way, the ugly way the copper casket ends it all now,
he lit up when he saw me,
the rich love too, and tremble, know damnation.

Hochprozentig – das Glas an den Silberapparat,
er wird nun stumm sein zu jener Stunde,
die nur wir beide wußten –
drollige Sprüche kamen aus der Muschel,
»in Frühstücksstuben entscheidet sich das Leben,
am Strand im Bathdreß hagelt es Granit,
das Unerwartete pflegt einzutreten,
das Erhoffte geschieht nie –«
das waren seine Stories.

Schluß mit der Promenade! Nur noch einige Steinfliesen,
auf die vorderste das Glas,
hochprozentig, Klirren, letzte Rhapsodie –
little old lady,
in a big red room –

V

Fühle – doch wisse, Jahrtausende fühlten –
Meer und Getier und die kopflosen Sterne
ringen es nieder heute wie einst –

denke – doch wisse, die Allererlauchtesten
treiben in ihrem eigenen Kiel,
sind nur das Gelb der Butterblume,
auch andere Farben spielen ihr Spiel –

wisse das alles und trage die Stunde,
keine wie diese, jede wie sie,
Menschen und Engel und Cherubime,
Schwarzgeflügeltes, Hellgeäugtes,
keines war deines –
deines nie.

High percentage – the glass by the silver receiver,
it will be silent now in that hour
only the two of us knew –
funny sayings came from the speaker,
'in breakfast-rooms life is decided,
on the beach in swimming-costumes hailstorms of granite,
the unexpected usually happens,
the hoped-for never – '
those were his stories.

Enough of the promenade! Only a few more paving-blocks,
my glass on the first,
high percentage, tinkles, final rhapsody –
little old lady,
in a big red room –

V

Feel – yet know, millennia felt –
sea and beasts and the headless stars
wrestle it down today as they did –

think – yet know, the most exalted
come in their own vessel,
are only the yellow of the buttercup,
and other colours play their game –

know all that and bear the hour,
none like this one, all the same,
humans, angels, cherubim,
black-winged, bright-eyed,
you never had that –
no such flame.

VI

Siehst du es nicht, wie einige halten,
viele wenden den Rücken zu,
seltsame hohe schmale Gestalten,
alle wandern den Brücken zu.

Senken die Stecken, halten die Uhren
an, die Ziffern brauchen kein Licht,
schwindende Scharen, schwarze Figuren,
alle weinen – siehst du es nicht?

VI

Do you not see that some are leaders,
many others turn away,
strange and tall and narrow creatures,
to bridges all on pilgrimage.

Stop the clocks, release the spigots,
the ciphers need no light or key,
vanishing multitudes, night-black figures,
all are weeping – can you see?

Du übersiehst dich nicht mehr

Du übersiehst dich nicht mehr?
Der Anfang ist vergessen,
die Mitte wie nie besessen,
und das Ende kommt schwer.

Was hängen nun die Girlanden,
was strömt nun das Klavier,
was zischen die Jazz und die Banden,
wenn alle Abende landen
so abgebrochen in dir?

Du könntest dich nochmals treiben
mit Rausch und Flammen und Flug,
du könntest –: das heißt, es bleiben
noch einige Töpferscheiben
und etwas Ton im Krug.

Doch du siehst im Ton nur die losen,
die Scherben, den Aschenflug –
ob Wein, ob Öl, ob Rosen,
ob Vase, Urne und Krug.

What does your retrospect lack?

1951

What does your retrospect lack?
The start was ill-begotten,
the middle quite forgotten
and the end an attack.

Why are garlands a-dazzle,
why melodies from the keys,
why are jazz-bands a-crackle
when every evening's a battle
you lose in melancholies?

You could have shown off your talents
with drinking and flame and fug,
you could have – but then you haven't,
potters' wheels empty and stagnant
and a little clay in the jug.

But in clay you see wasters only,
the fragments, the ashy plug –
whether wine or oil or roses,
whether vase or urn or jug.

Satzbau

Alle haben den Himmel, die Liebe und das Grab,
damit wollen wir uns nicht befassen,
das ist für den Kulturkreis gesprochen und durchgearbeitet.
Was aber neu ist, ist die Frage nach dem Satzbau
und die ist dringend:
warum drücken wir etwas aus?

Warum reimen wir oder zeichnen ein Mädchen
direkt oder als Spiegelbild
oder stricheln auf eine Handbreit Büttenpapier
unzählige Pflanzen, Baumkronen, Mauern,
letztere als dicke Raupen mit Schildkrötenkopf
sich unheimlich niedrig hinziehend
in bestimmter Anordnung?

Überwältigend unbeantwortbar!
Honoraraussicht ist es nicht,
viele verhungern darüber. Nein,
es ist ein Antrieb in der Hand,
ferngesteuert, eine Gehirnlage,
vielleicht ein verspäteter Heilbringer oder Totemtier,
auf Kosten des Inhalts ein formaler Priapismus,
er wird vorübergehn,
aber heute ist der Satzbau
das Primäre.

»Die wenigen, die was davon erkannt« – (Goethe) –
wovon eigentlich?
Ich nehme an: vom Satzbau.

Sentence-construction

1951

We all have heaven, love, the grave,
and that need not detain us,
that has been discussed and worked through in our Kulturkreis.
What is new, however, is the question of sentence-construction
and that is urgent:
why do we express anything?

Why do we rhyme or draw a girl
directly or in the mirror
or sketch on a smallish sheet of handmade paper
countless plants, treetops, walls,
the last as fat caterpillars with tortoise heads
pulling themselves along, strangely low on the ground,
in a well-defined configuration?

Overwhelmingly unanswerable!
It isn't a prospect of being paid,
many starve doing it. No,
it's an impulse in the hand,
directed from a distance, a position of the brain,
maybe a delayed saviour or totem animal,
at the cost of its content a formal priapism,
it will pass,
but today, sentence-
construction is primary.

'The few who knew any thing about it' (Goethe) –
about what exactly?
I take it: about sentence-construction.

The Goethe quotation is from the first scene of *Faust* Part 1, spoken by Faust to his
famulus Wagner, who had just expressed his desire to know about 'the world, [and]
man's heart and spirit'.

Verhülle dich

Verhülle dich mit Masken und mit Schminken,
auch blinzle wie gestörten Augenlichts,
laß nie erblicken, wie dein Sein, dein Sinken
sich abhebt von dem Rund des Angesichts.

Im letzten Licht, vorbei an trüben Gärten,
der Himmel ein Geröll aus Brand und Nacht –
verhülle dich, die Tränen und die Härten,
das Fleisch darf man nicht sehn, das dies vollbracht.

Die Spaltungen, den Riß, die Übergänge,
den Kern, wo die Zerstörung dir geschieht,
verhülle, tu, als ob die Ferngesänge
aus einer Gondel gehn, die jeder sieht.

Muffle yourself

1951

Muffle yourself with masks and with cosmetic,
screw up your eyes as if your sight were bad,
never let them see that you're a sceptic
and sadly deep beneath the easy lad.

In darkening twilight, pass the gloomy garden,
the sky a potpourri of fire and night –
muffle yourself, the tears, the exacting craftsman,
let no-one see the flesh that won the fight.

The fissures, lacerations, transmutations,
the core when your destruction's under way,
muffle, pretend the distant exhalations
of song are from that gondola in the bay.

Wir ziehn einen großen Bogen

Wir ziehn einen großen Bogen –
wie ist nun das Ende – wie?
Über die Berge gezogen
und vor allem die Monts Maudits.

Wir holen aus Cannes Mimosen
für eine Stunde her,
wir hängen an unsern Neurosen
sonst hätten wir gar nichts mehr.

Wir träumen von Sternenbahnen
und fleischgewordner Idee,
wir spielen alle Titanen
und weinen wie Niobe.

Das Ende, immer das Ende –
schon schießt ein anderer vor
und nennt sich Wächter und Wende,
Hellene – goldenes Tor.

Die Gräber, immer die Gräber –
bald werden auch die vergehn,
hier, sagt der Friedhofsgärtner,
können neue Kreuze stehn.

Wer altert, hat nichts zu glauben,
wer endet, sieht alles leer,
sieht keine heiligen Tauben
über dem Toten Meer.

Auch wir gingen aus, uns üben
zu Sprüchen und sanfter Tat,
doch es schleifte uns zum Trüben
und zu guter Herzen Verrat.

We draw a great arc

1951

We draw a great arc in existence –
and ask, how will it end? –
Over the mountainous distance
and the Monts maudits, my friend.

From Cannes we bring mimosas
that last no more than an hour,
we rely on our neuroses
to counterfeit staying power.

We dream of starry environs,
the idea incarnate in sleep,
we play at being Titans,
like Niobe we weep.

The ending, always the ending –
another promoted by fate
who claims he's a prophet ascending,
a Hellene – the Golden Gate.

The gravestones, always the gravestones –
soon they too will decay,
here, say the gravedigger's jawbones,
new crosses may stand one day.

Who ages has no need of visions,
who dies sees a void, no more,
and sees no holy pigeons
over the Dead Sea shore.

And we had good intentions
of preaching and gentle deeds,
but slipped to dishonourable mentions
and dashing good people's needs.

Wie ziehn einen großen Bogen
um wen, um was, um wie?
Um Wenden, um Wogen –
und dann die Monts Maudits.

We draw a great arc in existence
for whom, for what, don't you see?
For changes, for waves in the distance,
and then the Monts maudits.

Die Gitter

Die Gitter sind verkettet,
ja mehr: die Mauer ist zu –:
du hast dich zwar gerettet,
doch *wen* rettetest du?

Drei Pappeln an einer Schleuse,
eine Möwe im Flug zum Meer,
das ist der Ebenen Weise,
da kamst du her,

dann streiftest du Haar und Häute
alljährlich windend ab
und zehrtest von Trank und Beute,
die dir ein Anderer gab,

ein Anderer – schweige – bitter
fängt diese Weise an –
du rettetest dich in Gitter,
die nichts mehr öffnen kann.

The barriers

1951

The barriers are all secured,
the wall shuts off the enclave —:
your freedom you've assured
but whom did you save?

A weir by three tall poplars,
a seagull dips in the air,
that is the song of the flatlands,
you came from there,

in those days the sun would darken
your skin and bleach your hair,
you lived and fed through no bargain,
another paid your share,

another – be silent – bitter
the shuddering start of that tune –
you saved yourself behind barriers
that will not open soon.

Verzweiflung III

Sprich zu dir selbst, dann sprichst du zu den Dingen
und von den Dingen, die so bitter sind,
ein anderes Gespräch wird nie gelingen,
den Tod trägt beides, beides endet blind.

Hier singt der Osten und hier trinkt der Westen,
aus offenen Früchten rinnt es und vom Schaft
der Palmen, Gummibäume und in Resten
träuft auch die Orchidee den Seltsamsaft.

Du überall, du allem nochmals offen,
die letzte Stunde und du steigst und steigst,
dann noch ein Lied, und wunderbar getroffen
sinkst du hinüber, weißt das Sein und schweigst.

Despair III

1952

If you talk to yourself, you talk to objects
and of objects which are bitter to you,
another conversation's not in prospect,
death carries both, for both there's no way through.

Here sings the East, the West is out to swallow,
a trickle-down from common fruits and the trunk
of palms and rubber-trees, and then to follow
the rarest drops of orchid to make you drunk.

You everywhere, you prodigally choosing,
your last ten minutes and you rise to a peak,
another song, and wonderfully moving,
you sink away, know being, do not speak.

März. Brief nach Meran

Blüht nicht zu früh, ach blüht erst, wenn ich komme,
dann sprüht erst euer Meer und euren Schaum,
Mandeln, Forsythien, unzerspaltene Sonne –
dem Tal den Schimmer und dem Ich den Traum.

Ich, kaum verzweigt, im Tiefen unverbunden,
Ich, ohne Wesen, doch auch ohne Schein,
meistens im Überfall von Trauerstunden,
es hat schon seinen Namen überwunden,
nur manchmal fällt er ihm noch flüchtig ein.

So hin und her – ach blüht erst, wenn ich komme,
ich suche so und finde keinen Rat,
daß einmal noch das Reich, das Glück, das fromme,
der abgeschlossenen Erfüllung naht.

March: letter to Meran

1952

Wait for me and do not bloom too early,
then you can loose your tide-spray white and green,
forsythia, almonds, unrefracted sun superbly
in the valley shimmers, for the self the dream.

I appear collected, deeply uncommitted,
wanting substance, always without pretence,
prone to fits of sadness long persisting,
the diagnosis easily admitted,
if passing moments by-pass common sense.

So up and down – ah bloom for me in kindness,
I search around, finding no way out plain
to bring the Reich and fortune if it's pious
on the path to fulfilment once again.

An –

An der Schwelle hast du wohl gestanden,
doch die Schwelle überschreiten – nein,
denn in meinem Haus kann man nicht landen,
in dem Haus muß man geboren sein.

Sieht den Wanderer kommen, sieht ihn halten,
wenn ihn dürstet, wird ein Trank geschänkt,
aber einer nur, dann sind die alten
Schlösser wieder vor- und eingehängt.

To –

1953

It may be you were standing at the threshold,
but cross it you most certainly did not,
here no stranger has the freehold,
and all are strangers not born on the spot.

See the wanderer coming, see him stopping,
if he is thirsty he is given a drink,
but only one, and then familiar
locks are hung on doors and in the link.

Nimm fort die Amarylle

Ich kann kein Blühen mehr sehn,
es ist so leicht und so gründlich
und dauert mindestens stündlich
als Traum und Auferstehn.

Nimm fort die Amarylle,
du siehst ja: gründlich: – sie setzt
ganz rot, ganz tief, ganz Fülle
ihr Eins und Allerletzt.

Was wäre noch Stunde dauernd
in meinem zerstörten Sinn,
es bricht sich alles schauernd
in Augenblicken hin.

Away with the amaryllis

Things blossoming make me fret,
it's so easy and so fundamental
and lasts an hour or several
as dream and life after death.

Away with the amaryllis,
as you see, so thorough,
all fullness, depth and colour,
from initio to finis.

I admit no hours passing on,
with my precarious balance
things shudder apart in fragments,
in a moment they are gone.

Eingeengt

Eingeengt in Fühlen und Gedanken
deiner Stunde, der du anbestimmt,
wo so viele Glücke Trauer tranken,
einer Stunde, welche Abschied nimmt,

Trauer nur – die Sturm- und Siegeswogen,
Niederlagen, Gräber, Kuß und Kranz,
Trauer nur – die Heere abgezogen,
sammeln sie sich wo – wer weiß es ganz?

Denke dann der Herzen wechselnd Träumen,
andere Götter, anderes Bemühn,
denk der Reiche, die Pagoden säumen,
wo die feuerroten Segel blühn,

denke andres: wie vom Himmel erben
Nord und Süd durch Funken und durch Flut,
denke an das große Mammutsterben
in den Tundren zwischen Eis und Glut,

eingeengt von Fühlen und Gedanken
bleibt in dich ein großer Strom gelegt,
seine Melodie ist ohne Schranken,
trauerlos und leicht und selbstbewegt.

Hemmed in

1953

Hemmed in by feelings of the hour, reflection,
the hour you were attuned to call your own,
where so many joys in mourning learned their lesson,
that hour which says farewell in monotone.

Only mourning – waves of war and victory,
defeats and cenotaphs, embraces, bays
are only mourning – armies remake history
somewhere – none knows and no-one says.

Reflect on longing's various dream-dominions,
different gods, a different enterprise,
reflect on tall pagodas ringing kingdoms
alive with flame-red sails against the skies,

and other things: the inheritance from heaven
in North and South of desert and of flood,
the mighty mammoths' final Armageddon
in tundra wastes wiped out by ice and blood,

hemmed in by feelings of the hour, reflection,
inside you still a rushing torrent swelled,
its melody outsang attempted subjection,
no cause for mourning, light and self-propelled.

Auferlegt

Was Er uns auferlegt, ist ohnegleichen,
die Löwen lachen und die Schlange singt,
sie leben in gewiesenen Bereichen,
in die das Schicksal keine Reue bringt.

Was Er uns auferlegt, ist so verschlossen,
man ahnt es manchmal, doch man sieht es nie,
und was man sieht, ist schauerübergossen,
grau, übergrau, gesteigertes Cap gris.

Was Er den Tag entlang und auch die Nächte
uns auferlegt, ist einzig, daß man irrt,
das Tränen macht, kein Glück und keine Mächte
geben ein Etwas, welches Inhalt wird.

Was Er dir auferlegt in deine Hände:
ein Flockenspielen, das du nie gewinnst,
was Er dir auferlegt, das ist am Ende,
das ist um dich ein gläsernes Gespinst.

Laid on us

1953

What He laid on us is unexampled,
the lions celebrate, the serpent sings,
their existences are circumscribed and partial,
for them regret not something fortune brings.

What He laid on us is shut in covers
you sense from time to time but never see,
and what you see is always drenched in shudders,
grey, super-grey, intensified Cap gris.

What He in waking hours and in the night-time
has laid on us is simply: going astray,
which makes us weep, nothing in our lifetime,
no joy, no power gives meaning to the day.

What He laid on you to manage darkly,
a game with snowflakes that you never win,
for what He laid on you is the finale,
a web of icy glass to lock you in.

Was schlimm ist

Wenn man kein Englisch kann,
von einem guten englischen Kriminalroman zu hören,
der nicht ins Deutsche übersetzt ist

Bei Hitze ein Bier sehn,
das man nicht bezahlen kann.

Einen neuen Gedanken haben,
den man nicht in einen Hölderlinvers einwickeln kann.
wie es die Professoren tun.

Nachts auf Reisen Wellen schlagen hören
und sich sagen, daß sie das immer tun.

Sehr schlimm: eingeladen sein,
wenn zu Hause die Räume stiller,
der Café besser
und keine Unterhaltung nötig ist.

Am schlimmsten:
nicht im Sommer sterben,
wenn alles hell ist
und die Erde für Spaten leicht.

What's bad

If you don't know English,
hearing about a good English detective story
that hasn't been translated into German.

In a heat-wave, seeing a beer
when you haven't any cash.

Having a new thought
you can't wrap up in a line of Hölderlin's
like professors do.

At night, abroad, hearing waves breaking,
and telling yourself they always do.

Really bad: being invited out
when home has quieter spaces,
better coffee,
and there's no need for conversation.

Worst of all:
not dying in summer
when everything's bright
and the soil easy for spades.

295

Bar

Flieder in langen Vasen,
Ampeln, gedämpftes Licht
und die Amis rasen,
wenn die Sängerin spricht:

Because of you (ich denke)
romance had its start (ich dein)
because of you (ich lenke
zu dir und du bist mein).

Berlin in Klammern und Banden,
sechs Meilen eng die Town
und keine Klipper landen,
wenn so die Nebel braun,

es spielt das Cello zu bieder
für diese lastende Welt,
die Lage verlangte Lieder,
wo das Quartär zerfällt,

doch durch den Geiger schwellen
Jokohama, Bronx und Wien,
zwei Füße in Wildleder stellen
das Universum hin.

Abblendungen: Fächertänze,
ein Schwarm, die Reiher sind blau,
Kolibris, Pazifikkränze
um die dunklen Stellen der Frau,

und nun sieh zwei erheben,
wird das Gesetz vollbracht:
das Harte, das Weiche, das Beben
in einer dunkelnden Nacht.

Bar

1953

The lilac-vases shapely,
shaded lamps preferred,
GIs going crazy
hearing the singer's words.

Because of you (ich denke)
romance had its start (ich dein)
because of you (ich lenke
zu dir) and ... (du bist mein),

Berlin in grips and banding,
six miles narrow the town,
no air-clippers landing
when the fog is this shade of brown,

the cello is playing too meekly
for this overloaded world,
the hole we're in deserved Lieder:
as quaternary rot's unfurled,

yet the violinist conjures
Yokohama, Vienna, the Bronx,
two buckskin boots let thunder
universal honky-tonks.

The lights dim, fan-dancers sparkle
swarming, herons in blue,
hummers, Pacific garlands
keep women's secrets from view;

and now the commandment fulfilling,
a couple claims the night,
the hard, the soft, both living
their darkening delight.

Nur zwei Dinge

Durch so viel Formen geschritten,
durch Ich und Wir und Du,
doch alles blieb erlitten
durch die ewige Frage: wozu?

Das ist eine Kinderfrage.
Dir wurde erst spät bewußt,
es gibt nur eines: ertrage
– ob Sinn, ob Sucht, ob Sage –
dein fernbestimmtes: Du mußt.

Ob Rosen, ob Schnee, ob Meere,
was alles erblühte, verblich,
es gibt nur zwei Dinge: die Leere
und das gezeichnete Ich.

Only two things

1953

Having passed through forms, so many,
through you and we and I,
fulfilment not in any,
just the eternal question: why?

That is a childish question.
Inscribed in the late-growing dust
you saw only: learn your lesson –
sensible, sick, invention –
your far-determined: you must.

Whether roses or snow or pampas,
whatever could blossom or die,
only two things exist: blankness
and the designate I.

Melancholie

Wenn man von Faltern liest, von Schilf und Immen,
daß sich darauf ein schöner Sommer wiegt,
dann fragt man sich, ob diese Glücke stimmen
und nicht dahinter eine Täuschung liegt,
und auch das Saitenspiel, von dem sie schreiben,
mit Schwirren, Dufthauch, flügelleichtem Kleid,
mit dem sie tun, als ob sie bleiben,
ist anderen Ohren eine Fraglichkeit:
ein künstliches, ein falsches Potpourri –
untäuschbar bleibt der Seele Agonie.

Was ist der Mensch – die Nacht vielleicht geschlafen,
doch vom Rasieren wieder schon so müd,
noch eh ihn Post und Telefone trafen,
ist die Substanz schon leer und ausgeglüht,
ein höheres, ein allgemeines Wirken,
von dem man hört und manches Mal auch ahnt,
versagt sich vielen leiblichen Bezirken,
verfehlte Kräfte, tragisch angebahnt:
man sage nicht, der Geist kann es erreichen,
er gibt nur manchmal kurzbelichtet Zeichen.

Nicht im entferntesten ist das zu deuten,
als ob der Schöpfer ohne Seele war,
er fragt nur nicht so einzeln nach den Leuten,
nach ihren Klagen, Krebsen, Haut und Haar,
er wob sie aus Verschiedenem zusammen
das er auch noch für andere Sterne braucht,
er gab uns Mittel, selbst uns zu entflammen
– labil, stabil, labil – man träumt, man taucht:
schon eine Pille nimmt dich auf den Arm
und macht das Trübe hell, das Kalte warm.

Du mußt aus deiner Gegend alles holen,
denn auch von Reisen kommst du leer zurück,

Melancholy

1954

The butterflies and bumblebees and sedges,
they write, are signs that summer will be kind,
but maybe all the joys which hope alleges
are merely masking something less refined;
the sound of violins, as they replay it,
with trills and perfume, a dress that floats, my dears,
something that lasts, the way they say it,
distinctly questionable in other ears:
an artificial, lying potpourri –
it cannot fool the soul's deep agony.

And what of man – a good night's sleep, as may be,
yet shaving has exhausted him again,
before the post, the first long-distance query,
devoid of substance, the fire's out in his brain;
a more exalted, public undertaking
– there are such things, imagined sometimes too –
impossible in fact and muscle-breaking,
beyond hope, tragically closed to you:
let no-one say, the spirit has the power,
while flickering hints can rarely have their hour.

Do not attempt a clever explanation
that maybe the creator had no soul,
he's not concerned with individuation,
or suffering, cancer, skin and bone control,
he wove mankind from different bits of matter
which he still needs to use for other stars,
he gave us means of lighting our own reactor
– stable, unstable, stable – dreams and scars:
a pill at best will take you for a ride
and make the gloomy bright, the cold subside.

Everything you need must come from near you,
even from trips you get no lasting ease,

301

verläßt du dich, beginnen Kapriolen
und du verlierst dir Stück um Stück.
Von Blumen mußt du solche wählen,
die blühn am Zaun und halb im Acker schon,
die in das Zimmer tun, die Laute zählen
des Lebens Laute, seinen Ton:
vermindert oder große Terzen –
ein Kältliches verstarrt die Herzen.

Die Blumen so – dann zu Vergangenem
sich wendend oder Zukunft, wie sie wird,
da gehst du von Verschleiert zu Verhangenem,
einem Vielleicht zu einwandfrei Geirrt,
ein Hin und Her: einmal versiegte Güsse
und Noah strahlt, die Arche streift auf Land,
und einmal ist der Nil der Fluß der Flüsse,
Antonius küßt die braune, schmale Hand:
die Ruriks, Anjous, Judas, Rasputin
und nur dein eigenes Heute ist nicht drin.

Tiere, die Perlen bilden, sind verschlossen,
sie liegen still und kennen nur die See;
an Land und Luft: Gekrönte und Profossen –
noch eine Herme mehr in der Allee;
nur Äon schweigt, er hält die Perlengabe,
wo alles fehlt und alles zielt,
der Äon träumt, der Äon ist ein Knabe,
der mit sich selbst auf einem Brette spielt:
noch eine Herme mehr – man lasse sie,
auch sie führt zum Gedicht: Melancholie.

if you rely on things, they'll commandeer you
and you will lose them piece by piece.
If you want flowers, take the wilder choices
that bloom beyond the fence, half in the grain,
and put them in your room, and hear the voices,
life's music, in its modal vein:
minor or major thirds, unyielding –
a touch of ice will freeze all feeling.

The flowers so – then turn to the outdated
or to the future, what it yet may cost,
you move from what's obscure to what is fated,
from a perhaps to definitely lost,
a to and fro: the torrents once subsided
and Noah beams, the ark is touching land,
once on the Nile, the king of rivers, glided
Antony, to kiss a brown and slender hand:
the Ruriks, Anjous, Judas, Rasputin
and only your today is not therein.

Animals forming pearls are locked as guardians,
they lie quite still and only know the sea;
on land, in air: prize-winners and custodians –
another herm erected by decree;
Aeon alone can hold the pearl in silence
while others aim and miss and aim,
Aeon the boy is dreaming, self-reliant,
his own opponent in his quiet game:
another herm is due – superfluously,
it too leads to a poem: melancholy.

In einer Nacht

In einer Nacht, die keiner kennt,
Substanz aus Nebel, Feuchtigkeit und Regen,
in einem Ort, der kaum sich nennt
so unbekannt, so klein, so abgelegen,

sah ich den Wahnsinn alles Liebe und Leids,
das Tiefdurchkreuzte von Begehr und Enden,
das Theatralische von allerseits,
das niemals Gottgestützte von den Händen,

die dich bestreicheln, heiß und ungewaschen,
die dich wohl halten wollen, doch nicht wissen,
wie man den anderen hält, an welchen Maschen
man Netze flicken muß, daß sie nicht rissen –

ach, diese Nebel, diese Kältlichkeit,
dies Abgefallensein von jeder Dauer,
von Bindung, Glauben, Halten, Innigkeit,
ach Gott – die Götter! Feuchtigkeit und Schauer!

In a night

1954

In a night of no acclaim,
saturating rain and fog substantial,
in a place obscure of name
so small, unknown and hard to disentangle,

I saw the madness of all love and pain,
the deep contaminants of lust and loathing,
the histrionic show unleashed again,
and God protect us from how hands were groping,

feeling you up, all hot and unabluted,
and trying to hold you without knowing how
to treat a stranger, how darns are constituted
to mend the net that nothing will allow –

ah, these fogs, this cold depressing weather,
this sense of loss of self, obliteration
of ties, belief and dignity forever,
ah God, ye gods! dampness, precipitation!

Tristesse

Die Schatten wandeln nicht nur in den Hainen,
davor die Asphodelenwiese liegt,
sie wandeln unter uns und schon in deinen
Umarmungen, wenn noch der Traum dich wiegt.

Was ist das Fleisch – aus Rosen und aus Dornen,
was ist die Brust – aus Falten und aus Samt,
und was das Haar, die Achseln, die verworrnen
Vertiefungen, der Blick so heiß entflammt:

Es trägt das Einst: die früheren Vertrauten
und auch das Einst: wenn du es nicht mehr küßt,
hör gar nicht hin, die leisen und die lauten
Beteuerungen haben ihre Frist.

Und dann November, Einsamkeit, Tristesse,
Grab oder Stock, der den Gelähmten trägt –
die Himmel segnen nicht, nur die Zypresse,
der Trauerbaum, steht groß und unbewegt.

Tristesse

1954

Not only groves are homes to wandering shadows,
beside the open field of asphodel,
they wander amongst us, even in your legato
embrace while you still dream in cradled spell.

For what is flesh – made of thorns, of roses,
what the breast – of satin, of a curve,
and what the hair, the armpits, the ambrosial
depths the ecstatic eyes on fire observe?

It bears the once there were: the early lovers,
the once there was: when you no longer kiss,
nothing to hear, the whispered pleas, the hungers
spoken have had their season, nothing to miss.

And then November, loneliness, tristesse,
the grave, or crutch to bear grave's candidate,
no benediction from on high, the cypress,
the tree of mourning, stands unmoved and great.

»Abschluss«

Nachts in den Kneipen, wo ich manchmal hause
grundlagenlos und in der Nacktheit Bann
wie in dem Mutterschoß, der Mutterklause
einst, welternährt, kommt mich ein Anblick an.

Ein Herr in Loden und mit vollen Gesten,
er wendet sich jetzt ganz dem Partner zu,
verschmilzt mit Grog und Magenbitterresten:
sie streben beide einem *Abschluß* zu.

Ach ja, ein Abschluß, wenn auch nur in Dingen,
die zeitlich sind, besiegelbar durch Korn:
hier ist ein Endentschluß, hier ist Gelingen,
sie saugen lief das Glas, sie liegen vorn –

mir steht ein Meer vor Augen, oben Bläue,
doch in der Tiefe waberndes Getier,
verfratzte Kolben, Glasiges – ich scheue
mich, mehr zu sagen und zu deuten hier.

308

"Closure"

1955

Here in the bars where I often spend my evening,
devoid of purpose, naked as a child
in mother's womb, and safe in mother's keeping,
world-experience found itself beguiled.

A man, well-suited, with distinguished bearing,
turns, gives full attention to his mate,
softened by a grog-and-bitters pairing,
both attempting *closure*, blissful state.

Ah yes, closure, even in concrete matters
of temporary moment, sworn in schnapps:
a final signing-off, no life in tatters,
they drink deep, having everything under wraps –

for me a sea appears above it, azure,
but life-forms in the horrid depths pulsate,
distorted tentacles, some glassy danger –
I'm loth to interpret or to annotate.

Kommt

Kommt, reden wir zusammen
wer redet, ist nicht tot,
es züngeln doch die Flammen
schon sehr um unsere Not.

Kommt, sagen wir: die Blauen,
kommt, sagen wir: das Rot,
wir hören, lauschen, schauen
wer redet, ist nicht tot.

Allein in deiner Wüste,
in deinem Gobigraun –
du einsamst, keine Büste,
kein Zwiespruch, keine Fraun,

und schon so nah den Klippen,
du kennst dein schwaches Boot –
kommt, öffnet doch die Lippen,
wer redet, ist nicht tot.

Come

1955

Come, let's talk together,
who's talking is not dead,
already flames engender
panic in the head.

Come, we say: the colours,
come, the blue and red,
we look and listen by numbers,
who's talking is not dead.

Alone in your Sahara,
your grey and lonely life,
no bust in the empty parlour,
no dialogue, no wife,

already cliffs are looming,
your final sail is spread,
come and start communing,
who's talking is not dead.

Worte

Allein: du mit den Worten
und das ist wirklich allein,
Clairons und Ehrenpforten
sind nicht in diesem Sein.

Du siehst ihnen in die Seele
nach Vor- und Urgesicht,
Jahre um Jahre – quäle
dich ab, du findest nicht.

Und drüben brennen die Leuchten
in sanftem Menschenhort,
von Lippen, rosigen, feuchten
perlt unbedenklich das Wort.

Nur deine Jahre vergilben
in einem anderen Sinn,
bis in die Träume: Silben –
doch schweigend gehst du hin.

Words

1955

Really solitary,
you and words, alone,
no trumpets and triumphal entry,
something less well-known.

You delve into their spirit
to find a primal core,
year after year – no minute
reveals a fraction more.

Lamps burn as you listen
in a gentle human key,
from rosy lips that glisten
the word pearls artlessly.

Your years only turn yellow,
following a life apart,
still syllables seek their fellow –
but silent you depart.

Gedicht

Und was bedeuten diese Zwänge,
halb Bild, halb Wort und halb Kalkül,
was ist in dir, woher die Dränge
aus stillem trauernden Gefühl?

Es strömt dir aus dem Nichts zusammen,
aus Einzelnem, aus Potpourri,
dort nimmst du Asche, dort die Flammen,
du streust und löschst und hütest sie.

Du weißt, du kannst nicht alles fassen,
umgrenze es, den grünen Zaun
um dies und das, du bleibst gelassen,
doch auch gebannt in Mißvertraun.

So Tag und Nacht bist du am Zuge,
auch sonntags meißelst du dich ein
und klopfst das Silber in die Fuge,
dann läßt du es – es ist: das Sein.

Poem

What is the meaning of these compulsions,
half image, half word, half leitmotif,
what is in you, what convulsions
arise from a sense of quiet grief?

From nothingness a streaming together,
from single things, from potpourri,
from one place ashes, flames from another,
you scatter, douse, make formulae.

You know you cannot hope to tackle
everything, so plant a green fence
round this and that, be always tranquil,
defy the lure of doubting sense.

Thus day and night you must deliver,
your chiselled blocks no flight allow,
hammer building-joints of silver
then stop – you've made pure being now.

Aprèslude

Tauchen mußt du können, mußt du lernen,
einmal ist es Glück und einmal Schmach,
gib nicht auf, du darfst dich nicht entfernen,
wenn der Stunde es an Licht gebrach.

Halten, Harren, einmal abgesunken,
einmal überströmt und einmal stumm,
seltsames Gesetz, es sind nicht Funken,
nicht alleine – sieh dich um:

Die Natur will ihre Kirschen machen,
selbst mit wenig Blüten im April
hält sie ihre Kernobstsachen
bis zu guten Jahren still.

Niemand weiß, wo sich die Keime nähren,
niemand, ob die Krone einmal blüht –
Halten, Harren, sich gewähren
Dunkeln, Altern, Aprèslude.

Aprèslude

1955

You must be able to dive or learn to do it,
one day brings happiness, one day disgrace,
do not give up, you must not hide and rue it
if light was wanting in this case.

Hold fast, hold up, if one day in low spirits,
another overstreamed, another dumb,
uncommon law, not sparky little snippets,
not alone – something to come:

nature is set on making cherries,
even with April blossoms that are too few,
keeping back her stone-fruit berries
for good years to dedicate them to.

No-one knows how seeds attain their quorum,
no-one can guess the blossom's magnitude –
hold fast, hold up, live your portion,
darkness, ageing, aprèslude.

Herr Wehner

Dies ist meiner
dieser Her Wehner
der bei uns Hauslehrer war
früh an Lungenphtise verschied
nachdem er meinen jüngsten Bruder angesteckt hatte,
der starb an meningitis tuberkulosa.

Stammte aus Lissa
Sohn eines Schmiedes
ging immer in Holzpantinen
was bei uns unüblich war,
seine Braut Liska
war einen Pfingsten bei uns
Tochter eines Polizeimajors
also was Besseres
sie kicherten oft abends
wenn die Mücken summten
und wir schlafen gehn mussten
aber, wie ich später hörte,
war es wohl doch nichts Rechtes.

Dieser Herr Wehner
ist insofern meiner
als er irgendwo begraben liegt,
vermodert in polnischem Kombinat,
keiner der Gemeindemitglieder
wird seiner gedenken,
aber vor mir steigt er manchmal auf
grau und isoliert
unter geschichtlichen Aspekten.

Herr Wehner

This one is mine
this Herr Wehner
who was our live-in tutor,
and died young of pulmonary phthisis
after having infected my youngest brother,
who died of meningitis tuberculosa.

Came from Lissa
son of a blacksmith
always wore wooden clogs
which was not usual where we lived,
his fiancée Liska
stayed with us one Whitsuntide
daughter of a police major
and so of the better sort
they often giggled in the evenings
when midges were humming
and we had to go to bed
but, as I later heard,
there was probably something wrong there.

This Herr Wehner
is mine inasmuch
as he is buried somewhere,
mouldering in the Polish factory belt,
no member of the congregation
will remember him,
but he sometimes comes to mind for me
grey and isolated
as an aspect of history.

319

Kann keine Trauer sein

In jenem kleinen Bett, fast Kinderbett, starb die Droste
(zu sehn in ihrem Museum in Meersburg),
auf diesem Sofa Hölderlin im Turm bei einem Schreiner,
Rilke, George wohl in Schweizer Hospitalbetten,
in Weimar lagen die großen schwarzen Augen
Nietzsches auf einem weißen Kissen
bis zum letzten Blick –
alles Gerümpel jetzt oder garnicht mehr vorhanden,
unbestimmbar, wesenlos
im schmerzlos-ewigen Zerfall.

Wir tragen in uns Keime aller Götter,
das Gen des Todes und das Gen der Lust –
wer trennte sie: die Worte und die Dinge,
wer mischte sie: die Qualen und die Statt,
auf der sie enden, Holz mit Tränenbächen,
für kurze Stunden ein erbärmlich Heim.

Kann keine Trauer sein. Zu fern zu weit,
zu unberührbar Bett und Tränen,
kein Nein, kein Ja,
Geburt und Körperschmerz und Glauben
ein Wallen, namenlos, ein Huschen,
ein Überirdisches, im Schlaf sich regend,
bewegte Bett und Tränen –
schlafe ein!

6.1.1956

320

Can be no mourning

1956

In that little bed, almost a child's bed, Droste died
(on show in her museum in Meersburg),
on this sofa Hölderlin in the tower, in a joiner's care,
Rilke, George probably in Swiss hospital beds,
in Weimar the great dark eyes of Nietzsche
lay on a white pillow
to the last glance –
all lumber now or no more extant,
unidentifiable, unreal
in painless-eternal decay.

We carry in us seeds of all the gods,
the gene of death and the gene of bliss –
who could separate them: words and things,
who mingle them: torment and the place
they end in, wood and streaming tears,
for brief hours a pitiful home.

Can be no mourning. Too far, too distant,
too untouchable bed and tears,
no No, no Yes,
birth and bodily pain and belief
a pilgrimage, nameless, a slipping away,
more than earthly, that stirs in sleep,
and moved both bed and tears –
sleep now!

6.1.1956

Benn names German writers of great importance to him: Annette von Droste-
Hülshoff (1797–1848), Johann Christian Friedrich Hölderlin (1770–1843), Rainer
Maria Rilke (1875–1926), Stefan George (1868–1933), Nietzsche (1844–1900). This
was his last poem.

Wie sehn die Buchen im September aus

Wie sehn die Buchen im September aus
am Oeresund, dem Gardasee des Nordens,
an dem soviel Rittersporn blüht
wie sonst in ganz Europa nicht zusammen
und drüben Sverige,
das stolze Land.

Armer German sitzt am Wasser
fragt er etwas auf Deutsch
spucken ihn die Leute an,
fragt er französisch,
verstehn es die Leute nicht
u dänisch ist eine schwere Sprache
weich u süss wie Schlagsahne

Alter German,
lange auf Galeere gerudert,
wer auf Galeere sitzt
sieht die Wasser von unten
kann die Ufer nicht beobachten
die Möven nicht verfolgen
alles Schiffsbauch
Schimmelzwieback
Fussfessel,
Schlick Impressionen
für hohes Leben

How do the beeches look

Nachlass

How do the beeches look in September
on the Oeresund, the Garda of the North,
with larkspur blooming in a profusion
the whole of Europe cannot match,
and Sweden over there,
the proud country.

A poor Deutscher sits by the water,
if he puts a question in German
people spit at him,
in French
they don't understand
and Danish is difficult
soft and sweet like whipped cream.

Old Deutscher,
long chained in the galleys,
those who row galleys
see the underside of water
cannot watch the shore
or the flight of gulls
nothing but ship's belly
mouldy biscuit
ankle irons,
slime impression
not the high life.

Von Bremens Schwesterstadt

Von Bremens Schwesterstadt
bis Sils-Maria –
ich hab das Alles satt,
die Vita mia,

weiss Gott, ich weiss nicht mehr,
was ich geschrieben,
ein Zug von d'outremer
hat mich getrieben,

doch jetzt kein Hafenglück,
man kehrt nicht wieder,
man sieht aufs Meer zurück
und senkt die Lider.

From Bremerhaven

Nachlass

From Bremerhaven pat
to Sils-Maria –
I've had enough of that,
the vita mia,

I've no time to spare
for what I've written,
a wind from outremer
has kept me driven,

but now no harbour calls,
return is blighted,
the travelled seascape palls,
you close your eyelids.

Epilog 1949

I

Die trunkenen Fluten fallen –
die Stunde des sterbenden Blau
und der erblaßten Korallen
um die Insel von Palau.

Die trunkenen Fluten enden
als Fremdes, nicht dein, nicht mein,
sie lassen dir nichts in Händen
als der Bilder schweigendes Sein.

Die Fluten, die Flammen, die Fragen –
und dann auf Asche sehn:
»Leben ist Brückenschlagen
über Ströme, die vergehn.«

II

Ein breiter Graben aus Schweigen,
eine hohe Mauer aus Nacht
zieht um die Stuben, die Steigen,
wo du gewohnt, gewacht.

In Vor- und Nachgefühlen
hält noch die Strophe sich:
»Auf welchen schwarzen Stühlen
woben die Parzen dich,

aus wo gefüllten Krügen
erströmst du und verrinnst
auf den verzehrten Zügen
ein altes Traumgespinst.«

Epilogue 1949

1949

I

The drunken floods are falling –
the hour of a dying blue
and the corals withdrawing
round the island of Palau.

The drunken floods are going,
not yours, not mine, a scam,
they leave you holding nothing
but the images' silent I am.

The floods, the flames, the enigmas –
and then from the ashes hear:
'Life is building bridges
over rivers that disappear'.

II

A substantial ditch of silence,
a towering rampart of night
surrounds the rest and movements
you chose to live and fight.

Prophetic and retrospective,
the strophe is not gainsaid:
'On what looms esoteric
did the Parcae weave your thread,

out of what brimming amphorae
pours your diminishing stream,
your features wasted restoring
an ancient patterned dream.'

327

Bis sich die Reime schließen,
die sich der Vers erfand,
und Stein und Graben fließen
in das weite, graue Land.

III

Ein Grab am Fjord, ein Kreuz am goldenen Tore,
ein Stein im Wald und zwei an einem See –:
ein ganzes Lied, ein Ruf im Chore:
»Die Himmel wechseln ihre Sterne – geh!«

Das du dir trugst, dies Bild, halb Wahn, halb Wende,
das trägt sich selbst, du mußt nicht bange sein
und Schmetterlinge, März bis Sommerende,
das wird noch lange sein.

Und sinkt der letzte Falter in die Tiefe,
die letzte Neige und das letzte Weh,
bleibt doch der große Chor, der weiterriefe:
die Himmel wechseln ihre Sterne – geh.

IV

Es ist ein Garten, den ich manchmal sehe
östlich der Oder, wo die Ebenen weit,
ein Graben, eine Brücke, und ich stehe
an Fliederbüschen, blau und rauschbereit.

Es ist ein Knabe, dem ich manchmal trauere,
der sich am See in Schilf und Wogen ließ,
noch strömte nicht der Fluß, vor dem ich schauere,
der erst wie Glück und dann Vergessen hieß.

Until the rhymes are partnered
as the lines decide they should be,
and ditch and rampart are answered
in the wide grey landscape set free.

III

A grave by the fjord, a cross by the golden entrance,
a stone in the forest, by a lake are two,
a song complete, a choral sentence:
'The skies are changing their stars, farewell to you'.

What you have borne, the madness, the new thunder,
will bear itself, you must not fear to know,
the butterfly lives to the end of summer,
a long time still to go.

And should the last one flutter, to darkness sinking,
the last decline, the last taboo,
the great choir still exultantly is singing:
the skies are changing their stars, farewell to you.

IV

A garden in my mind I sometimes visit
East of the Oder, where wide plains await,
a ditch, a bridge, I'm standing in a thicket,
blue lilac, ready to intoxicate.

A boy I sometimes see control the rudder
on a little sedgy lake, I mourn him yet,
before the floods began that made me shudder,
promising joy, but better to forget.

Es ist ein Spruch, dem oftmals ich gesonnen,
der alles sagt, da er dir nichts verheißt –
ich habe ihn auch in dies Buch versponnen,
er stand auf einem Grab: »tu sais« – du weißt.

V

Die vielen Dinge, die du lief versiegelt
durch deine Tage trägst in dir allein,
die du auch im Gespräche nie entriegelt,
in keinen Brief und Blick sie ließest ein,

die schweigenden, die guten und die bösen,
die so erlittenen, darin du gehst,
die kannst du erst in jener Sphäre lösen,
in der du stirbst und endend auferstehst.

A saying there is too I often remember,
it promises nothing, simply tells you so –
a thread it is in this book's texture
and stood upon a grave: 'tu sais' – you know.

V

The many things that you have sealed so deeply,
that you have borne within you all your days,
no conversation unlocked them indiscreetly,
no letter and no revelatory gaze,

good or evil, they are always silent,
your daily struggles, all that gave you pain
only in the one sphere can be lightened
in which you die and, ending, live again.

PROSE

Brains

1915

Whoever believes it is possible to lie with words
might think that was happening here

Rönne, a young doctor who had previously done a lot of dissection, was travelling through South Germany towards the North. He had spent the last months doing nothing; his two-year placement in an institute of pathology meant that about two thousand corpses had passed through his hands without thinking, which had left him exhausted in a remarkable and inexplicable way.

Now he sat in a corner seat facing forward: this is wine country, he decided, fairly flat, with a succession of scarlet fields passing, smoking with poppies. It is not particularly hot; a blue floods the sky, damp and wafted up from lake shores; every house leans on roses, many a one quite submerged. I shall buy a book and a pencil: I shall write about as much as possible to stop it all flowing away. So many years I have lived, and everything has sunk into oblivion. When I began, did it stay with me? I no longer know.

Then in many tunnels his eyes lay ready to leap up and capture the returning light: men were working in the hay; wooden bridges, stone bridges; a town and a car crossing hills to stop before a house.

Verandas, wards and coach-houses, built on top of a mountain range in a forest – here Rönne was to deputise for the doctor-in-chief for a few weeks. Life is so all-powerful, he thought; this hand will not be able to delve to the bottom of it, and looked at his right hand.

There was no one on site apart from staff and patients; the place was high up; Rönne had a solemn feeling; illuminated by his solitariness he discussed official matters distantly and coldly with the nurses.

He let them do everything; turning levers, attaching lamps, switching on motors, using a mirror to shine light on this and that – it did him good to see science divided up into a series of manipulations, the coarser ones of a blacksmith, the more precise ones worthy of a clockmaker. Then he took his own hands, moved them over the x-ray tube, adjusted the mercury level of the quartz lamp, enlarged or narrowed a gap through which light fell on a back, pushed a funnel into an ear, took cotton wool and let it lie in the passage and concentrated on the effects of this procedure on the ear's owner: how ideas developed of helpers, healing, a good doctor, general confidence and well-being, and how the removal of fluids could affect the psyche. Then an accident arrived and he took a small piece of wood cushioned with wadding, pushed it under the damaged finger, wound a stout bandage around it and considered how this finger seemed to have been broken by a jump over a ditch or an unnoticed root, by wildness or indiscretion, in short, with how deep a connection to the course and the destiny of this life, while he now had to take care of it like something far away or fugitive, and he tried to catch the sound in the depths when, just as pain set in, a more distant voice might be heard.

It was the practice in this institution to release those with no chance of recovery back to their families, while concealing this circumstance, because of the mass of documentation and dirt which death brings with it. Rönne walked up to one such and examined him: the artificial opening at the front, the back with bedsores, and in between a little decayed flesh; congratulated him on being successfully cured and watched him padding away. He will now go home, thought Rönne, consider the pain as a tedious accompaniment of recovery, adopt the concept of renewal, give his son advice, educate his daughter, support bourgeois values, take on his neighbour's general view of things, until night comes with blood in the throat. Whoever believes it is possible to lie with words might think that was happening here.[1] But if I could lie with words, I would probably not be here. Yet did I lie when I said to this man: Good luck!

One morning he sat at his breakfast table in shock; he was feeling so deeply: the doctor-in-chief would go on leave, a deputy would come, get up at this time and eat his bread roll: you think you are eating, and breakfast is having its effect on you. Nevertheless he went on issuing whatever questions and orders were necessary; tapped one finger of his right hand against one of the left, then a lung appeared under them; walked past beds: good morning, how's the stomach? But it could occasionally happen now that he would walk through the wards without asking each patient the regulation question, whether about the frequency of his coughs or the temperature of his

---

1 In his letter to F.W. Oelze dated Berlin, 23 January 1946, Benn glossed this remark by adding: ' – but one cannot lie with words, they submit to the man who lives and plays with them'.

intestines. When I walk through the rows of prone figures – this occupied him too deeply – I keep falling into two eyes, being noticed and thought about. I am being associated with friendly and serious objects; maybe I am taken in by a house they are longing to return to, maybe a piece of tanner's bark they once tasted. And I also had two eyes once with glances that ran backwards; yes indeed, I existed: without questions and composed. How did I get here? Where am I? A little fluttering, a dissipation.

He tried to think when it might have begun, but no longer knew: I am walking along a street and see a house and remember a castle like this in Florence, but they only appear to correspond and are extinct.

Something from above is weakening me. There is no steadiness left behind my eyes. Space surges so endlessly; surely once it flowed towards one point. The bark that held me together has decayed.

Often, when he had returned to his room from such rounds, he turned his hands to and fro and looked at them. And once a nurse noticed him smelling them, or rather, moving his head above them as if he were testing their air, and then joining the lightly curved surfaces together, open upwards, by the little fingers, and then moving them together and apart, as if he were breaking open a large soft fruit, or bending something in two. She told the other nurses, but no-one knew what it meant. Until it happened that a largish animal was slaughtered in the institute. Rönne arrived, apparently by chance, as the head was being cut open, took the contents in his hands and bent the two halves apart. Then it struck the nurse that this was the movement she had observed in the corridor. But she could not make a connection and soon forgot about it.

But Rönne went through the gardens. It was summer; adders' tongues rocked the blue of the sky, the roses were blooming, headed with sweetness. He sensed the pressure of the earth: right up to the soles of his feet, and the swelling of forces: no longer through his blood. But he preferred to go along paths which lay in shadow and had many benches; often he had to rest from the boundlessness of light, and felt himself the victim of a breathless sky.

Gradually he began fulfilling his duties only irregularly; and especially if he was expected to express an opinion about something to the manager or the matron, if he felt that now it was important on his part to voice a contribution about the matter in question, he really broke down. What should one say about some event? If it didn't happen one way, it would happen a little differently. The post would not remain vacant. But he only wanted to watch what he saw quietly and rest in his room.

But when he was lying down, he was doing so not as someone who had only arrived a few weeks ago, from a lake and across the mountains; but as if he had grown up with the place where his body now lay and had been weakened by all those years; and from head to foot was covered with something stiff and waxy, like a deposit from the bodies which had been his daily companions.

In the time that followed too he was much occupied with his hands. The nurse who worked for him loved him very much; he always talked to her with such entreaty, although she did not really know what was at stake. He often began with a certain mockery: he knew these strange structures, he had held them in his hands. But then he would relapse again: they lived according to laws which were not ours, and their fate was as foreign to us as that of a river we are sailing on. And then completely extinguished, his glance already benighted: this was a matter of twelve chemical elements which had not come together at his command and would separate without asking him. Where would they go, should one say? Some breeze was blowing over them, that was all.

He was not facing any thing now; he had no power over space, he said once; lay on his bed almost the whole time and hardly moved.

He locked his room door behind him so that no-one could burst in on him; he wanted to open and confront with composure.

Hospital vehicles, he ordered, might drive to and fro along the highway; he had observed that the sound of moving cars did him good: it was so far away, it was like before, travelling to an unknown town.

He lay always in one position: stiffly on his back. He lay on his back in a long chair, the chair stood in a straight room, the room stood in the house and the house on a hill. Apart from a few birds he was the highest animal. So the earth carried him gently through the ether and without disturbance past all the stars.

One evening he went down to the halls where patients were lying: he looked along the rows of chairs, where they were all quietly awaiting a cure under their blankets; he looked at them lying there: all from their home country, out of sleep full of dreams, of going home at evening time, of songs from father to son, between happiness and death – he looked along the hall and went back.

The doctor-in-chief was recalled, he was a friendly man, he said one of his daughters had been taken ill. But Rönne said: you see, in my hands I held them, a hundred or a thousand; many were soft, many were hard, all very prone to melting away; men, women, over-ripe and full of blood. Now I always hold my own in my hands and have always to investigate what is possible for me. If at birth the forceps had pressed a little deeper into my temple …? If I had been hit repeatedly on a particular place in the head …? What is it about brains? I always wanted to fly up like a bird out of the ravine; now I live outside in the crystal. But now please set me free to go, I'll swing again – I was so tired – this way is on wings– with my blue anemone sword – in the midday cataract of light – in fragments of the South – in decomposing clouds – atomising stars – my temples dissolving.

The birthday

1916

Sometimes an hour, you are there; the rest is what happens.
Sometimes the two floods rise up into a dream.

By degrees a doctor had reached more than twenty-nine years old and in general thought there was no point in summoning up feelings of a particular kind.

But, as old as he was, he did wonder about this and that. An urge to find the meaning of existence confronted him repeatedly: who fulfilled it: the gentleman striding along with an umbrella under his arm; the woman knitting as she sat by the elder-tree, the market over, in the evening breeze; the gardener who knew all the names: cherry laurel and cacti, and for whom the red berry in the dead bush was last year's?

He was born in the North German plain. In Southern countries, of course, the sand was light and loose; a wind – that had been proved – could carry grains around the entire world; here was the dust grain, big and heavy.

What had he experienced: love, poverty and x-ray tubes; rabbit-hutches and just now a black dog standing in an open place, occupied with a big red organ swinging to and fro between its back legs, comforting and prevailing; children stood round about, ladies' glances sought the animal, teenagers changed their position to see the action in profile.

How had he experienced all that: he had harvested barley from the fields, on wagons, and that was great: stooks and baskets and horse-harness. Then a girl's body was full of water and had to be drained and sluiced. But above everything hovered a quiet, doubting As if: as if you were really space and stars.

And now? It would be a grey insignificant day when he was buried. His wife was dead; the child wept a few tears. She was a teacher now and had to spend the evenings marking. Then that was over. Influencing brains as subject and object at an end. The conservation of energy came into its own.

What was his first name? Werff.

What was his whole name? Werff Rönne.

What was he? Doctor in a whore-house.

What time was it? Twelve. It was midnight. He was becoming thirty. In the distance a thunderstorm was rumbling. The cloud was bursting into May woods.

Now it is time, he said to himself, for me to begin. In the distance a thunderstorm is rumbling, but *I* am happening. The cloud is bursting into May woods, but the night is *mine*. I have Northern blood, I shall never forget that. My fathers ate everything, from troughs and cattle-shed. But I only want, he encouraged himself to say, to go for a walk. But then he wanted to summon up something symbolic, but failed. He found this in its turn meaningful and pregnant with future import: maybe metaphor was already an attempt at evasion, a kind of vision and a want of fidelity.

*

Through motionless blue mist, driven inland from the nearby sea, Rönne strode out next morning on the way to his hospital.

This lay beyond the town and all paved streets. He had to walk across earth that was soft, letting violets through; dissolved and penetrated, he swayed as he trod.

There from gardens the crocus threw itself at him, the candle of early mass in poetic speech, and especially the yellow variety, which to the Greeks and Romans had been the epitome of charm, no wonder it transported him into the kingdom of heavenly things. In pools of crocus juices the god bathed. A wreath of blossoms kept intoxication at bay. By the Mediterranean the fields of saffron: the tripartite scar; flat pans; horsehair sieves above fires, light and open.

He drove himself further: Arabic za-fara, Greek kroke. There was a Corvinus, King of Hungary, who had known how to avoid saffron stains when eating. The dye came nearer without any trouble, the spice, the flower-meadow and the Alpine valley.

Still deep in the satisfaction of drawing such plentiful associations, he came across a glass shield bearing the words *Maita Cigarettes*, illuminated by a ray of sunlight. And now by way of Maita – Malta – beaches – shining – ferry – harbour – mussel-eaters – depravities – came the bright chiming sound of a slight splintering, and Rönne tottered in a kind of happiness. But then he entered the hospital: an unyielding stare, an uncompromising will: to link the stimuli and

341

sensations meeting him today to the store he already had, not leaving any out, tying in each one. He imagined a secret structure, something of armour and eagle's flight, a kind of Napoleonic longing, such as the conquest of a hedge behind which he was resting, Werff Rönne, thirty years old, a doctor.

Ha, not so easy today, open your legs and down from the chair, young lady, the thin blue artery from the hip into the bush, we must make a note of that! I know temples with these arteries, narrow white temples, tired creations, but I will note this one, snaking, a little branch of violet blood! What? If the conversation should turn to small arteries – I stand there ready armed, especially on little skin arteries: At the temple?? O gentlemen!! I have also seen them on other organs, thinly snaking, a little branch of violet blood. Should I sketch it for you? This is the way it went – should I get up? The entry point? The portal vein? The ventricle? The discovery of the circulation of the blood – – – ? Do you see, any number of impressions to be considered? They whisper: who is this man? Standing there composedly? Rönne is my name, gentlemen. I occasionally collect such little observations; not uninteresting, but naturally quite unimportant, a small contribution to the great structure of knowledge and recognition of reality, ha! ha!

And you, ladies, we know each other! Permit me to create you, dress you up in your essences, with your impressions within me, the leading organ has not decayed, it will be shown how it remembers, you are already getting up.

You address the part you love. You look into its eye, give soul and breath. – You have the scars between your thighs, an Arab bey; they must have been large wounds, torn by the sinful lip of Africa. – But you sleep with the white Egyptian rat, its eyes are rose-red; you sleep on your side, with the animal on your hip. Its eyes are glassy and small like red caviar eggs. In the night it is attacked by hunger. Across the sleeping woman climbs the animal. On the bedside table stands a plate of almonds. It climbs quietly back onto the hip, snuffling and hesitating. Often you wake up when the tail snakes across your upper lip, cool and slender.

He stood there for a moment checking within himself. But he stood there full of power. Remembered image ranged by remembered image, between them the threads rustled to and fro.

And you from the house of pleasure in Aden, brooding on desert and Red Sea. Over the marble walls at every hour runs bluish water. From gratings in the floor rise clouds from fumigatory plants. You know all peoples of the earth by their loving. What you long for is a modest house on the Danish Sound. After final peaks of passion, billiards, with boys in light suits playing alongside. – And you, in the brothel through which the war has passed, between dishes and leather daily burst in a hundred ways under unknown limbs or also under bundles of haemorrhages and shit.

He stood transfigured before himself. How he played it out, ah played! rainbowed! greened! a May night quite unnameable! He knew them all. Opposite them he stood, clean and original. He had not been weak. Strong life bled through his head.

He knew them all. But he wanted more. He wanted to approach a very daring territory; there was probably a conscious life without feelings, or had been, but our inclinations – he remembered this sentence most clearly – are our inheritance. In them we experience what is granted us: now he wanted to love one of them.

He looked along the corridor, and there she stood. She had a birth-mark, strawberry-coloured, from the neck across one shoulder to the hip, and in her eyes, like a flower, a purity without end and around her lids an anemone, motionless and happy in the light.

What might her name be? Edmée, that was ravishing. What then? Edmeé Denso, that was celestial; that was like the call of the woman newly preparing herself, the one to come, the longed-for woman whom the man was in course of creating for himself: blonde, and bliss and scepticism out of sobered brains.

So: now he was in love. He explored what was happening inside: feeling. He needed to create superabundance in face of nothingness. To drive bliss and torment into midday, into a bald grey light. But now there had to be flutterings! Those were strong sensations he was up against. He could not stay in this country –: Southernnesses! a commanding position!

Edmée, in Luxor a flat white house or in Cairo the palace? Life in the city is serene and open, the light is famous, glowing with clarity, and suddenly night falls. You have countless fellaheen women to serve you, to sing and dance. You will pray to Isis, lean your brow against pillars whose capitals at the corners bear those flat heads with the long ears; stand amongst long-legged birds in ravines of sycamores.

For a moment he searched about. Something like Copts had come to mind, but he was not able to develop it. Now he was singing again, the soft man in his happiness.

Winter comes and the fields grow green: a few leaves fall from the pomegranate bushes, but the corn shoots up before your eyes. What do you want: narcissi or violets shaken into your morning bath when you rise late; in the night do you want to wander through little Nile villages, when onto the winding streets great clear shadows are cast by the bright Southern moon? Ibis cages or heron houses? Orange gardens, yellow-flaming and sending clouds of juice and haze over the city at midday; a carved frieze from Ptolemaic temples?

He stopped. Was that Egypt? Was that Africa around a woman's body, gulf and liana around the shoulders' flood? He searched in different directions. Did anything remain? Was there anything he might add? Had he created it: passion, sadness and dream?

But what a peculiar current in his breast! Excitement, as if he were streaming away. He left the examination room, strode through the hall into the park. He felt pulled down, down onto the turf, easily mown down.

How tired it has made me, he thought, with what force! Then he was penetrated by the knowledge that fading was the fruit and weeping the pain –: shocks! gaping distance!

The park was glowing extravagantly. A bush on the turf had leaves like ferns, each fan large and fleshy like a doe. Round every tree in blossom the earth lay closed, a pail to water it and meet its every need. Sky and blossoms: softly, from eyes, came blueness and snow.

As he sobs, Edmée grows ever nearer! A marble parapet hammered by the sea. To the South assembled lilies and barques. A violin opens you, deep into your silences –

He flashed up a glance. He was trembling: against the grass stormed radiance, damp from a golden hip; and earth mounting the light. To and fro moved a tongue of temptation; from its plumage showers of blossom escaped the magnolia into a breeze rubbing past.

Edmée was laughing: roses and bright water.

Edmée was walking: through steep paths, amongst violets, in a light from islands, out of osmium-blue seas, bordering blocks of stone and star; doves, fieldfares, hacked silver with their wings.

Edmée was tanning, a bluish oval. She was playing by palm-trees, she had loved a great deal. Like a shawl she carried her genitals coolly

344

through the movement of her warmed steps, her hand heavy on her hip, harvest-yellow, beneath corn and seed.

In the garden, commingling. The flowerbed echoed no more of colours, buzzing of bees browned the hedge no more. Extinguished were direction and slope: a blossom floating stopped and stood still in the blue, hinge of the world. Crowns were dissolving softly, chalices collapsing, the park sinking in the blood of formlessness. Edmée spread herself down. Her shoulders became smooth, two warm ponds. Now she was slowly closing her hand around a shaft, ripeness in her abundance, mown in brown, at her fingers, under great sheaves of transfigured bliss – –:

Now he was streaming within, now a tepid dissolution. And now connections were getting tangled, the flesh of his self sank –:

Steps echoed across the slope of a valley through a flat white town: dark gardens closed the lanes. On cornices and architraves, which in their decay presented gods and mysteries, distributed through a Florentine country, lay drops of bright blood. A shadow staggered amongst limbs which said nothing, amongst grapes and a herd; a fountain played, a splintering game.

On the turf lay a body. From cellars spilled a vapour, it was mealtime, pipes and grease, the bad breath of someone dying.

Upwards looked the body: flesh, order and conservation were calling. He smiled and closed himself again: already vanishing he looked at the house: what had happened? What path had mankind taken to this point? It had wished to create order in something which should have remained a game. But in the end it had still remained a game, for nothing was real. Was he real? No; only everything possible, that's what he was. He bedded his nape deeper in green foliage; that smelled of thyrsus and Walpurgis-nights. Melting through midday, brooklike pebbled his head.

He offered it up: the light, the strong sunlight ran unstoppably between his brain. There it lay: scarcely a molehill, ripe, scratching inside was the animal.

*

But what of the Marollen District,[1] he asked himself soon afterwards? Behind the Palace, around whose pillars laurel stands, lanes break

1   In Brussels, below the Palais de Justice; Benn calls it Morellenviertel.

into the depths, down the slope descends house by little house.

One-eyed men idle round carts of snails. They lay down money. Women notch the shells open. A circular cut and the flesh hangs down pink. They dip it in a cup of broth and bite. The woman coughs, they have to move on.

Soothsayers using transference of ideas ceaselessly ring shrill bells especially aimed at women and have batteries.

Gipsy women in front of barrows, rays, flat, violet and silver, their heads hacked off; some cut in half, incised and hung up to dry; between them crooked dried fish, coppery and iridescent.

A smell of burning and stale fats. Countless children are relieving themselves, their language is foreign.

What of the Marollen District, Rönne wondered. I must endure it! Up! Down! I swore never to forget this image: the summer which struck a wall of bushes, flaming with plumage, with bunches of twigs, biting with dense blue fleshes, against a wall which did not stream, the damp blue tendril!

He chased down. Around the high lane it all ran together: little houses, burrowed under by long narrow caves which were spitting out bones, young ones strutting, old ones ripe, genitals high girded.

What was being sold: clogs for necessities, green dumplings for the self, anchor-brandy for bliss. What body and soul most needed, tins of ointment and madonnas.

What was happening: little children before kneeling figures, only just having sprung from their breast; hoarse voices, decayed over burnt stone; a man digging unimaginably deep into his pocket; skulls, a desert, bodies, a gutter, stamping earth, chewing: I and you.

He fled deeper down the lane. But there: a little memorial: to the founder of a youth seminary: the soul of man, the community system, the extension of life and the town council strutted full beard and propagation. The structure revealed itself: trials of proficiency were rendered, in fact repeatedly, investigations undertaken which led to conclusions.

Where had his South gone? The ivy cliff? The eucalyptus, where by the sea? Ponente,[2] coast of sunset, silver-blue the wave here!

He ran into a den of thieves: he battled with drinks, hot, brown. He lay on the bench so his head hung down from gravity and blood.

2   The French name of a warm wind along the north-western coasts of the Mediterranean Sea.

346

Help, he cried, a commanding position!

Chairs, objects for gentlemen who, with knees bent, wanted a support under the backs of their legs, were drying dully and Northernly. Tables for conversations like this: So, how are things, mischievous and masculine and around the thighs, ran respectably through time. No death hurled the weepy mademoiselle, every time the hour struck, into nothingness. Shopkeepers scraped their feet; no lava over the dead rocks of the road!

And he? What was he? There he sat between his impulses, the rabble was happening with him. His midday was mockery.

The brain welled up again, the dull passage of the first day. Still between his mother's thighs – that's how he happened. As his father rammed, so he rolled down. The lane had broken him, back: the whore was screaming.

He was on the point of going, when a sound happened. A flute struck on the grey lane, between the huts a song, blue. There must have been a man playing it. A mouth was active in the sound which rose and faded away. Now he began again.

Casually. Who told him to play? No-one thanked him. Who would have asked where the flute had gone? But he marched in like cumulus: drifting his white moment and already drifting away into all ravines of blue.

Rönne looked around him: transfigured, though nothing had changed. Except for him: full to the lips with happiness. Crash on crash, thunder on thunder; the sail soughing, the mast ablaze: Between little basins hummed the dock in its length: grandly glowing the *harbour complex*.

Above the cliffs light is climbing, already taking on shadows, the villas shimmer and the distance is full of mountains. A peg of black smoke darkens the jetty, while the tiny ferryboat battles with the curly wave. Across the rocking landing-stage hurries the busy facchino;[3] hoyo – tirra – hoy sound the calls; life's full flood pouring out. The ship's belly points towards tropical and subtropical climates, salt-mines and lotus rivers, Berber caravans, yes even the Antipodes; a plain edged with mimosa empties red resin, a slope between chalk-marl the oily clay. Europe, Asia, Africa: bites, deadly reactions, horned vipers; on the quay the house of pleasure steps to meet the new arrival, in the desert the sultan fowl stands silent –

3 Porter.

347

It was still standing silent, when the *olive* happened to him.

The agave was beautiful too, but the taggiasca[4] came, delicately oily, blue-black, melancholy by the Ligurian Sea.

Sky, rarely clouded: a tumble of roses; beyond all bushes the blue gulf, but the endless light woods, what a shadow-heavy grove!

A sheet spread out around the trunk meant work was coming. A mixture of horns, claws, leather and wool rags, fed every fourth year. But now men, otherwise dedicated to skittles with eager passion, were beating the crowns, suddenly turned to the fruits.

Weevils in the old wood. A burnet-moth flickering from the myrtle. A little press is being turned, a slate cellar crossed in silence. Harvest is near, blood of the hills, around the grove, bacchantic, the city. - If *Venice* came, he ran over the table. He felt lagoons, and a dissolution, sobbing. The song from the old days of Doge Dandolo echoed dully, he flew like dust into a warm air-current.

An oar-stroke: a deep breath: a barque: support for the head.

Five bronze horses, given by Asia, and around the columns singing: sometimes an hour, you are there; the rest is what happens. Sometimes the two floods rise up into a dream. Sometimes a rustling: when you are shattered.

Rönne listened. There had to be something deeper. But evening came quickly from the sea.

Bleed, rustle, endure, he murmured. Men were looking at him. Oh yes, he said, their freckles, their bald necks, with hair prickles over their Adam's apple – under my crucifixion, I want to sink like the sun.

He paid quickly and got up. But at the door he took another look back at the tavern's darkness, at the tables and chairs which had caused him so much suffering and would do again and again. But there, from the ribbed shaft of the table centrepiece by the woman with leaky eyes, glowed from great legendary poppy the silence of untouchable country, reddish, dead, consecrated to the gods. That, he felt deeply, was the way he must follow forever. Surrender entered him, a loss of last rights, quietly he proffered his brow, its blood gaped aloud.

It had grown dark. The street accepted him, over it the sky, the night's green Nile.

But across the Marollen District echoed again the sound of the

4 Italian olives from the north-west coastal region.

348

flute: sometimes the two floods rise up into a dream.

There a man was hurrying away. There someone was swinging himself into his harvest, reapers were binding him, giving wreaths and sayings. There someone was moving, glowing from his fields, under crown and plumage, out of sight: he, Rönne.

Diesterweg

1918

He stepped out, released, in the procession of decorated masks,
past tutelary spirits, dipping his foot into a fountain,
indicating how happiness flowed away.

The war lasted three years. Since he was fit for service, the doctor in question also lived in deep orderliness. He got up in the morning as his profession demanded; the time of day supplied what was required for his thoughts: blood and bodies, rubbish and cinders; in the distance a single goal: yes, completely emptied of his own life, he had even forgotten his name: his arm was the important thing, the knife; he also had a saw.

However, now and again recently, for example, when he was struck by a smell from a garden that was drooping, or from a woman in flames and trumpets, his other life would reappear, with a nuance or possible transition inviting him to stay, or the swing of an echo, so that he looked up this way and that from the heap he lay in.

At meetings in the casino or discussions of a freer character, he looked around for it inquisitively. For he also remembered, and had recently read again, that this great struggle was not for material goods, no, it was for the defence and preservation of a culture, whose identifying concept, as far as he could discover, was the personality, whether defined biologically as the unique and unrepeatable occurrence of organic synthesis, or portrayed and considered ethically as an irreplaceable human value, or artistically as a free-born and beautiful act of defiance.

If he looked around on such occasions, firstly the doctor-in-chief would be there whose task it was to open proceedings, and who would start with a few witty remarks to the effect that few laurels were to be garnered here, since rumour had it that an audit was likely to be presented which might cause a little surprise here and there concerning the payment of outstanding contributions.

A smirk accompanied these friendly words from the chairman, which expressed the requirement for what might be called a superior spirit in the military hospital, naturally a somewhat annoying but in the circumstances unavoidable issue, to be met calmly and with a little humour.

And indeed they met with great success. In a display of unanimous solidarity, the proposal to meet the debit with a single extra payment was met with general approval as the most sensible way forward, yes, a few voices almost sounded as if they were experiencing a kind of elation and deeper community as they indicated that this common fate sounding for them all could only bring them closer together and elevate their comradeship and make the whole atmosphere even cosier.

But just then a trouble-maker – apparently – stood up. The doctor observing him shivered in anticipation, because that face was twitching and tense. Now battle would begin. Push against push, smoke and flames and, even if torn and wounded, an attitude thundering out against colourless nothingness.

He began with the agenda, probably as a background, the angle from which he would set the bait. That this was in fact the second point on the agenda, he claimed. That this was out of order, he suggested to the others. This needed to be said, he could not forbear to remark.

So here was a challenge to the existing state of affairs. Contradiction appeared and was an obstacle; spirits had to take sides, the watershed was there, naturally demanding.

The examining doctor gazed across the meeting. Yes indeed, here was crisis and the nub of conflict. Freedom of opinion, here was its place; the expression of quite individual existence here in its place!

And in fact, in the further course of things this or that opinion would be expressed and many a conviction represented, before in each case the moment of compromise emerged, which would finally rise to social intercourse, making the evening into a memory of beautiful, in the context of the peculiar external circumstances, quite exceptionally closely unifying hours. No-one was holding back from talking about very personal matters, where his fiancée came from, the badly cut suit, deferred payments, man opened up to man then, barriers fell, hearts ran over. And if towards the midnight hour song arose like: Friends, drink deep of foaming barley from the muses' city early, then each man felt again deeply the great common bond which embraced them all, and the seriousness and grandeur of contemporary events.

Then, deeper than ever before, the doctor felt how life was *happening* here. How here in a narrow space at an abandoned post the human being sat, who opened up, satisfied himself, closed down: he felt the established limits, the security of what had been given form.

He looked along the tables again, and every man who came to meet him was a ball of validities and fulfilment, had a name, and the life of his imaginings played this way and that. Whether he, receiving news from his neighbour, was partaking of the state of things that had already been established, or whether he, as it were lost, was filling the moment with content from his own thoughts – in any case they were sitting cleanly on their chairs, collected and transfigured by the mission of their form.

Then it started: he brooded, he sought, he bent himself far back. And suddenly he also saw the night in which they were all sleeping, and the dream, unchained and confused, against which reality measured itself.

Then he was felled by how far to the side he stood, and he felt pressure to involve himself too. He felt the call within him for a dam, a hurdle, he strove to attain the perfection he felt here. He brooded, he sought, he bent himself far back. For his part, he was watering, was dripping with earths and rivers, and finally was suffering too much: I will name myself Diesterweg, he said to himself, I will step in, I will have a name again, and Diesterweg will happen as well.

As well as what? Firstly the suit, Diesterweg, to cover his nakedness and make walking agreeable and because of the hairy pelt he had lost here in this misty land! Then he would snuffle a little mucus in his nose, regularly, rhythmically, that is engaging: a bit ill-educated, thinks his superior, but a simple family, not formal, a practical man!

A collector's sense! Delight in comparisons! Organic spiritual life! This is a beginning.

But the doctor, solidly, gripped everything at the root. Previously Diesterweg had probably asked on a few occasions why one man was called Mahn and another Matzke. They had opinions and disagreements, and their lived experience was the basis. But now Matzke arose before him, Matzke whose little hammers beat out progress.

Consider those dark epochs in past centuries also, said a new voice, in contrast to us: no worries, free research, water on tap all the way to the pineal gland: and this was Matzke, his profile became sharply established as rejector of the Middle Ages. Altogether: Romance culture as a whole, one heard a third mouthpiece of opinion, honesty and compulsory inoculation is the main thing –: now it was to be the turn of the man who could see into the future.

There: He has some sort of ironic character, remarked a new gentleman, and he meant Matkze.

This hit Diesterweg like a blow. So Matzke had absorbed something or worked something out for himself to a degree which allowed a colleague to express an opinion about it. Not to overstate it – he made an impression. He had real characteristics. He opposed something – in short, as the gentleman had just remarked – he was not merely someone, no, there was something about him.

Diesterweg looked down at himself. He had long wanted to have something about him. He reflected. Maybe it could be achieved with a tic, perhaps a certain movement of the hand; perhaps a short, quick wipe on the cheek with the index finger, a nervous wipe – ah yes, that was it: a nervous wipe, subconsciously, lost in thought, a kind of natural compulsion, highly personal; no-one could challenge what was his alone, at most it might rather be found somewhat revealing, already a slight loss of control, but in any case a strong characteristic, it would be Diesterweg, a nervous wipe on the cheek with the index finger.

He spun the thought out further. He could already see himself transferred from here. He would appear in a new circle. He imagined going to eat for the first time, laughing and drinking, and all the while he would have this little movement of his, as a man who behind this nervous wiping might be hiding an unusual personality, at ease with itself richly and strongly enough to accept the attention of a watching environment to a perhaps revealing, because compulsive, finger movement.

He dreamed on. He would return here, where he was now of little account. Tanned by a sun of quite indeterminate intensity, in adventurous colours, perhaps with a scar and indulgent as to coat and shoes. It would be Diesterweg, but a different one, who was made by a life, perhaps on islands or voyages, from veiled periods when no-one was near him. That was where this wiping of the cheek came from. All the indeterminacy whose traces he bore, campaigns over the sea and Southern battles engraved on his ripened brow and perhaps complicating it a little.

Confused by deeds carried out by his arms, by the rustle of actions he created. Things of the day no longer veiled his gaze; that returned to suddennesses that had formed him, to shudders and defeats which he had faced.

The new Diesterweg, the Southern one. All these poor things of his day – merely the game on a fan, delicate and painted into disappearance. He was the gentleman with the tic, the commanding one before whom reality was defeated; by a grove in which a sacrifice smoked, and in a meadow full of garlands.

With deep glances he looked through the room: this was the human being, the stranger who gave his name; yet he could foresee the waves of occurrences, throwing out forms to let its basins play, and drinking in when its limbs were fulfilled.

Here people ran, snatched at poor property. But he wandered in the foam of blossoms; of light, from shadows, between columns standing on lions over the face of temples – the flight of blossoms. He stepped out, released, in the procession of decorated masks, past tutelary spirits, dipping his foot into a fountain, indicating how happiness flowed away.

Then he stopped by a basin across which an ageing source was discharging. There was a mark, a little scar from the thousandfold lips of boys drinking as they ran out of groves, once as the world that was ending began –

Those are realities, it bursts upon Diesterweg, and these gentlemen are dealing in entirely personal matters! Armed with everything necessary to discern the connections, that is illogical, they cry in a reproachful tone, and are neat and prompt.

By taking prophylactic measures they make individual beings secure, but what they saved in their hundred years – there you see, gentlemen, down there, at the bottom where the pine trees stand: the row streaked with metals – back, back, lemur battalions! A swindle, the whole drive! O the nymph's brow of our first human being!

The gentlemen are somewhat disconcerted, however do not take any further notice of him and tackle jointly the observations put forward by the other side in the sense of the discussion.

If the graves are ready and the stenches shovelled under, Diesterweg exaggerates his train of thought, a piece of shrapnel remains as a charm on their watch-chain – memories of life, chatting about grandchildren, boudoir confidences – but the blind, the cripples coming out of the battles – come to me, we will slash the

354

gentleman to pieces who uses a noun like a knife to eat fish with.

The gentlemen step back a little, their conversation has spread out, its content belongs partly to the past, childhood events woven in with pain, photographs shown: this valley, this hill.

Incontestable, Diesterweg ventures, too incontestable! Show me the pictures, gentlemen, *let us step into a country which the camera cannot show.* Where the plagues, the epidemics, where starvations rustle, where a nameless pack loafs on the shores and the rivers overflow. Or where chinchilla. The day stands in winter redness, the slope in hoarfrost, the auks' cry breaks on dead seas, or where harpoons.

He sat down at a table and the talk took off. While there were food smells, opinion played its part again, previous experience created the ground for personally coloured attitude.

It emerged especially clearly that a stay in foreign countries gave words increased weight and any comparison with tropical latitudes stifled any opposition in the bud.

As for the success of the conversations, often no harmony was to be achieved, often there was neither victor nor vanquished.

Diesterweg looked through the window into the greyness which was evening. Weighty ruin lay over the forms he knew to have once included hills, the sky too had surrendered and the earth was flowing: that was chaos, formlessness. Now he was back in the room and around him the beings croaked about his edge, no, he felt their breath boiling and the flanks hot.

It came from the distance and entered him like a dream. It is dust talking, he felt; the desert cast it out. Then ever more fully, the hour surrounded the house; a pulsation of mist, dissolved and pressing, a gust of wind murmured at the wall, trying to find what it held.

Something was happening; no-one knew what. The gentlemen were excited and flying, they reared up with proposition and response, grew jagged with attitude and raw with personal matters.

Already the windows were bending into the room, it seemed to Diesterweg, and the gentlemen: they stepped from one foot to the other and seemed to be treading water, as if they were separating out and establishing themselves, each one within himself, and there one was moving the flat of his hands up and down over his outlines and around his skull, to see whether he was falling apart.

But by the window, it seemed to Diesterweg, stood the white of an eye, the hot track of a whistle sounded around the house – that is the demon, screamed Diesterweg, he will take everything he once divided into water and land – and prepared for his last bout. There was the room and there were the tables. There were the doctors, there was the gentleman. There was the human being struggling to create himself, forcing himself into forms in fear of the universe, there was humanity, which bore consciousness but had never suffered it – and there was he who had. He had suffered it, he had lived it. He was made invulnerable by his compulsions, he bore his structure like a pelt, he threw it off, he smiled, his temples a little pale from the happiness of downfalls.

He pushed his chair away and stepped out.

Who is stepping out, he was just wondering. Could it be Diesterweg, a doctor who has performed his service, excellently and precisely? Who is sinking down, who is being drawn into the night, it has no stars, it has no voice, into the dumb, the unsayable night?

Diesterweg was considered sick and was sent back to Berlin.

He arrived on a day when snow lay across roof and street, though near to melting. It was soon after the beginning of the year, but towards evening there was already a trace of renewed light in the West.

He took an apartment which looked onto a lively square. He worked during the day, but around five in the evening he would stand at the window of his apartment, which he left dark behind him, and breathed into his very blood how long the brightness lasted, deployed by snow and the cold, how there was a pressure from extinguished light-sources. He took it as a grant to him. In this city where he was nothing, where he as a nothing fought with other nothings for bread, for clothing, for a place in the tramcar, he felt for the first time for many years one thing: the drift. Let machines be whatever they are, and humanity and knowledge, but one thing at least is sweet: to feel in your neck, in your eyes, which protrude a little, in your nostrils that flare, how light begins.

He strolled through the city, which he had not seen for a long time. He entered the building where he had begun his career. He walked through the rooms where the books were kept, upstairs, downstairs, work by work. That had been his intoxication, conquering them all; now he went through the rooms and thought: all the words in the world.

He stepped up to a bookcase and took down the volume which

356

seemed to him the deepest and worth all the others put together, and which no-one yet knew except him: *Development is always complete*, he read, *and yet never at an end* – put it back and stepped out.[1] It is dripping over the spheres, he thought, and inexpressible is the hour when all words are forgotten, I carry them in my dream, the world.

He felt into the light, into the tip of this light which came out of the park, which curved itself into soft down. He felt them, the days which were beginning, trembling with little crocus, all their sobbing and slipping away. He strode past a statue: a nag dumbly trampling centuries, a suit of armour before which dynasties burst – yet for example La Colonna, he thought, and the castles and basalts, now shepherds live in the hills, the fields are silent and fevers drift. Evening enveloped him and swallowed what was Diesterwegish. I want to go deep into myself, sang one voice, I my heart and my crown, I my shadow and my brightness –

Mixed with coolness from awakened forest –: I see hours, a series, great, everywhere and through all days, in the wine of early morning, in the entablature of night –

Already through the shadows' namelessness –: irretrievable one, the hour calls to glances which fill and lose themselves, from breath to breath and from feature to feature.

1 The quotation is from Semi Meyer (b. 1873): *Probleme der Entwicklung des Geistes* (Leipzig, 1913).

The garden of Arles

1920

That is pure yellow. *It dissolves like chicory. Now God
cannot be far away. What God is nowadays: tablets or
the original seed-head with potash or coquero*

In his apartment in Berlin sat a philosophy tutor and wrote: The
whole of humanity can be divided into those driven towards description
or towards metaphysics, Homer or Simmel, age-old eddies –
now on what flood?

Three vases full of garden-heart roses veiling the autumn from his
brow: the whole of humanity can be divided into those drawn to
singularity and those drawn to universality, is what I can see now the
synopsy?

It was afternoon, he looked up. On the street people were walking,
including a solicitor he knew, who was small, nimble, grey and well-
dressed and was dusting down his coat.

Many men are dusting down their coats at this moment, suggested
the man at the desk, it is not an occurrence unique to the solicitor.
He is doing something simultaneous yet again, you have only to stand
up, and there immediately is one of the basic supports of this immense
tension between stabilisation and the unquestionably distant, always
terrible this fatal antinomy of the urge to set something up against
retreat into the absolute.

Leaning back in his chair he thought of Ephesus. Suddenly the
Caystrus valley was there, through which ran the royal road of the
Persians – now the sea had withdrawn from the bay which once lapped
Artemisium, now the cypress stood between ruins and in the lagoons
in interlaced reed was a crowd of fishermen collecting mussels.

It had been here that the self began, in whose last flames the flowers
were now drifting about him. Here the smoke had risen, between
these dressed blocks, perhaps, where now the horses' heads were slowly
blurring, of the small breed which stood immortal on the Parthenon.

Or had it been in Tyrrha, which sank away in olives? Perhaps
here, having escaped from the city, where every man was equal and
a fellow-human ruled, a democrat, a popular tribune, perhaps here,
between roses and silent wine, he[1] had written that they are no longer

1 Heraclitus (540–475 BC), pre-Socratic philosopher, sometimes called the Obscure.

358

the same rivers, even if we step into the same rivers: εἶμέν τε καὶ
οὐκ εἶμεν.[2]

Remarkably chaotic century, there had been only two like it up
to the present time. A swinging of battles across Asia and the Aegean
Sea, a shuddering in brains and gestures between Ionia and the moth-
erly city, a conflagration of numbers and of curves on vases and
triangles for first-born children of that other kingdom.

But now to develop what was only a shadow within him, now to
portray, in the single hour granted him tomorrow, the history of this
Western self, in such a way that his listeners could see how unavoid-
ably, how unconditionally, how with total validity this change was
taking place today towards what at present he could only term hyper-
aemian metaphysics:

Gentlemen, he would say, when you wake tomorrow, the man
now addressing you is on the way to Batavia. He is leaving Europe,
he is circumnavigating your continent, once more brushing along
the mesh of the widely spread veil of its sensations and products, once
more being touched by the hem of its widely developed civilisation,
deployed like a fan whose segments intersect retrospectively on an
island south of the Ionian Sea.

If he sails through the Levant he is brushing the Syrtes, seeing a
flat, unexpressive country. Sandbanks full of melon, palm, fertilised
by human hand, a fellaheen woman baking durra bread outside a
hut of river mud and chopped reeds, but that is not river mud, that
is Nile mud, that is ovarian mud from primal Europe, there they
landed, the first Occidentals with trees from Lebanon for the
Pharaohs' harbours, and brought home from the Nile Valley the
signs for the sacrificial vessel, bees, and the palace.

He fell silent in the presence of this Minoan kingdom: around huge
internal courtyards labyrinthine war-palaces towering, frescoes,
feasts, faience fanned by warm winds, a hectic dream of games,
masques, contests – blown away, trampled by the Thracian cohorts
– on incised stones and sarcophagi one last solemn liturgy – yes, he
remembered a painted vase or some kind of oil vessel from that time,
whitish-yellow on a reddish ground, a female acrobat walking on her
arms, with her breasts held in her hands, and shooting an arrow from
a bow held by her feet – and now it seemed remarkable to him that

2 We are, but we are also not.

this had survived through so many centuries, as it were devoid of meaning, the plant frond and the acrobat.

Drive towards meaning or drive towards things, he repeated, ancient eddies, now on what flood? On this one, he looked up and saw his listeners before him, who would sit before him tomorrow, most in bits of old uniforms, needy, hungry, inelegant, sons of farmers, sons of clerks, sons of this painstaking people which had been seduced by the great Western intoxication of the nineteenth century into that dream of power, into that dream of a happiness proclaimed by Mill, the Englishman. 'An existence as far as possible free from pain and as rich as possible in pleasures both in point of quantity and quality'[3] – seduced and now defeated sons, eating husks in a dead land.

But he wanted to rouse them, he wanted to teach them to despise this century of stale categories, he wanted to be the wave that would carry them to the distant tragic shore with the silent altars and the falling frieze of temples.

'Do you not feel, gentlemen, how the hour glows, do you not sense, as if in the flame of noon through which pollens drift and the South Seas move, sense in your brain, in your blood or in the faltering of your verticals, something like the approaching rush of a great dream?

If I could spread it over you, if I could magic you into the vision of the only self, throughout the history of humanity repeatedly the only cosmically representative self, if I could magic you into the vision of its great, painful and deep happinesses, as into a time of roses, into a narcissus blossom, it is again drawing near from the kingdoms where fate holds sway.'

Whether it was the abundance of his material that excited him, or the end of summer, the deeply autumnal nature of the flowers that drove him on, he had completely lost that murderous compulsion to fix his thought conceptually, to annul matter in favour of the unitary idea, around him the hour was streaming, the unforeseeableness of time, when everyone knew it was over, and no-one knew in which direction it was turning, in the middle of the chaos of his own discipline, the lack of success in its history, the senselessness of this battlefield for sense.

Heraclitus, he wrote, the first lonely creator, clouds are sailing out from your desert, from your country full of ruins. Dark one, how

---

3   John Stuart Mill (1806–73), *Utilitarianism* (London, 1863), chapter 2.

green grew your valley and full of the noise of the source: the absolute is the dream.

There is a scratching, a brushing, a rustling like a mole through the earth, throwing up hills as a result of some damaged instinct; a snuffling, a spreading, a decking-out of lips at the goading of an opponent, falling on a blood-line that must be seized.

Nineteenth century, he wrote, campaign for booty through singularities, concretism triumphant, broken now like no other, under the law of stylisation and of synthetic function – law, validity, truth, shouts from a thousand Pilate gobs, yet it wanders, waddles, abuses itself, womanises, it is flat and steep and both at the same time, the self is beyond the logos and sickness is upon the world.

Inextinguishable by system, immovable by law that dominates matter, yes yes the upper lip, no no the lower lip: unhealthy the word, prisoners' tattoos on the arm, out of the bagno in Toul, life sentence, with the green cap, inescapable, to the catacomb –

Breakthrough from the zone of thought into that of being, last impulses of what has validity in time towards eternal timelessness, feverish jactations of the individual into the unconditional – yes, there were two suns in the picture, in vortices between the cypresses, and a cornfield, on which the sky was screaming down –: a flat forehead, a fleeing brow, a criminal's forehead: the idiot of Arles.

If he could walk through Marseilles and Marseilles is a strange city. Everyone there wants a bastide, a little house in the country, white, especially against the desert paleness of the Crau. Called the French Sahara, against which he always wore dark clothes, a dark smock, that was central, that was different, that was a central point of concentration, rotation around the man from the Drente brook.

If he could walk through Marseilles, calades, the little streets of steps; nothing but innumerable, flat white houses, no city wall, no maximum dose, in boundless numbers – a completely dissolute city.

And sunflowers, naturally always sunflowers, to provoke anyone, firstly always next to the railway and then lapping, shuffling, oiling, olive oiling directly with bright yellow.

He knew this when he got up, he knew it who painted in Provence under that sky, a sky above olives and wine. He painted, he was possessed by the impossibility of remembering; he was crimson with blindness,

361

he crashed it down and he forgot and so created what was endurable.

The man in Algiers[4] knew about it too. Out of a complete forgetting of yesterday he created the novelty of that hour – 'ah, Michel, happiness is like spring water from the Ameles, which, as Plato relates, could not be kept in any vessel' – between pomegranate and oleander, in the glare of the desert, on a cliff in Kabylia he wrote this to Daniel and Dionysus – but the man who shattered it all had to come from the North.

Kant, he thought, diadem-spider, lascivious with value, slave-market, martiniquais, schematisable reifications, wire-skeined, netting all fish and flight-values into the skull's weir-baskets –

Kant, he thought, manufacturer in Golden Sections, matter's great incurver, acrobat of connections, harasser – by systematic methods – into cosmos triumphant –

Kant, he thought, comfortable affair, scholar's study, silhouette from the eighteenth century, starry sky above the jabot – collapsing continent. Stock made from rats' tails, the rats sounding out the wreck, headlong – fleeting – transatlantic.

The desert is growing, he thought, woe to the man who conceals deserts. Leaping off in Egypt, Nile-self, shit-bead thousands of years old, enough of on-the-one-hand and on-the-other balances, swindled upwards with Europe's empires, together into the breaches – spray out your aroma of law, bleed away your validity cypress.

Up with palm-wine that kills the palm! Up with the Bedouin-I maybe in the tropic region, let us consider these simple meals of sorghum flour, of maize in the delta, I mean the *up-front* I that faces things without a thought.

Let us consider the fellaheen-I: broad beans play a major part there, I mean the lettuce-, radish-, colt's-foot-I, with local headmen add a meat diet.

Gentlemen, I must say, you have fallen victim to a quite subtle swindle, a swindle of law, a swindle of conclusions, a swindle of rounding-off – highly paraboloid!

He stood by the window and looked along the street, which stood there so cleanly, with house-front, gas-lamps, waste-pipe, ventilation-flap, spick and span, oiled, stuck together, with a parting on the bald

---

4 André Gide (1869–1951). The following quotation is from his novel *L'immoraliste* (1902), partly based on his experiences in Algiers, though not set there. Benn was to meet Gide in Berlin in 1931.

head of the noun-man – behind it all he dimly felt the country, the wide bread-fruit, the hewing – , this view of the world conditioned by group-formation and the sequence of changes, this four-thousand-year-old swindle of the allegedly continuous self – cramp-irons, he cried, cramp-irons, settled in the North, Kant-crown, who is knocking the hoar-frost from your brow – there were two suns in the picture in vortices between the cypresses and a cornfield on which the sky was screaming down – there is a garden in the distance, leap-garden and lemur-self.

O olive gentle, agave mantle, the greenness and the rocky pale; from ruined blisses, from break-heart whispers, your drink, your meal. O olive scatter, agave shatter away the light of some star-stream, already a roundness is growing at the gable of my eyes and deploying doves in the music of my lids, so early in the morning and with blossoms in the reeds – treeless island of my dream.

Antinomies, sprinkled in browns, once stretched out into Northern discursiveness, here they graze exhausted into falling blood. Along the foliage, the infected foliage, from lines of cut corn, graves for all happiness, from skies, fatally towering skies, go pools of autumn, go ponds of decay.

From antithesis-cleft, from brain-rip, from monistic interlopers: lemur-I, anointed with smoke from the herds, breadfruit-tree titans, ape transcendencies, a violet Zion.

Sky is the flood, land the flame, where its gulfs descend ablaze; a mixture, on a ridge, Yggdrasil stands to the right, pines to the left – this is the place where the eye created.

Free-eye. Algiers-eye. Sweet brow of unremembering. Bird's-eye. Polyphemus gaze under all the shepherd temples, deaf to ecstasy, hissing into the self – by way of Tyrrha, through the Eleatics, through Hegel's identity and Troeltsch's dynamics stepping up to the curve of cross-section, dynamo standing at an angle to the wind of things – to the diagonal motif, into the garden of Arles:

there can create himself, exhausted, with meadows, with the bar of Iris which brooches the town. It is time for mowing, against dande-lion, against taraxacum, as surrogates for tea and coffee, now I must hurry, summer is becoming foliage, soon decay can come and bring veils.

Crazy this umbellate steppe, quite crazy these necks or clubs, this hydrocephalus of yellow, this sultan's tent-square of uniform colouration, this elephant's thick-skinnedness – in short that is *pure yellow*.

It dissolves like chicory. Now God cannot be far away. What God is nowadays: tablets or the original seed-head with potash or coquero (coca).

My God of betel, my bitter little burning on the palate, my little thirst-quencher, what a garden! ganja more likely, a niffy gamble, garnering pregnant earth, jumble with a reed tendency, colour zigzag.

Now willow there, to skewer it; no, cypress, sore from tears. No, tree, treeness, the most general, the most inclusive, the greediest: from Lap pine to araucaria, the most explosive, the summation.

And always no house. Why house? House would disturb. Beloved house, table-and-bed house, home-house, soundless concept-house – but its white white wall: samum[5] of light, split into spray-white, into Orinoco-wide white, oppositional throw of the material to cause rocketing spark-white, *exploded* chromatic system with white geysers – o postman between hebephrenian valeurs! Respectable pouch at the belt, containing: factual letter values, and into his full beard rolled: a padded cell; still staring fixedly from an animal face at the edge of being, from Ephesus to Einstein this heavy antinomy, the bow of the yoke entirely Spinoza: determinatio est negatio – Yet the sunflower motif, that is transition, that is gentle song, Ionic tragedy, at the edge of the abyss the beat of a butterfly's wing: O olive gentle, agave mantle, the greenness and the rocky pale; from ruined blisses, from break-heart whispers, your drink, your meal. O olive scatter, agave shatter away the light of some star-stream, Arlesian garden, lemurs marching, treeless island of my dream.

The city fell apart in blocks of destruction, thunder struck the market, the naked blood. There stood the poacher, the attacker, the night-owl, dissolving in corruption.

The peoples coupled, the young trees crackled: the herds went mad biting hide, flesh drove on blindly, horse-like, sleep as if in scarlet roses. Transitoriness makes me shudder, I am pierced by this high heaven of defection, the treachery of those covered by aprons – where is God's harrow for the seed of loyalty?

Everywhere I look is Peru: with steaming jungles and the biggest rubber forest in the world; deserts are there, on which rain falls once every nine years, a native people, Inca or from Tahiti, vanished,

5   Dry wind in the Sahara.

wiped out, dried up or drowned, in Tiahuanaco on Lake Titicaca: the temple there is larger than life, in ruins, like a cake of dung from a part of humanity with crumbling hangings, with undecipherable symbols on a temple gate –: no sound, no saga, no echo, no sign – the temple there is unique and confused.

That is Arles. Everywhere gulls from the sea, from flight. Everywhere waves rise as if around sites which are being extinguished.

An island consecrated to the moon is there, but foliage mourns by the rivers – end, end – in garlands of roses, as Adonai with a thyrsus, in pine green, on hills and slopes: – nevermore, nevermore.

Where is Hadrian's skull, capturer of cities, kings and lands, where is Hadrian's sweet skull, over which bliss flowed from udders, where is the fat, soft bath skull – gone like junk, with a slug of fennel under the tongue.

Or where is the snake – near the sea the windows overlook is said to have been a trace of its path – , or where else is the snake which stabbed the Egyptian queen, granddaughter of so many kings, the Asian Venus who came to Bacchus?

That is Arles: Arles made of Doric triumphs, earth's dressed blocks, the meadow of Zeus – words in metamorphosis, a scatter of values – shadows and ashes – ποταμοὶ – ποταμοί.[6]

6 Rivers, rivers.

An extract from *The modern self*

… Gentlemen, no biography of the self has been written, but if you immerse yourselves in the history of the relationship between the world and the self, you will see this development with great clarity: the strengthening of a feeling of independence in the individual subject. The self, at first placing itself completely in the external world, hardly distinguishing in its world-view between the position of its own person and the living creatures that surround it, collects and gradually concentrates the subjective feeling of life into the consciousness of an individual existence.

But this, the individualism of the Attic epoch and the Hellenistic period, still entirely objectivistic like the whole world-picture of the period, comes to perfection in two parallel streams of development as modern consciousness, in the sense of being the bearer of the purely phenomenal world.

Running parallel to the change of world-picture, starting with the thoroughly pluralistic understanding of the world in animism: the world split into countless objective individual existences which include the self, an individual being like the others, which does not occupy a place distinguished in any way, via polytheism's gradually sharpening distinction between gods and spirits: the multi-faceted, incalculable, capricious behaviour of spirits opposed to the somehow lawful actions of gods, all the way to the unitary idea of monotheism: parallel to the world ruled by *one* will, *one* law, animated by *one* life-principle, runs a developing sense of human life, in which the self forms within, bit by bit, that idea of subjectivism, that the whole external world is given to it as an inner experience.

You know the way from the obscure and mostly lost work of Heraclitus via Marcus Aurelius's book on himself, from the lyrics of Gregory of Nazianzus and Augustine's confessions down to the great revolt of the Renaissance, when the self gave up feeling itself merely 'as a corporation or else some other form of generality' (Burkhardt); you have before you the obscure mass of subjectivistic motifs from medieval Christian mysticism, you remember the fundamental doubts of Descartes that there was any reality, the neo-occasionalism of Malebranche, for whom all true knowledge possible to us is restricted to the understanding of ideas and their relationships, the psychologism of Locke and his followers, Kant's division of things in themselves and appearances, finally having before your eyes, as a quite orgiastic finale, modern positivism's relativisation of time and space.

Here it is then, this self, bearer of all experienced content, formed to anticipate all content that can be experienced. Beginning and end, echo and flue for itself, conscious into every last cranny, a priori banned from experiments, cosmos, peacock's tail of discursive escapades, god unlaunched by hellebore into a murmuring sound; – consciousness like cakes of dung, passions cerebrisms; consciousness to the point of dreading sunlight, sex intrinsic; consciousness, a cliff with the king's inscription, sick with the mystic thou of syntax, last great letter: Persian, from Susa, Elamitic, threatening plains subjected to violence: inheritance and end and Achaemenids.

Eye extinguished, pupil looking inwards, nowhere persons any more, but only the self forever; ears malformed, listening into the shell, yet no eventuality, only being forever; over-ripe, putrescent, like a giraffe, uncircumcisable, without belief and without doctrine, only consciousness eternally senseless, eternally beset by anguish –: from the coasts to the beaches, from the deserts to the belts, across the seas, onto the great ships, through the breezes, between the seabirds of the Azores, between the flying fish, through the Gulf Streams by way of New York's most shining woman –: damned sunburnt moaning, cowboy ramrodding, prairie rape, if possible in underclothes, snowy linens, sticking out a bit, where California's great fruit and Canada's glowing thrust of summer –, or from poisons, the last, which eat away mucous membranes, to the abyss which brings extinction.

Waking: sniffing: for the Southern word: into the dance: for the Ligurian complex – deadly, Northern, misty curse, Western funèbre.

Brightest Greece, Taine's Hellenes, how strong the neck and how proud the breast. Foot, frugal, young race, shepherds living on three olives, a clove of garlic and an anchovy head; sleeping on streets, the women on the roofs, bright winds, happinesses with a nothing – , their gods, who do not die, whom the winds do not shake, whom the rain never soaks, whom the snow does not reach, 'where the aether opens without a cloud and the white light runs on insubstantial feet'.

Brightest Greece, Taine's Hellenes, poor frugal young race and suddenly: from Thrace, Dionysus.

From the Phrygian mountains, from Cybele's side, while torches burn at midnight, with shattering brass instruments, with incursions of deep flute-sounds from the lips of staggering Auletes, with maenads swarming around in fox-skins and horns, he steps into the plain, which surrenders. No hesitation, no question: the nightly one walks over the heights, spruce in his hair, the bull-shaped one, adorned with leaves: after him now, heads to be swung now, hemp to be smoked now, and now the unmixed drink –: now wine and honey already in streams – now: roses, Syrian – now: fermenting corn – now is the hour of great night, of intoxication and dissolved forms.

There is one hearth for hashish in the world, between Haiti and the Abipones, there is one cry, from an island at the mouth of the Loire to the Tlinkit Indians after the crossing, after the epiphanies. There is one dance between the two kingdoms of brothers, which you see in an embrace: you hold the torch lowered to the ground and you the poppy stalk, you are dreaming and the other has gone before.

It is midday over the self or summer, there is a silence of fruits, across all the hills, a silence of poppies. There is a call; echo's call – that is not a voice, not an answering voice, no happiness, no call.

Now a hurrying in the grove, through the lentisk smoking, it is long after the Adonia, it is summer, Pan is glowing.

'Where are you, whose shadow goes before me, through yellow meadows, through meadows of cuckoo-flower, red-thorn country and elder-filled villages, where are you, I saw you down by the water, between the elms, at the edge.'

'Where is water, the sea is there. There was water without dolphins, where cooing, now it is summer surely, I brushed a thistle, a breath of honey lingered on my hand. The myrtle singing – rosemary, sage, lavender storming her dream; the land smoking, the island burns like resin – where is oleander, to follow the brooks?

Where are you? I am lonely, I am always on pastures, in quail country at my nets, in forests, where herbs intertwine, weasel and Orion's star – '

It is midday over the self or summer, there is a silence of fruits, across all the hills, a silence of poppies. There is a call; echo's call – that is not a voice, not an answering voice, no happiness, no call.

But there are fields over the earth, they bear nothing but flowers of intoxication – stop, Narcissus, the Moira are dead, you speak to humans as to the wind – , how far you felt, how far you splashed, became your own Lyaean image.

Narcissus, Narcissus, the forests are silent, the seas are silent around shadow and tree: – you, earth, clouds, sea, around your shoulders, shouting for procreation, hungering in your fists, to tear yourself pieces out of the body of the world, forming them and forgetting self deeply into them, from all the need and shame of solitariness – then: over the lids the breath of the tree, then: cooing, then: between asphodels you see yourself in the Stygian flood.

Extracts from *Lyric self*

1927

… In the sea there are living creatures of the lower zoological system covered with cilia.[1] Cilia are the animal sense-organ before differentiation into separate sense-energies, the general organ of touch, the basic connection to the marine environment. Imagine a human being covered in such hairs, not only the brain, but the entire organism. Their function is specific, their reaction to stimuli sharply isolated: it concerns the word, especially the noun, less so the adjective, figures of speech hardly at all. It concerns the cipher, its printed image, the black letter, and nothing else.

… Perhaps words are already approaching now, words mixed up, not yet recognisable in clarity, but the cilia can feel that out. There might be a friendly leaning towards blue, what happiness, what a pure experience! Think of all the empty, exhausted metaphors, the unsuggestive preambles for this one colouring, one can call up into one's heart the Zanzibar sky above bougainvillea blossoms and the sea of the Syrtes, think of this eternal and beautiful word. I do not say blue at random. It is the ultimate Southern word, the exponent of 'the Ligurian complex', of immensely exciting power, the principal means of 'pushing through contexts', after which self-ignition begins, the 'fatal beacon', summoning them to stream forth the distant kingdoms, to take their place in the structure of that 'pale congestion'…[2]

Words, words – nouns! They have only to open their wings and millennia drop from their flight. Take anemone forest,[3] between the tree-trunks delicate, small plants, and, yes, further away fields of narcissus, smoke and mist from all the calices, the wind blossoms in the olive-tree, and over marble steps fulfilment climbs interlaced into a distance – or take olives or theogonies: millennia drop from their flight. Botanical and geographical worlds, peoples and countries, all the historically and systematically lost worlds, here their blooming, here their dream – all the mind's frivolity, sadness, hopelessness become sensible from the strata of a cross-section of concept.

1 Cilia: delicate hairs.
2 The words in quotation marks are self-quotations.
3 The two words in English represent a single compound noun in German.

Ah, never enough of this experience: life lasts twenty-four hours, and if there is a high-point, it was hyperaemia! Ah, back again and again into this furnace, into the stages of placentary spaces, into the preliminary steps of the sea from a primal vision: tendencies to regress with the aid of the word, heuristic states of weakness caused by nouns – that is the basic procedure for interpreting everything: every IT means destruction, the tendency of the I to be blown away; every YOU means destruction, the miscibility of forms. 'Come, all gamuts are roaring out ghosts, form dissolves' – that is a sight into the hour and the joys when 'Gods fall like roses' – gods and gods at play.

Hard to explain the power of the word that dissolves and joins. Foreign by nature the power of the moment from which constructs press in under the form-summoning might of nothingness. Transcendent reality of the strophe full of destruction and full of return: the frailty of individuality, and cosmological existence in which its antithesis is transfigured, it bears the seas and the heights of night and makes creation into a Stygian dream: 'Never and always'.

How Miss Cavell was shot

1928

I wish to give my account of Miss Edith Cavell, who was shot as an English spy by the Germans in autumn 1915. I saw her and spoke to her more than once at that time, was required by my job to attend her trial, ordered as a doctor to be present at her execution, certified her death and laid her in her coffin. I do not know if there is anyone else still alive who witnessed both the trial and the execution; neither the Gouverneur who ordered the execution nor the diplomat who entered a plea for mercy saw and heard the proceedings take effect. The occasion for my present statement is the showing of the Cavell film in London,[1] which will reawaken her memory in all countries. No question, she will appear as a legendary figure in the history of the victor nations. Her legend will form independently of the historical and materially effective facts of the occurrence in which she played a leading role, and, far from believing I might be able to correct, clarify or amend the history of her country, I shall simply recount what I can remember. And I remember her, it must be said at once, as an active player who paid for her deeds, as the brave daughter of a great people which was at war with us.

I had been Senior Doctor in the Brussels Gouvernement since the first days of the occupation. One evening in late autumn 1915 I receive the order to await a car at a certain spot next morning to be driven to an unnamed place. I am joined in the car by two military lawyers, one to attend officially, the other out of interest. We drive through the dark streets to the *Tir national*, the Brussels garrison's shooting-range at the edge of the city. The car stops. The ground is sloping. We climb down into a hollow with soldiers lining the route. At the end of the slope there are two details of twelve men each in two rows facing the butt, over which grass is growing. In front of it two new posts, white planks rammed into the earth.

We stand and wait. Now a car drives up. Out steps a Belgian, a civilian,[2] with a Catholic priest. The Belgian is about forty, an engineer, married, father of two children, compactly built, lively movements, unfettered, a flat cap on his head – accomplice of Edith

1 Herbert Wilcox's silent film *Dawn* of 1928, starring Sybil Thorndike, was withheld from presentation in London for a time for fear of offending the Germans.
2 Philippe Baucq, usually described as an architect.

Cavell. With incomparable vivacity, with almost detached ease he strides down the hill to where the soldiers are standing, takes off his cap, with an inimitably chivalrous movement stands before the squad which will shoot him, says the words 'Bonjour, messieurs, devant la mort nous sommes tous des camarades' – is interrupted by the duty military lawyer, who presumably fears a provocative speech. From now on the delinquent remains standing, quietly, knowing he will die, perfect deportment.

Now the second car arrives. Miss Cavell gets out, beside her a Protestant priest, a well-known Berlin pastor who has kept company with her during the last night. Edith Cavell is maybe forty-two years old, has grey to white hair, no hat, in a blue tailored dress, her face lean and mask-like, walking stiffly and jerkily, with severe muscular hindrance, but without hesitation, without stopping she walks down to where the posts are. A moment's pause, she and the pastor; a few metres from the white plank; she talks quietly to the pastor, and what she said to him he later related to me: she is happy to die for England and sends her salutations to her mother and brothers, who are in the field in the British army. Other women are making greater sacrifices: their husbands, brothers, sons; she is giving only her own life – o my country, over there across the sea, o my homeland, which she salutes. A quiet parting from the pastor.

The last act. It lasts hardly a minute. The company is ready, the military lawyer reads the death sentence aloud. The Belgian and the Englishwoman have their eyes bound with a white cloth and their hands tied to the posts. One order for both: Fire, from a few yards away, and twelve bullets which hit their marks. Both are dead. The Belgian has sunk down. Miss Cavell still stands upright against the post. Her wounds are mainly in the chest, heart and lungs; she is completely and absolutely dead in an instant; quite wrong to say that she struggled under the shots and had to be finished off with a shot to the head. In fact she was indubitably dead during the order to fire. Now I walk to the post, we take her down, I feel for a pulse and close her eyes. Then we lay her in a small yellow coffin which is standing to one side. She is to be buried immediately, the place to remain unknown. There is a fear of demonstrations because of her death or a national procession from the city, therefore swift action and then silence and secrecy about her grave.

The political background to this execution was as follows: the position of the German army of occupation in Belgium had been extremely difficult during the first few months. A densely populated country, the quickly vanquished army had been small and its active component transported to England, so there were still men in the country. There was as yet no trench warfare or skirmishes or a proper offensive this way and that, artillery was thundering from the front in Flanders, now nearer, now further away, the Allies could come back at any moment, a continual knife-edge. A smallish occupying force of Landsturm men along the railway-line from Aachen to Brussels, the only supply route for military base and fighting armies. A weak, inactive German troop held the capital, the beautiful, impulsive, excited, hate-filled capital; at its head a mayor who was openly acting contrary to the ordinances of the German commandant; the populace in absolutely unmasked hatred; the national colours and cockades as big as your palm on hats and in buttonholes, on umbrellas and ties; raids at night, danger in the streets, soldiers forbidden to go out alone, attacks on railway-lines, blowing up tunnels, attempts to hit troop transports, that is to say unsafe position, undecided war.

The country criss-crossed by organisations of the enemy powers. To keep watch on the opposition, to collect national forces, for active operations. In addition a secret information service of inexplicable precision: each step forwards or backwards taken by the German front known in minutes and obvious in the expressions of people on the streets, everything we did, every military occurrence at base immediately radioed on to the Allies. But above all the activity of collection, recruitment and organisation of Belgians capable of carrying arms and their transport by night in stages across the Dutch border and to the depots of the Entente.

Numberless espionage cases before the German military courts, and more and more it emerged that women had been in action, had apparently worked out the plans, carried out the operations. Women were not shot, women were taken to Aachen, given work to do, and after the war were destined for rewards and fame as heroines. The husbands had all been harmless and had done the cooking. In the women glowed a fire, they were the heads of the organisation. The weaker sex – could one carry out a sentence against them?

There were about twenty accused in the case against Edith Cavell, with the Englishwoman as leader. This was one such organisation. Its special activity had consisted of collecting Englishmen and

374

Frenchmen who had remained after the battles of autumn 1914 in Northern France and Belgium, some wounded and some who had escaped, looking after them, hiding them, and transporting them to Holland together with Belgians capable of fighting. Their system had proved itself. It had been based in Miss Cavell's house in Brussels. Miss Cavell, as an Englishwoman long known to the German authorities in Belgium, remained in the city as organising impulse. Miss Cavell had been living in Brussels for some years, being a lady nurse by profession, had trained women to work in kindergartens, had been for a time a nurse in the St. Gilles Hospital, and on the outbreak of war had arranged and developed her quarters for these political aims as a Red Cross ambulance station. Her illegal work ran from August 1914 to summer 1915, when she was arrested.

Now the trial began. Interesting conspirators, a social mix: the Belgian Princess Croy, the French Countess Belleville, intellectuals, lawyers, a pharmacist couple from Namur, engineer Baucq, whose shooting I have just described, finally poor coal-workers from the Borinage region who had been engaged for a few francs a night to lead groups through the woods. Adventurism, patriotism, insolent contempt for us, les Boches, accusations amongst and against each other from the conspirators, despair, fainting, national incitement, all these things were played out before us during the two days of the trial.

Damning evidence was given by: agents of our counter-espionage service, self-incrimination amongst the accused, original handwritten documents, and Miss Cavell's confession, which I heard from her own mouth: that this organisation of hers, in the months in question had collected, armed and led across the Belgian–Dutch border about three hundred enemy soldiers and Belgians capable of fighting. This trial was no court-martial extortion, indeed the accused were supported by defence lawyers of their own choice, that is to say Belgian barristers. The facts could not be denied. I remember well the bitter and despairing cries of the co-accused workmen who had been seduced by the principal defendants, especially Miss Cavell, into taking on the duties mentioned above by bribery and the threat of being denounced to the national committees. I remember too the brilliant pleas of the Belgian barristers, some of whom spoke German, who did not attempt to counter the objective facts, but, using amazing references to Prussian history, emphasised the purity of the defendants' motives and begged for mercy. Miss Cavell herself, who was heavily burdened from many sides by her co-accused, behaved with extreme restraint, spoke quietly and very little, kept her stiff impenetrable expression, did not leave a lively impression. Others, Countess Belleville, were the most fanatical I have experienced in their hatred, insults against the tribunal, and their nationalism.

Seven of the accused were sentenced to death, the remainder given severe prison sentences. The sentences against Miss Cavell and engineer Naucq were carried out, he having been already sentenced to death by another tribunal. I had been ordered to attend the proceedings, since the presence of some medical aid had been thought desirable in view of the large number of accused, the probably long time the trial would take and the severe sentences expected. I was only called on once, to bring round a woman who had fainted. The rest of the time I listened and in the pauses spoke to the accused. Those are the facts.

How is the shooting of Miss Cavell to be judged? Formally it was correct. She acted like a man and was punished like a man by us. She had taken action against the German armies and they had crushed her. She had entered the war and the war had destroyed her. The French also shot a woman spy. I believe that today's woman not only understands this consequence but demands it.

Should she have been pardoned? From the logic of the military system this could not happen. Think of these three hundred enemy soldiers now on the other side. Think of this belligerent company shooting at our soldiers. Think of three hundred rifles on the Yser or at Langemarck, set up by Edith Cavell, that mowed into our lines. What court-martial would not have been obliged to condemn her to death, what Gouverneur who felt responsible for his troops could ever pardon her?

In liberal circles it is usual to characterise the execution of Edith Cavell as the cruel act of avenging militarists. Last summer, on the occasion of the execution of Sacco and Vanzetti, a Berlin newspaper wrote that this judicial murder in America should be condemned like the German one of Miss Cavell. My opinion in our case, however, is that war cannot be opposed[3] if there is lifelong celebration of the dynasty, agreement to the payment of army wages, admiration of accounts of battles, and then denunciation of the general who used

3 Benn altered this phrase in manuscript in a copy of the original newspaper publication of
   the text in the possession of his third wife to read: 'I understand that war is opposed, but…'.

a cannon and the Gouverneur who gave the order to fire; that is foolish wherever it happens, here or over there.

And finally, not to deny the final measure to that brave daughter of the English people, who now rests amongst the kings in London and whose name has been given to those cliffs in America:[4] what would she think about a story that takes place within a liberal atmosphere and bourgeois humanism? The great phenomenon of the historical process, both as a whole deep and contradictory, as it is tragic and absurd in detail – could it be created and borne by a humanity which counts on pardon? No, world history is not a foundation for happiness, and the door-posts of the Pantheon are streaked with the blood of those who act and then suffer, as the law of life commands.

4   Mount Edith Cavell is in Canada.

Primal vision

1929

An incomparable clarity came upon me when I saw I had passed the high point of life. I looked into the day, which without being special was one of those days in the return of times, beginning of November, slightly cool, insignia of autumn on the street, played out tepidly and without consideration by the earth.

I was struck by a lightness which moved me. That was probably the way things were, and I among them, all of us transparent in the world's descent. A coming and going, pressure and denial, and between them untouchable the path of being. The beginning inconceivable, the end a legend, stagnant water, steaming, the today and here. Distant and dissolved the days of youth, the passages of violence, the sickness of the great flight. Distant and dissolved that thicket and terrain, 'nous n'irons plus aux bois, les lauriers sont coupés'.

A strange report can be read from the century when antiquity was growing old. It seemed to the people in the Roman Empire as if the rivers were becoming shallower and the mountains lower; on the sea Etna could no longer be seen from as far away as before, and the same was heard said of Parnassus and Olympus. The cosmos, in the opinion of observers of the natural world, was in decline as a whole. It was this downward direction, spatially speaking, which I experienced so keenly. Tree-trunks could be looked through anywhere, and where previously it had been possible to listen, shouts and cries had become inaudible. I had a topographically wide view across the terrain, and in a remarkably plastic way was covered by space with a proximity from far away.

It was like this in the country when I undertook Sunday outings there, and the same in the city, where my apartment hovered above everything. Above the decade, today, after the end of the war. Above the forty years since Nietzsche, the end of the psychology of instinct. The hundred years since the first gas-lamp was lit, that famous year when Europe welcomed: a continental rail network, international steamer cruises, the telegraph, photography, improved microscopes, and the means of attaining artificial sleep.

Yes, this city,[1] certainly not of dew and birdsong, but, rather, full

---

1 Berlin.

of the pressure of objects, in my space how silent and easy it was! Outside, when you noticed, what living and moving, what chaos, what paradoxes: ancient and experimental things, stadia and neuroses, atavisms and ambivalence. Bizarre epic moments: collectivism, but even fruit barges organise themselves, and market stalls produce dividends; five proletarians in one bed, but toy dogs, in pairs, must match the look of their mistress, perfumes, truffles, and dishes made of palm marrow. Poetry and philosophy: one fifth of secondary-school pupils go to school without breakfast because they are poor, but the institutes in Dahlem are spending millions on a boarding-house for visiting foreign scientists. The starry sky: rocket-ships to the moon, projectile aviation to the stars, and the last droshky travelling from the Wannsee to Fontainebleau, with kith and kin following in the dog-cart; two waiters in white tie and tails walking from Brandenburg to Geneva to lay a wreath on the union memorial; three Hindus are on their way here, cycling around the world – all these are actual and notable things, full of reality, but in my rooms they became soundless and stilled.

Of these rooms, three overlooked the street, one the courtyard. The courtyard was invaded by a music café I often listened to, intoxicating melodies. Sometimes, at night when I went into my bedroom, music was still playing. I would open the window and put out the light. I would stand and breathe the sound. Stand for a long time. I looked into the night which promised nothing more for me, nothing more than the twilight of my heart, a heart growing old: vague air, greying emotions, you give to someone and are forfeit, but giving and forfeiting lay far away.

The red glow of the city fell into the other rooms. Since I did not see Nineveh with its ground of jasper and ruby, since I did not see Rome in the arm of the Antonines, I would watch this one, it bore the myth which began in Babylon. A mother city, a womb of distant ages, of new shudders caused by dance-steps and injections. What books of hours and sequences were to the epochs of monks, and speculations and cosmogonies to the centuries of rationalists, came today from the pliancy of women dancers, with the murmurings of their knee-joints they opened up the expression of existence to whole migrations of peoples. And I saw that thing we do not know driving though their flesh and stone. It ripped foundlings from the fields and drove communal blocks onto different rails, it smeared asphalt

379

through their forests for a humanity which was reproducing itself. A mass of humanity which had doubled its living weight in the last century, was growing each year by twelve million individuals, and in less than a century would repeat the process da capo. Thus gigantic centres, over-population. Bread more expensive than the flesh of children. Melons into the gutters, potatoes into the flower-bed – the world would grow into that far beyond my time, far beyond my spaces, far beyond the hour I was standing in this November night, its glow there, its silence here.

After years of struggle for knowledge and the last things, I had come to the conclusion that these last things probably do not exist. No small responsibility for this conclusion came from my having become acquainted with an oldish man who had introduced himself to me one evening in company as a fellow-countryman of mine, an ear-specialist with his own clinic, Bavarian consultant physician, as he remarked in his first sentences, and mentioned people we both knew. A few young people who had often visited his parents' house, good-for-nothings, layabouts, journalists, drunks – long since vanished. He had met one again years ago and had wanted to try and help him get a job on a newspaper, but the man in question had not even turned up at the agreed time, then made an appearance at his house in a far from sober state, so that, in his very words, he 'had him shown out', and a few weeks later the man had succumbed in delirium.

He revived the past in this way, and in deportment, dress, and influence was definitely superior to the dead man, also by far in fame, the possession of a clinic and military rank, indeed he put everything about the man into the shade; but had the friend of my youth died completely unfulfilled for that reason, without standing for anything, useless, the enormity of life never having shone through his course, his capacity to feel intoxication and instinct, his indifference to individual properties, his fleshly decay, from which rhythm he too had sunk into the depths, certainly after years of angelic purity, but had this man here described a greater arc, was he borne through the ear-clinic by more mysterious experiences? I was undecided, and incapable of granting that conclusion. Since life had been fully at work in the dead man's history, it must have manifested itself in what, measured against the consultant physician, had been a lower form. And I was unable for the moment to say what kind of manifestation this had been.

It was the unity of life, I was coming to think, which I felt I had to defend against attack. Life wants to preserve itself, but life also wants to perish, I understood this chthonic power. If I directed my thoughts to the animal kingdom, the class, the appearance and death of types, naturally overflowing seas had washed away whole parts of the race in what geologically was a short time, and cataclysmic torrents of ash from volcanic eruptions had stifled great animal communities; but precisely the dying-out of types, the disappearance of unities had never been caused by these geological occurrences. The dying-out of types and no less the simultaneous appearance of new ones came to have more and more the status of fact in the history of the world, creating the impression of a unitary inner cause. Thus in the history of the world, butterflies and honey-sucking insects appeared at the same time as flowering plants, with certain reef-building corals the echinoderms and crabs that lived in community with them and disappeared when they disappeared. No relation to elementary events, no apparent connection with changes of milieu, no obvious explanation, a phenomenon only interpretable from within. A disappearing formal tension, ageing, a decrease in numbers and the space required for life seemed to be expressing itself on the one side, a bursting forth and being on the other; a polarity in the impulse to make forms, an inner tension between characteristics seemed to be present; being seemed to rest in bowls held by the gods, now there was more water, now more land, here a coral and there a mollusc, resting at the foot, rising and falling around the figure of man, streaming out animals and splitting off plants, he, inescapable amidst the forces of further events, the bowl-bearers and their distance –: to them too the dead man would have succumbed, and in wider connections his series of forms descended into the gape of an early grave.

An insignificant cause, purely personal trains of thought; but the occurrence led me to look more closely at this man, this gentleman at the peak of his time, the leader of broad strata, the bearer of the positive idea, the causal-genetic thinker. I saw him before me with his instruments, the ear funnel, the pincers, germ-free and nickel-plated, far behind him the Moorish epoch, the age of cutting hernias and stones, the Galenic darkness, the mystical mandrake. I saw his clinic, polished and brushed, far removed from the physic-gardens and distilling-ovens of medieval urinoscopy. His sonorous and voluminous organ enveloped me plastically with its suggestive and hypnotic charm and completely suppressed those discussions and songs of the walas I had read about, the Cimbrian priestesses who, in white leather garments and a brazen belt, had been responsible for their so-called healing arts. Only when I reflected that humanity had lasted so long, despite obstetrics having been practised until recently under the clothing and in mysterious darkness, had lasted so long despite all the leprosies and plagues, epidemics, worms and bacteria which our representative had stepped forward to fight but a relatively short time ago, probably only then did my thoughts turn to that remarkable hypothesis of the latest American eugenicist which suggested that, for the majority of men, the time of death should be considered as determined by heredity, indeed they reckoned that for eighty per cent of humanity sickness had no decisive influence on the length of life, but that heredity was responsible for this part of human fate as well. And, further, when I found a confirmation of this hypothesis in certain statistical peculiarities: that the ideal length of life as calculated by modern science, that is to say the normal mortality figure, this standard figure checked over five-year periods in one century in an area of two hundred and seventy-six districts, say in England, which I was studying, had already proved to have been the case in the first third of the nineteenth century, thus during a time long before what is called the triumphal march of modern biology, it could happen that, when I called to mind the ear-specialist and his pincers, more generally the relation between sickness and humanity, I could not prevent the rune-covered staffs of magicians and the sacrifices performed by our ancestors at sacred sites pressing forward into my understanding.

At any rate, there he stood before me: the biologist, the germ-cell Marxist, the aniline exporter, the investigator of villa synthesis, who emerged as a lamb and spoke as a dragon. The age of Bacon, the adult age of thought, the cast-iron century which did not make gods with an axe but devils with mineral ores: four hundred million individuals crammed into a tiny continent, twenty-five races, thirty languages, seventy-five dialects, inter- and intranational tensions of exterminatory intensity, here battles for an hourly wage of tuppence, there a golf tournament at the Carlton Club in blossom-drenched Cannes, princes in the gutter, tramps as dictators, orgies of vertical trusts, fevers of profit: the limited riches of the continent to be assessed economically, that is to say with additional duty.

Dissolution of classic systems from the Urals to Gibraltar. *High capitalism*: earthquakes in Southern Europe, a great time for building-firms and interior designers; iron and steel agents fresh from a blessing on Mount Athos descending on the Mariza Valley! On the face of it mourning the victims, while calculating the profit margins; the leading article on earthly frailties drawing sound economic conclusions from geological faults! *Socialism*: regulated food supply, bodily immortality, healthy survival –: social security's dream of the Hesperides.

And over there stood the great country with the Philadelphia myth, the man whose skull was smashed in with a piece of lead piping because he was wearing a straw hat on the 14th of May. Holy Aloysius of Delaware, the virginal martyr who tried to wear a straw hat out of season. – Who had more in the bank at thirty: Dempsey or Hölderlin? – 'Where are the leading citizens of New Salem?' asked Lincoln as he entered the city. Answer: 'New Salem has no prominent citizens, everyone is prominent here', and there they stood: an honest avowal of racial equality from ice-cream to the cut of the trousers.

Idols of unity, schemata in formation dancing, staple goods, religious ceremonies under floodlights, the eucharist with jazz, Gethsemane as a record high, Christ as the successful entrepreneur, social lion, advertising genius and founder of modern business life, who at the wedding in Cana knew how to save the day with a mediocre Jordan wine, the born manager who, even at a time when there was no call for a new religion, could invite the rich man Nicodemus to dinner. For the dollar was the will of God, property morally positive; therefore Bible-study to counter a falling market, the Pentateuch to counter the property barons. The keep-smiling prophet of the New World and the aniline metaphysician of the Old, with Shakespeare crossing the Atlantic like cables in code about oil shares and the exegesis of petroleum. Mitropa a knockout – the new type: spattering the earth with his marks: the suspension bridge from Manhattan to Fort Lee, to be completed in 1932, 1067 metres long, carried by four cables each 914 millimetres in diameter, thicker than in any cable bridge built so far; in the Brooklyn Bridge built in 1888 the diameter was only 400 millimetres – a difference of 514! With flights and missiles he compromises zeniths, he conquers space and time, strange space, strange time, driving-belt categories, price-fixing concepts, he *corrects* space and time, primal history.

This my century! If it could have been my century – ah, it was the aeon, history, the horde, Aurignac, growth in darkness, the licentiousness of the night of creation. Once the green plants of the coal forest, once the triumphal marches of vertebrates into the seas of prehistory, once this race, from the glacier edges of Asia, with memory veiled on retrospect, restless and itself shortening earth's periods.

Some kind of mass lay hidden, and something was driving it towards realisations of a compulsion. Age-old impulses! The strongholds of diluvial industry in France and Austria, very near to those of today: Creuzot and the Škoda factory – brilliant skills! The laurel-leaf tip of the Solutré culture – the pinnacle of technical stone-working! In the warm middle of the Intermediate Ice Age the beauty from Willendorf, primary instinct for style, constructive autochthony. In the loess sites of Central Europe, besides nine hundred mammoth remains, twenty-five thousand artefacts! As the Magdalenian moved from stone-cutting to bone-carving, a greeting for the dawn of a new age, the silver strip was the Quaternary hunter with his horn harpoon.

Stimulus and repression. Technical today, mechanical yesterday. The first dugout canoe of greater consequence for society than submarine and Fokker; the first arrow more deadly than phosgene, installations with running water were common in antiquity, no less lifts, pulleys, clocks, flying-machines, automata; monomania in tunnels, corridors, pipes, aqueducts –: termites with agoraphobia, compulsions to grasp.

Driven masses. Intracranial tumours into the gutters, bacilli into the flower-beds, yolk-sacs in the push of distances. Inheritance in excesses and intoxication, astral burning, oversea decay. Crises, mixtures, third century: Baal with lightning and scourge of the Roman god, Phrygian caps on the Tiber, Aphrodite in the Lebanon – realities in balance, floods in transformation.

Age-old impulses of an ageless mass in the sound of the seas and the falling of light. Life wants to preserve itself, but life also wants to perish, stimulus and failure – games of the night. The individual lost, down with the self. Out of heavy-duty indifference, out of a tiredness of character, a dream-downfall of conviction, ah, work: a phantom for the subdued; greatness: a spectacle for gawpers, death-rattles for gold teeth; on science, banal method of hiding the facts, religion, invective – dithyrambs of youth, down, down!

I saw the self, the gaze from its eyes, I enlarged its pupil, looked into it deeply, looked out of it deeply, the gaze from such eyes: almost weak in expression, sensing rather, sensing danger, an age-old danger. From catastrophes that were latent, catastrophes that lay before the word, frightful race memories, hybrid, in animal form, sphinx-pouched from the primal vision. I recalled the sayings of certain deep sages, that it would be an evil thing to give expression to everything they knew. I thought of the strange propositions that one should cease from searching for those last words, whose sound, if once pronounced, would make heaven and earth totter. I felt for the breath of masks, my throat rattled in runes, I forced my questioning into demons, sick with sleep and brutal, with mythic instincts, in anti-verbal instinctual threats from prehistoric neurons; I began to comprehend, I was granted the vision: monism in rhythms, mass intoxications, compulsion and repression, Ananke of the self.

An incomparable clarity came upon me when I saw life as it were conquered. Thence the fleet of a thousand ships, I asked with the dialogues of the dead from late Rome, in the underworld and whitening before the eyes of the beholder, the bones of famous shades, the jaw of Narcissus and Helen's pelvis, thence the fleet of a thousand ships, the death of countless numbers, the destruction of cities. Thence the heroes, the founders, the sons of gods, Tuisko and Mannus, and the songs that were sung to them. Of none remained more than an outline and a breath: life was a fatal and an unknown law; man, today as once before, could do no more than accept his lot without tears. Once the green plants of the coal forest, once the triumphal marches of vertebrates into the seas of prehistory – return was everything.

Return and this hour of night. I stood and listened. I stood for a long time and breathed in the sound. Life wanted to preserve itself, but life also wanted to perish – long rhythms, a long sound. The night had long breaths, could collect and disperse at play. It gave, it streamed out and lingered back; meanwhile the gods were only silent, Daphne trembled in the laurel, the herms slumbered by Amphitrite's sea.

And over everything lay swooning and dreams. That thing we did not know moved the logs: hearth fire, early coffins, old men's chairs to and fro. Ancient living, twilight and poppy, towards the downward stair, the murmuring of withdrawn waters.

385

An extract from *On the problems of being a poet*

1930

... The self is a late mood of nature. Here, however, we approach complexes without utility and without history, deeply nihilistic in the tension of a dark longing. Now out of an age with all the coarse weight of powers, with opportunistic psychology at the temples in wreaths of thorns, between crowns of creation delivered by industry, humanitarian ideals to the point of compulsive neurosis, sexual workshops as if on madonnas only –: in its agonies the self rips it down, with its tears it summons the ancient flood, beckons to the mouth which lives from the hand, grasps its knife and dances on the cutting edge, conjures up the monsters spawned by Tartarus –: back, o word: once a cry of lust into the distance; come down, o self, to congress with the universe: to me, you host of banished soldiers: visions, intoxications, peoples of early times.

Ecstasy, sweet, which brings it distance; voice, wholly dark, which sings of early times. Now it sees the world more comfortingly than day could imagine, now it sees on the world the many and the one, woven together, without burden. It sees a red feather, an eagle's feather, blowing above the mescal plant. An eagle's feather and the fire-tender bending his head to the prairie. In the tent there is red earth, at the entrance wood for the fire, now the leader waves the cloth impregnated with mushroom juice, now with a bone pipe he imitates the cry of the eagle which is approaching from a great height. Now many eagles, with outspread wings, each feather drawn separately, a beautiful sight! Now on the arm of one rattling a gourd, a little person with a blue cap, just placed there by the earth-maker god. Splendid things, all night long, visions until morning, orgies of surrender, feelings of community – peyote cult of the Arapahos.

A doctrine is passing through the world, of ancient origin, the theory of surges of passion. Native to India particularly, Brahman means ecstasy, swelling of the mind. The realities of that country: the broad rivers, the great beasts, the famines –: protect yourself against them in other ways, win control over them through spells and discipline: in hallucinations one sees reality, in prayer one attains power over the gods, he whose dreams of bliss do not come true will taste the fruit. The yoga system: the praxis of introversion, propaedeutics for voluntary stupor –: four hundred million men for millennia –: a propensity of the soul.

It sees features of the self: the schizophrene with the deep stratum. Between the orbital arches, prelogical, emotional reflection, for millennia, for many, many millennia, much, much longer than our intellectual history based on the theory of opposition, the human race lived through magic causality and mystic participation.

Yes, the self is darker than our century thought. No, the brain is not the Enlightenment's little practical thing, to sketch its existence as civilising. The brain, which has held creation above water for so many millennia, is considered deep even by the mothers. Life, which originates in abysses and organises itself for a while before disappearing in the inferno, life will tear open its jaws against these hordes of civilisation which regard the sea as a food tube because of its oyster-beds and fire as a beer-warmer under their asbestos mats. Because it allows these small fruits to multiply, because it allows these water-colours to be painted high on their basalt walls with flecks of their semen, it is far from having bowed over the book of homilies. The day will come when the Monts Pelés[1] will stifle these fruitful settlements with their lava and oceans will submerge this mouldy melioration without bellowing – o lovely day of nature's penitence, when two blubber herds come to blows with fish-bones on an ice-floe again over sealing places, o return of creation, when varnished double hordes anoint their lip-wedges and in masks with hooked beaks bring the sacrifice accompanied by the call of the totem animal.

The self, enlarged in antiquity, unloading its hyperaemia – the art of poetry seems quite related to it. But what does that mean, what does that say, what is excluded, what is it compelled to aim at? A step into the dark, a theory of pure nihilism for all for whom positivism means happiness, opportunity and progress, a step beyond every ideology as a lyrical hormonising of historic systems, beyond every reality as the harbour for the shouts of quantum querulants, a step from refugee misery to a god of the hour. What remains as transcendence for a non-metaphorical race, as reality with symbols of madness, canon of naturalness and hieroglyph made of phantasms, matter without ideas, and yet the medium from which to drink the magical –: it is the *body*, with its terrain inaccessible to free will, on

1 Montagne Pelée in Martinique erupted in in 1902.

387

which we live with double tongue, with its only two-thirds inborn, one-third unborn being, its regions equally unexplored in dreams and in waking, a shadow kingdom from which there is no return, Stygian country by which the gods swore.

From far away, a dream lies in it, an animal, from far away it is laden with mysteries, coming from those early peoples who still carried the primal times within them, the origin, with their feeling for the world which is still so completely foreign to us, their puzzling experiences from precognised spheres, in whose bodies internal consciousness was still prone to change, the constructive powers of the organism still free, that means accessible to consciousness as to the centre of the organism, experience still flexible, while today it has long been withdrawn from our choice, that of a biological type different from ours, archaic masses, an early stratum, which still understood the animal in the totem with a warm wound.

The body is the last constraint and the depths of necessity, it carries presentiments, it dreams the dream. The disposition of creation to swell is completely obvious: thus it laid down its correlates and in states of intoxication demands form. Everything is formed from its hieroglyph: style and perception, everything is provided by it: death and carnal pleasure. It concentrates the individual and indicates the places where it is less strict, germination and ecstasy, for each of the two kingdoms one intoxication and one flight. There is – and here I come to the end of this hyperaemian theory of poetry – only one Ananke: the body, only one attempt to break through: swellings, phallic and central, only one transcendence: the transcendence of sphygmic bliss.

Only the solitary man and his images exist, since now no Manitou redeems into the clan.[2] Mystic participation is past, through which by sucking and drinking reality was imbibed, but the memory of its totalisation lasts forever. Only the solitary man exists: in compulsive repetitions under the individually fated law of becoming in the play of necessity he serves this immanent dream. His social preconditions do not worry him: amongst men, he as a man is impossible, as Nietzsche says of Heraclitus, and his life is a cause of laughter. Let others, between the lines and without division, speak of things which only happened later, portray relationships which are transitory, live

2   A reference to Native American beliefs.

on questions which are quickly resolved, he will return always and forever for whom all life was merely a call from the depths, old and new depths, and all that's transitory merely a simile[3] for an unknown primal experience, which is seeking for memories within him.

A dark, inviolable figure. His great animal is the crow: 'they caw and swoop towards the city, it will snow soon – woe to the man who has no place to call home'.[4] And when it snows, he sinks, everything gives him back, midnight, mothernight: 'That you cannot end makes you great, and that you never begin, that is your fate; your song turns like the firmament of stars, beginning and end forever the same.'[5]

---

3 A quotation from the concluding *Chorus mysticus* of Geothe's *Faust*.
4 A quotation from a poem by Nietzsche.
5 A quotation from a poem in Goethe's *West-östlicher Divan*.

An extract from *After nihilism*

1932

... The only higher, that is to say tragically struggling, human being is the only subject of history, he alone is anthropologically fully developed, we are not talking about complexes of pure instinct. After all it will be the superman who overcomes nihilism, if indeed not the type portrayed by Nietzsche wholly in the sense of his nineteenth century. He portrays him as a new type, biologically more valuable, in racial terms advanced, vitalistically stronger, eugenically more complete, more justified by durability and maintenance of the species, he sees him as *biologically positive*, that was Darwinism. Since then we have studied *bionegative* values, values which rather damage the race and endanger it, but which are part of the process of differentiation of the mind, art, creative genius, signs of dissolution in the religious sphere, degeneration, in short all the attributes of productivity. Thus we do not rank the mind as part of a healthy biology, nor of the rising graph of positivism, neither do we see it as eternally languishing in life's tragic struggle, but we *rank it higher than life*, superior to it in construction, as a forming and formal principle: intensification and concentration seem to be its law. This entirely transcendent attitude may enable nihilism to be overcome, in fact artistically exploited by our learning to see it dialectically, that is to say as a provocation. To let all the lost values be lost, to let all the dead chants of the theistic epoch be dead, and to let all the weight of nihilistic feeling, all the tragedy of nihilistic experience be made subject to the formal and constructive forces of the mind, to breed ethics and metaphysics of form that are quite new for Germany. Many things suggest that we are facing a general and decisive anthropological change, in banal terms a shift from internal to external, a migration of the last substance of the species into a process of forming, a transfer of powers into structure. Modern technology and modern architecture certainly indicate this direction: space no longer considered in philosophical and conceptual terms, as in the Kantian epoch, but as dynamic and expressive; the feeling for space no longer gathered together in lyric solitude, but projected, turned out of the mould, realised in metallic form. Many things, like expressionism, surrealism, psychoanalysis, suggest we are moving in this direction, that we are *biologically* approaching a re-awakening of myth and *cortically* a restructuring through discharge mechanisms and pure expression. Our resistance to the purely epic, a streaming-in of external material, explanations, psychological cover-ups, causality, development of milieu, as opposed to our desire for direct connection, cutting, organisation, pure conduct, all say the same. The last substance of the species requires *expression*, leaps over all ideological gear-changes and takes possession of technology nakedly and directly, while civilisation turns in content back to myth – that seems to be the final stage. The ancient and eternal human being, the primary monist, aflame before his final incarnation, an image beneath the gold helmet: how many rays still shining between the runes, how much brilliance still at the edge of shadows, how manifold: with links to states of intoxication and to breeding, with tensions from rise to finale, he, in his memory the elementary synthesis of creation and in his brain the progressively cerebralised analysis of his historic mission, casting away Europe's normalised masses, brushing Yucatan's white ruined stone, the transcendent colossi of Easter Island, reflects on his ancestors, primal men, the Proselenes,[1] reflects on his immeasurably ancient but always single-mindedly murderous anti-dualist, anti-analytical battle and raises himself up to one last formula: the constructive mind.

'An anti-metaphysical world-view, yes – but if so, then an artistic one', this saying from *The Will to Power*[2] would then take on a truly final sense. It would then take on for the German the character of absolutely fundamental seriousness, as an indication of a last way of escaping his losses of value, his diseases, intoxications, obscene riddles: the goal, belief, overcoming, would then be united in the concept: the law of form. It would then assume for him the character of a popular duty, fighting, fighting the battle of his life, to work towards acquiring the really unconquerable things whose possession was already achieved, without any struggle, by more ancient and more fortunate peoples in their youth by reason of their dispositions, their boundaries, their heavens and seas: a feeling for space, proportion, the magic of conferring reality, being bound to a style. Thus: aesthetic values in Germany, the culture of art in a country where one is brought up to dream and worry so much? Yes, absoluteness

1 Prehellenic inhabitants of Arcadia.
2 Nietzsche, *Der Wille zur Macht*, published posthumously in 1901.

of form achieved by breeding, form whose degrees of linear purity and stylistic spotlessness must certainly not be allowed to be inferior to the concentration on content achieved in earlier epochs, up to the very peaks of hemlock cup and before the cross, yes, only from the extreme tensions of formalism, from the final intensification of constructivism, progressing to the limit of immateriality, could a new *ethical* reality be formed – *after* nihilism.

Extracts from *Speech to the Prussian Academy of Arts*, given on 5 April 1932 on the occasion of his admission as member of the Sektion für Dichtkunst

... A new level of cerebralisation seems to be in preparation, more frigid and icy: dividing existence of the self, history, the universe into only two remaining categories: concept and hallucination. The *decay of reality* since Goethe exceeds all measure, to the extent that even long-legged wading birds, if they became aware of it, would have to take to the water: the dry land is shattered by pure dynamics and pure relativism. *Functionalism* is the thing now, you know, movement without a bearer, non-existent being. Process as such surrounds a veiled and crazy utopia, as does the economy as such, as do a flora and fauna of factory monads, all of them huddled behind functions and concept. The old realities space and time are functions of formulae; health and sickness a function of consciousness; imaginary quantities are everywhere, dynamic phantoms, even the most concrete powers like the state and society can no longer be comprehended in their substance, always only process as such, dynamics as such ...

... If new species came into being once, as fossils show, since the arrival of *Homo sapiens* they no longer do. The whole of the last hundred years has throbbed with this question, in a thousand bioculture laboratories, in a thousand breeding farms there were attempts to engender new varieties which would establish themselves, but organic matter will not provide anything more. Ageing, relaxation of creative tension, decline of productive impulses, across whole organisms and individually: the physiological insolvency of man is the subject of discussion from Vladivostok to Frisco, and instead skulls are swelling in size, brain volume is increasing: progressive cerebralisation and its effects, no-one deals in concepts without punishment, eugenicists foresee that because of cranial increase babies will no longer be able to pass through the birth canal, they will demolish the pelvis or die –: over-specialisation in the chief organ is a frequent starting-point for the disappearance of species ...

Concept and hallucination, I said, are the mechanisms for expression in the new stage of cerebralisation, no longer the purely epic manner of seeing things, Apollonian monotony and mere decoration as a line of development. What is meant by hallucination is known to all today. Expressionism, Surrealism belong to it, Van Gogh's formula: 'I expect only the excitement of certain moments' – Violante of Assy's kingdom of intoxication[1] will always stand as the beginning – Klee, Kandinsky, Léger, the whole South Sea episode, none relies on logical and empirical, but on hallucinatory and congestive mechanisms ...

... If transcendence still exists, it must be animal in nature, if rootedness in something beyond individualism still exists, it must be in the organic sphere. This self that lives on loss and finds frigidity, isolation of the various centres, no continuity, no biography, no centrally observed history, and if from a certain stage of organisation onward it tries to confirm its own existence, no other reality than its own instincts, only the organic mass can confer transcendence, the transcendence of the early stratum. Primitive peoples are rising again in late ones ... So the body, suddenly, is the creative force, what a change of direction, the body transcends the soul – what a paradox, countering millennia, but no doubt that here might be an anchorage for our variant, a concretisation of its vagueness, and both content and rhythm for its style. But we cannot escape the question: what do we experience in these states of intoxication, what arises in this creative joy, what takes form in its moment, what does it catch sight of, on what sphinx does its expanded vision gaze? And the answer has to be: here also it basically sees currents streaming to and fro, an ambivalence between image-making and the removal of form, gods of the moment who dissolve and make forms, it sees something blind, nature, it sees nothingness. This nothingness we see behind all figures, all turns and twists of history, concepts, behind stone and skeleton. That would constitute the situation of the self, I have not prettified it, you ought to take part in it, but now we are faced with the decision: *is that nihilism?* Probably, from the standpoint of every material, selective, historical idea of man, there is nothing worth saving in the old truths, the old contents, but from the standpoint of our investigation of what is productive, in my opinion: no. Precisely because the situation is one of extreme tension, so unavoidable, downright challenging, the thought suggests itself that this is no special situation, that the mind has never breathed anything but this ambivalence

1   A character in Heinrich Mann's novel *Die Göttinnen* (1903).

between making forms and dissolving, has never experienced itself in any state but that of differentiating between forms and nothingness, we see the productive impulse busying itself to find a base, a way of being, an ordering vision *against* this naturalistic chaos, we stand before a kind of law, the law of the form-demanding power of nothingness, and here our investigation stops: this seems to be the law of productivity. The form-demanding power of nothingness; thus above all something formal, its huge force determined by its depth, its content by the changing contemporary basis of this nothingness. Not at all logicising, not at all hovering in the air or speculative, rather bedded in what is most original in anthropological make-up, the formal principle here discovered and developed, together with its contemporary content supplied by waves of *progressive cerebralisation*, this basic concept for the whole incipient epoch provides a particularly well-founded perspective in respect of the style which is to come: given the no longer preventable collapse of reality, frigidisation and the ever-growing pressure of concepts, a radical offensive will be prepared on the part of the old still substantial strata, and the civilising final epoch of human existence, from which without any doubt all ideological and deistic characteristics will have vanished, will be at the same time the epoch of a great hallucinatory-constructive style, in which the elements of tradition, of creative beginnings will appear again in consciousness, in which once more, with a final vehemence, alone amongst all physical figures, *metaphysical* being will appear: man differentiating himself from chaos by means of creating forms for images and visions.

Eugenics I

1933

He who wishes to rule for a long time must apply eugenics widely

No-one can doubt any more, as my recent essays have perhaps indicated, that behind the political events in Germany there stands a historic transformation without foreseeable boundaries. The cultural varnish of one epoch is cracked and falling away. Inherited force is bursting into the light through the joins of what is organic, the human gene from the defects in old centres of regeneration. Values, genuine past values, are sinking into the shadows, past achievements are being transformed and are losing face –: centuries grown from seed are at an end.

The unexpected historic transformation is taking shape firstly in political form under one central concept: the total state. The total state, contrary to the crossbred pluralistic state of the past epoch, arrives with the proclamation of a complete identity between power and mind, the individual and the collective, freedom and necessity, it is monistic, anti-dialectical, lasting and authoritarian. It is the highest-bred executive concept known to Western history; amongst past cultures Egypt and Yucatan came close to its position. What is new, rebellious but at the same time synthetic about the transformation is shown in the specific concept of the leader. The leader is not the epitome of power, certainly not intended as a terror principle, but as the supreme intellectual principle. Leader: that means creativity, in him are collected responsibility, danger and decision, as well as the whole irrationality of the historic will first becoming visible through him, further the huge threat without which he cannot be imagined, since he does not come as a model, but as an exception, he summons himself, one can also say, he is summoned, it is the voice from the burning bush that he follows, must approach and behold the great face. In our case, to this leader the masses have also given themselves incrementally: in a ten-year struggle carried on in public before the eyes of all, they have together conquered the Reich, no power could hinder them, no resistance hold them back, there was absolutely no other power there – , in this too we see the elemental, inevitable, ever-growing mass of a historic transformation.

A historic transformation will always be anthropological. Indeed, every political decision taken today is a decision of anthropological and existential nature. Here begins a separation of epochs which touches the substance of things. What is the nature of the human being? Everything follows from the attitude to this question. Until recently the human being was a creature of reason and his brain the father of all things, today he is a metaphysical creature, dependent and framed by origin and nature. Once his interpretation of history was as progress in the civilising sense, now the link stretches backwards as mythic and racial continuity. Equally he was by nature good, needing no redemption, no inner process, merely a little social polish, today he is tragic, with original sin, in need of purification, support and strong legislation for his own refinement and the protection of the community. Until recently he was good and surrounded by countless good pacifists of the individual and national sort, now he becomes great through the concept of the enemy, only the man who sees enemies can grow. The nineteenth century saw his constitution empirically, just wait – a few more institutes, a few extra professors – and some kind of intellectualist theory would clarify his family tree, today he is no longer seen morphologically, but symbolically, sprung from intoxication and fed by instincts. His highest aspiration was to come close to nature experimentally, erecting above it his own world of brackets and numbers, in the present hour he approaches it in contemplation and receptivity, back in that old inner state of readiness: participation. All these things are expressions of profound anthropological transformation.

It seems to me certain that once again a new man will emerge from this transformation in Europe, half as a mutation and half as a result of eugenics: German man. He will not rise up against anyone, but he will differ from both the Western and the Eastern type. All the preconditions for his appearance are present: behind him a quarter-century of fundamental crises, genuine convulsions, disturbances such as no other people in the world has undergone, and in the last decade a growing consciousness of the biological dangers, in the sense that a people which becomes conscious of its dangers generates genius. He will differ from both the Western and the Eastern type because his intellectual ascendancy, both inwardly and in blending processes, has given itself up to both directions, their being and their methods, for two or three generations. From the East it took over that dissolution, that melancholy distance, blurring of form, feelings of panic which rise from the landscape, from anxiety and instinct – Dostoevsky-darkness; from the West via Sils-Maria[1] the felt nearness of Latinity, the sense of space, proportion, fanaticism of expression, artistic gospels within general European decay, 'art as the real task of life, art as its metaphysical activity' (Nietzsche). So from the East came substantive nihilism, origin Turgenyev, *Fathers and Sons*, 1862; from the West giving meaning to all content only through form, seeing only form, origin Flaubert, almost exactly in the same year. The suppression of content, the forcing up of every still effective experience into the formal sphere, this became the basic feature of the whole epoch, apocalyptic and ruinous: surrender of all realism, transference of all substance into form, into formula, in this gigantic shadow-march of diminutives, ciphers, foreign words as accomplished by the modern natural sciences, especially chemistry and physics, and which created a really new world of concepts above the old nature-friendly one: the functional world. This became an existence to be experienced in reality, present and fruitful, it allowed the recent decades to lead a physically disturbance-free professional life, authorised by the state, weighed inwardly, between institutes and experimental laboratories – , here lies the historic, bourgeois, even professional basis of *intellectualism* and also its end. Seen as a whole, probably established to repel mythic, introverted, biologically ancient relics and begun with great productive energy, it is ending as a neurosis, a space neurosis, as repression, but its history shows that during the last decade it did not occupy an unnatural and so to say frivolous place among us, but that, like industrialism and the big city, it belonged to the Ananke of the twentieth century. As such and with both its sources, the panic and the sublimated type, it will stand at the cradle of the new German man.

What will be his other features? Half as a mutation and half as a result of eugenics, as I said above, how much nature and how much mind, more centaur or more from the test-tube, that is our question, and once again, here in spiritual realms, we encounter the word *eugenics*, which causes many to think that, as a result of certain legislative pressure,[2] it is inherently a moral burden on the new man,

1   Nietzsche had a house in Sils-Maria.
2   The Nazi *Law to prevent the propagation of children with hereditary diseases* was passed on 14 July 1933.

stripping him of any inner distinction, and so in his defence we must examine this concept in detail and from its own history.

For where we would all be without this eugenics of nations is with the white bulls of Mithras or Baal's golden calves. For it has emerged that the greatest national terrorist of all time, the finest eugenicist of all peoples, was Moses. The eighty-year-old, the stutterer, who persuaded the Israelites, weakened by five hundred years of forced labour, to begin their march to freedom, allowed the old, the Egyptians, the fleshpot materialists, the stem of Korah[3] to perish, literally and precisely, in order to lead only the young, the good material, to Canaan. His law was: quantitively and qualitatively superior rising generations, a pure race –: from this law came his brutal measures against both his own people and the foreign tribes they met: beatings, severing of hands, stoning, shooting, burning to death to prevent racial mixing. This law led to the destruction by his order of a race, the Medianites, who had brought with them 'the plague', a venereal disease, in the following manner: after only the men had been killed, he was angry that the women had been left alive and had them slaughtered too, with the exception of the virgins, who according to the Bible numbered thirty-two thousand, so at a rough estimate some one hundred and fifty thousand – think about it – on suspicion of having gonorrhoea. For the same reasons of racial hygiene he decreed the total destruction of all tribes met with in Canaan, the host country they had usurped, forbade treaty-making with them, showing them mercy, intermarriage. That was Moses. And seven centuries later Ezra appears, the real founder, lawgiver, leader of the people of the Torah, and forbids not only future mixed marriages, but demands that men who already have foreign wives drive them out of the house and marry fellow-members of the tribe, as portrayed in detail in the last chapter of the Book of Ezra. A modern-day historian of the Jews says of these measures: '[they had] a tenacity that is often hard, but for that reason historic significance and influence – ', but is silent about the ejected wives. Now I do not advocate repetition of these measures, they are a matter for exact racial research and psychopathology alone, but it does seem to me very remarkable, almost sensational even, to consider that without these monstrous eugenic measures, which no-one has criticised so

3 Numbers 16.

far, two religions with dominion over the largest part of the inhabited earth, Christianity and Islam, or monotheism as such, would probably never have developed. It seems to me to follow from these facts, which have so far received no public attention at all, that racial eugenics is very ancient, at home in all circles of history, that it certainly does not constitute a moral burden on a people from the outset, and does not only occur in the horde stage (the people around Solomon's palace and temple was definitely cultured, and Ezra lived five hundred years later), but that it arises from profound political instinct: he who wishes to rule for a long time must apply eugenics widely.

The decisive question for us is: what will become of nature and eugenics, what should be bred, what is demanded by the people's genius, what is demanded by the present hour, what must be brought into being? A century of great battles will begin, armies and phalanxes of Titans, the children of Prometheus tear themselves from the cliffs, and none of the Parcae will interrupt her spinning to look down upon us. A century full of destruction is already here, thunder will mate with the sea, fire with the earth, so relentlessly will the final families of the white race attack each other. One thing remains: *brains* must be bred, great brains to defend Germany, brains with canine teeth, teeth of thunderbolts. *Criminal, to see the new man as a dreamer*, to envision him into the future instead of hammering him into shape; he must be able to *fight*, and will not learn how from fairy-tales, ghost stories, chivalric love-songs, but under arrows, amongst enemies, from thinking. There will be no more peace in Europe, attacks on Germany will start: from the West, from the East, from liberalism, from democracy – , therefore brains with horns, whose horns are like the horns of unicorns, and with them he shall push the people together to the ends of the earth. This saying from the Psalms[4] is not intended militarily, but militantly. A militant transcendence, a legal framework of high restraining laws, eugenics with intoxication and sacrifice for an existence of changeless depth, hardness from tragic feeling, form from shadows! Eugenics to oppose the new man's destructive aspect: disappearing worlds, music, the procession of Norns: all this closed up, Nordic, swords above. Once again the white race, its deepest dream: deformation and creation of form, once again in the

4   In fact, Deuteronomy 33.17.

North: the victory of Greek man. Then Asia, the new Djingis Khan. That is the perspective.

Militant transcendence –: the new German man, never purely earthly, never purely formal as long as he is young, very like the children of Prometheus when he ages, amongst all types the nearest to ripeness. Not intellectualist, but with an extreme potential for thinking, for self-regulation in constructive thought. Not artistic, but always ready for defence against any power, placed into realms which only surrender to contemplation and withdraw from realisation. From these realms comes justice, from them the swords. Everything as yet in waves, in drifts of shadows. Still scarcely a hand to divide the night, no eugenicists rising early. Where are they all, who not only have the call, but were selected by the nation across many decades to bear witness for it in the hour of need, the Olympians, the nectar-drinkers, the great achievers, the exalted deliverers of panegyrics on international occasions, the prize-winners, the Nobel laureates, the pilots, when it is the time to launch out and be something for Germany? Ah, they are sure to have other ideals, 'secret Germany', that was so convenient: many probably want to wait and see how the hare runs first, later they will join in and maybe overtake it, are far ahead, and then are eagles again, old-fashioned models, these hares –:

So there we are: when the eagles dreamily hide their grey heads between their wings, and the owls, instead of daring a flight, press closer to the tree-trunks in the dark, it is left to the bats to carry life through the night until the morning hands it over to bigger creatures, and to them I pass on my thoughts. I know they will come. I can see the black multitudes who built Littoria,[5] the city on marsh and fevers; I hear Faust finally say to the moment: to stand on free ground with free people.[6] I know this people will become free, this people that does not want happiness but to apply eugenics; remember, they all want mines, coal deposits, colonies, victories, possessions, and here is a people that knows it cannot possess all those things, and is determined nevertheless to rise up to itself from a great inner vision. I know this people will become free and its great minds will come with words that mean something again, status amongst the peoples and fruitfulness. In their sounds will be everything we suffered, the

5 A new city planned by Mussolini; building began in 1932.
6 Goethe, *Faust*, Act V.

unearthly and the transient, the inheritance of our suffering in thought. I know they will come, not gods, and as human beings only half good, but out of the purity of a new people. Then let them sit in judgement and tear down the posts and smash up the walls which have been poorly whitewashed and where profanation has been the price of a handful of barley and a crust of bread – they alone. I know they will come, I am sure, it is their footsteps echoing, I am sure, the sacrifices that fall are for them – I see them approaching.

Extracts from *Expressionism*

1933

… Between 1910 and 1925 in Europe there was practically nothing but the anti-natural style, and there was no reality, or at most caricatures of it. Reality was a capitalist concept. Reality meant plots of land, industrial products, mortgage registry, everything which could be distinguished with prices for middlemen. Reality meant Darwinism, international steeplechases and anything privileged. Reality also meant war, hunger, historic humiliations, injustice, power. The mind had no reality. It turned to its inner reality, its being, its biology, its construction, its intersections of the physiological and the psychological, its creativity, its radiance. The way to experience this, to ensure its possession, was through intensification of its productive aspect, somewhat as Indians do, through ecstasy, a certain kind of inner intoxication. But seen ethnologically, ecstasies are not disreputable, Dionysus came amongst the sober shepherd people, this unhysterical mountain folk staggered along in his Orphic procession, and later Meister Eckhart and Jacob Böhme had visions. Ancient chance meetings! Of course there were Schiller, Bach, Dürer, these buried treasures, sources of nourishment, rivers of life, but they demonstrated a different kind of being, grew from a different anthropological tree, had a different nature; but nature was *here* with us too, the nature of 1910 to 1925, identity between mind and the epoch.

… This last great art movement in Europe, this last creative tension, so full of destiny that a style struggled into being from it, how remarkable the rejection it engenders today! This Expressionism was basically unconditional, the anti-liberal function of mind at a time when novelists, whom Germans call epic writers, were throwing Germany scraps, in endless sagas providing the most insipid psychology and the most pitiable bourgeois world-view, while composers of popular hits and cabaret clowns in their pubs and dives were doing the same with their putrid rhyming witticisms. At least a struggle was evident, yes, clear historical law. The question with which a hundred and fifty years ago Kant ended one epoch in philosophy and introduced a new one: how is experience possible, was taken up in the aesthetic sphere where it signified: *how is it possible to create form?* Creating form, that was no artistic concept, but signified:

403

what a puzzle, what a mystery, that man makes art, that he needs art, what a unique event in the context of European nihilism! That was nothing less than intellectualism and nothing less than destructive. Putting the question certainly fitted the world of twentieth-century compulsions, in its tendency to make the unconscious conscious, to understand experience as nothing more than science, emotion as perception, the soul as psychology, and love as no more than neurosis. It had to resolve reflexes from the general analytical mania for making things easy, the ancient bounds of dumb rule-following, to loosen in an individualistic sense long ago hard-won automatisms of the physiological and organic kind, to uncover ever more penetratingly that 'it' which in Goethe, Wagner, Nietzsche had been mercifully covered in night and dread. But putting the question signified true readiness, true experience of a new existence, radical and deep, and also in Expressionism led to the only intellectual achievement which abandoned this now pathetic circle of liberal intellectualism, shook off the purely utilitarian world of science, broke through the analytical atmosphere of big business, to tread that difficult inward path to the creative strata, the ancient images, the myths, and, in the midst of that dreadful chaos of collapse of reality and reversal of values, to struggle compulsively, legally and with serious means, towards a new image of man. Today it is easy to label that as abnormal and destructive and foreign to people, with this magnificent national movement at work creating new realities, undertaking new consolidations, new insertion of substance into wholly defective layers, having as it obviously does the moral rigour to lay the ground from which a new art can arise.

… Art, what an enormous problem! For countless generations Western humanity has taken great interest in art, measured itself against art, checked consciously or instinctively all cultural, legal, cognitive fundamentals against its mysterious nature, its multifarious impenetrable being, and now it is suddenly supposed to be exclusively popular in everything it does, without taking into consideration this people's situation, whether in bloom or decline, profoundly at rest or in a time of revolution. Eyes have been closed to the fact that a popular and anthropological loss of substance has occurred which no longer permitted previous epochs' absorption in concrete subjects, but has severely attacked art as abnormal and foreign to the people, for now seeking its subject-matter in its own internal nature. The elemental, amazingly rigorous nature of this striking choice of style was not realised, but its very real difficulties were shrugged off by saying repeatedly: that is purely subjective, incomprehensible, irresponsible, and above all, again and again, 'purely formalistic'. These criticisms sound extremely paradoxical in the mouths of contemporaries who did the same thing with modern physics, blowing it up publicly into such a balloon of alleged philosophical significance and praiseworthy insight, that readers of morning and evening newspapers demanded their daily dose of atom-splitting. This monstrous science, which consists of nothing but unimaginable concepts, artificial and abstract formulae, the whole thing in the Goethean sense a completely senseless artificially constructed world. Ideas which can only be understood by eight specialists in the whole world, of whom five dispute them, are consecrated, together with houses in the country, observatories and Indian temples; but if a poet labours over his particular experience of words, a painter over his personal colour preferences, that has to be anarchic, formalistic, even an insult to common people. Clearly, art floats freely through the air, drifts down like a snowflake, falls like dew, tumbles to earth quite outside time, its compulsions, its cultural and intellectual structure; arrogant snobs foreign to the people are messing around. Clearly art, which costs no-one anything, must only offer what was taught in schools twenty years ago, but science, which costs the state, the regions, the public, the taxpayers huge sums, can potter on with its specialist humbug to retirement age with steady wages and widows' and orphans' pensions. Our new Germany will certainly not make that mistake, the people who lead it, themselves indeed artistically productive types, know too much about art, about the hybrid nature of all synthetic efforts not to know that art has a specialist side, that this specialist side must appear particularly in certain critical times, and that art's way to the people cannot always be the direct one of an unmediated transmission of vision to the public. In fact no-one, even those who see nothing aesthetically positive in Expressionism, will contest its identity with its time and that time's unquestioned achievements, its style not felt to be foreign to the people: it was the complete counterpart in the aesthetic sphere of modern physics and its abstract interpretation of the universe, the expressive parallel to non-Euclidian mathematics, which abandoned the classic space-world of the last two thousand years for unreal worlds.

... The Expressionist in particular experienced the deep factual necessity demanded by the practice of art, its professional ethos, the morality of form. He wishes for discipline, since he was the most fragmented; and none of them, whether painter, musician or poet, will wish for a different end to the myth than Dionysus coming to his end and resting at the feet of the clear god of Delphi.

Expressionism, then, was art, Europe's last art, its last ray, while all around the long, superb, harrowed epoch was already dying. The epoch with art, gone for ever! The early Greeks had as yet no art, there were sacral and political stone-carvings, commissioned odes, ritual arrangements, it starts with Aeschylus, then two thousand years of an artistic tendency, now it is over. What is starting now will no longer be art, it is more, it is less, we will soon come to what we suspect. If I still speak of art in what follows, I mean a phenomenon that is over.

... They [Expressionists] had no instinct for politics, there may have been surprisingly many biologically negative variants amongst them, morally defective too, even a few criminal cases, that has been shown, and I will not mince words. But in face of such summary verdicts labelling them as deserters, jailbirds, crooks, degenerate, undisciplined, worthless shares, deceitful stock manipulation, does the question not arise inevitably: did not art perhaps always look like that? There was probably never any art which came into being through civil cultivation, not since Florence, none which did not succumb to some recognised variety of the tree of knowledge, with spectators murmuring approvingly, in the last centuries art was always counter-art, always birth. Later, when the epochs come to a close, when the peoples are dead and the kings lie at rest in the chamber and in the anteroom the servants slumber forever, when the empires lie fulfilled and the ruins are crumbling between the eternal seas, everything will appear in order, as if they all had only needed to reach up to bring down the great shining garlands lying ready, but once, everything had been equally fought for, hung with blood, expiated with sacrifices, torn from the underworld and disputed with the shades. Perhaps today too much time is spent considering the defects, and not seeing that here too a few works will last, and a few men who with this expressive method raised themselves, their spirit, the liberated, anguished, shattered existence of their decades into those spheres of form, in which the artist, he alone, above sunken metropolises and ruined empires, consecrates his epoch and his people to human immortality. I believe so and am sure that those I see coming will believe it.

... What will be forged politically will not be art, but a new and clearly recognisable species. I have no doubt that politically we are heading in the direction of that Ghibelline synthesis, in which, Evola[1] says, Odin's eagles are flying towards the eagles of Roman legions. This eagle as heraldic emblem, the crown as myth and a few great brains as inspiration to the world. Mythologically that means: the return of the gods of Odin's race, white earth from Thule to Avalon, with imperial symbols: torches and axes and the breeding of super-races, solar elites, for a half magic and half Doric world. Endless distances to be filled! Not art, ritual will evolve around the torches surrounded by fires. I see three great epochs of genius in German man: around 1500 the countless painters, including some of the greatest outside the Mediterranean world. The seventeenth and eighteenth centuries resound with music. In the eighteenth poetry begins, the long mountain range raises itself and extends to today, Expressionism is the utter finale, perhaps the Maladetta Group and the Monts Maudits, the naked inferno, but it belongs to the chain. Latency for two or three generations, and the fourth epoch begins, again the heady stirrings – near and hard to grasp – is god.[2]

Here stands the species: mind and deed, transcendental realism or heroic nihilism, the scars of the individualistically tragic era cannot be completely removed, but as a whole more bedded in happiness than we were, the individual is compact, less Faustian than is common. A fusion of Southern architecture and lyric poetry from the land of mists; the tall stature of the sons of Atlas; their symbolic works will be great songs, oratorios in amphistadia, beach choirs of sea-fishermen, shell symphonies in chalk halls with the horns of the first huntsmen. Limitless distances filling up, a great style is preparing itself.

Here stands the species: it looks back in time: *our* century, twilight of the gods, Ragnarök – , 'human' times, liberal times: all things presented respectfully and twice daily, nothing seen as a whole or in general. Everything is unbounded, ideological and no-one is obliged

1 Julius Evola (1898–1974), right-wing Italian philosopher.
2 A quotation from Hölderlin's *Patmos*.

to be part of it. But one group is hammering out the absolute – forfeit to it, but overcoming it intellectually – into hard, abstract forms: picture, verse, flute-song. Poor and pure, never taking part in bourgeois successes, fame, the fat of servile consumers. Lives on shadows, makes art. Also the little group before the last transformation of worlds: lived for art, that means: lived in readiness for death and lived on Germany's devout blood.

Extracts from *Mind and soul of future generations*

1933

The concept of eugenics, the breeding of a people, which is playing so large a part here now, points in two directions, one critical, the other productive. The one strives for the elimination of what is not wanted, the other for the raising of fertility in the desired population. Allied to this second thought is the idea that, when numbers of live births in good genetic material increase, a wider band of chances of talent in the new generations can be promoted, and also, using conscious methodical selection and treatment of original partners, a certain direction of talent, type and formal environment. This last would also tend to mould ideas, to invigorate aspirations, acts of will, power aims, whether of an intellectual or political nature, whose point of departure would be the world of ideas and thoughts of the leaders. One must note from the outset: eugenics as such does not exist, the forms of degeneration, like the disappearance of species, arise in nature, eugenics goes against nature, outwits nature, is moulding, political decision-making, world-view, a statement of values, an act of will.

One cannot consider the concept of German eugenics purely nationally, its depth is enhanced when it is seen against a racial background. In our case, the white race. An old race, the leading one for three millennia; the transfer from the high cultures of the East to the West occurred in Crete, the Minoan empire was the first centre, powerful 1500 years before Christ. Since then the Mediterranean has held sway, later the North too: Denmark, England; the empires on the Atlantic: Portugal, Holland, the primacy of power moved around, but dominion belonged to Europe.

Now it is the four states Italy, France, England and Germany which have worked out the past centuries, and on whose shoulders today lies the hegemony of the white race ... Of these only Germany remains unfulfilled as a people, only recently becoming a Reich, an enormous racial melting-pot, sixty per cent Nordic , with the rest Eastern and Dinaric, a mixture that began fifteen hundred years ago but is not yet definitive, with a history always full of tensions but no solution, full of tendencies, but also always full of losses, and now it has passed through a quarter-century of fundamental crises, real convulsions, disruption not felt by any other nation in the world –:

here possibilities are present, ferment, readiness, pliancy, a kind of eugenic latency, here present, as recent events have shown, is also that inner fire, restlessness, surrender to ideas which point to a disposition for breeding, and might include the possibility of planning a new European type. Here then, in the Reich, of the great peoples of the continent only here, might be found the possibility of forming a new synthetic variant, a new superior type, and what might be bred here would probably also be the last inheritance and the last grandeur of the white race.

In the problem of eugenics it is relatively easy to identify what the people must unburden itself of in order to move towards a definitive future. This problem is the subject of much international discussion today. Especially in America, where there has been much very radical thinking in this direction. According to the report of an American eugenic commission, an annual rate of four hundred thousand sterilisations until 1980 will be required to remove by then the fifteen million poor-quality persons from the reproductive cycle. In Germany, Lenz, a ground-breaking researcher in this field, considers ten per cent of sterilisations in every generation to be eugenically correct. Grotjahn considers the proportion of unsuitable persons to be far higher, at nearly a third, that is to say of persons to be removed from the reproductive process.[1]

... It must be made clear that the following is not derived from official statement and political essays, but from publications from scientific circles. According to these, eugenics offices should be set up within the country, which as advisory and supervisory authorities would list and register the whole population according to a points system, calculating totals from an accurate study of ancestors and the personal constitution of each individual. This points system will then form the basis for marriages ... Genius is known not to be inheritable, even if in very rare cases children do display it, as a rule a family's development of talent breaks off if it produces a genius ... Is a sound body in itself a guarantee of fulfilled humanity? Is mere health enough to lead a people to greatness in universal history? Life and mind: that has been the basic question of our time for decades: as opponents or as an interactive community, what are the decisive values of human existence: the biologically natural and healthy, or

34 Fritz Lenz (1887–1976) and Alfred Grotjahn (1869–1931), German eugenicists.

eugenics of the mind? ...

We may probably suspect that there is no race without mind. That therefore eugenics applied to race also always means eugenics of the mind. Only the mind – mind as the faculty to take decisions, a sense of measure, rigorous judgement, sharp examination – physically educates a people or one of its members, to the point where it is possible to speak of race and breeding. The Greeks certainly loved and developed the body, but they also developed dialectics, rhetoric, historiography, tragedies and the first stirrings of individualism. It will therefore probably be necessary to introduce intellectual and moral breeding first of all, and this procedure probably means no more than setting the people in motion, since only from the people, from the people's own new experience and belief can the critical and procreative will begin to take effect. Everything Germany is experiencing today will certainly feed that will: its unity, political union and metaphysical community, as well as the idea of its as yet unfulfilled destiny, which is Germany's alone among all the peoples of Europe, further the discipline of its present leadership and the unyielding will of self-forming – all this will rise into the reality of a new great form of mind and body: German breeding.

An extract from *The people and the writer*

1933

... Even today I cannot help wishing for 'a stronger practical link between people and literature' only in the sense that literature should not become more popular and easier to understand, but that the state should provide public bodies, academies, universities, seminars to persuade the nation to see in literature true transcendence with its own rules, the profound mysterious hieroglyph of the people's actual nature. A state which tried it, as the new German state is doing, even if it should not succeed, would receive lasting fame. But one must be clear that there are obviously quite enormously complex relations between people and literature, much more complex than with all other arts, as history teaches.

Doric world
An investigation into the relationship of art and power

1934

I. *A world in a light that is often described*

Beside the Cretan millennium, that millennium with no battles and
no men, though there were young pages carrying tall amphorae, and
little princes in fantastic head-dresses, yet without blood and hunting,
without horses and weapons, beside that Pre-Iron Age in the valley
of Knossos, those open galleries, walls dissolved by *trompe-l'oeil*, that
delicate artistic style, colour-glazed ceramics, Cretan women's long
stiff skirts, narrow waists, brassières, feminine palace steps with broad
low risers suited to the tread of women – past Mycenae, lies the Doric
world. Beside the matriarchal splinter of the Hittite race, female
rulers and women's processions, lies the Aryan man and bearded
gods; beside flower-paintings and stucco reliefs, lies composition on
a grand scale and monumentality, this world which looms into our
movements and on whose remains our excited, shattered, tragically
questioning glances linger: continuous being, yet always in its place;
variety, yet in order; cliff-cries, Aeschylean gloom, yet in the form of
verse and divided into choruses; order is always there, allowing us to
look into the depths, capturing life as proportioned space, forging
it, seizing it with chisels, burning it onto a vase as a procession with
bulls – , the order in which the material of the earth and the spirit of
man, still intertwined and conjoined, and each as if demanding the
utmost from the other, developed what our now so disturbed ways
of seeing are searching for: art, perfection.

If we look back on European history and choose as our formula
that it was made by peoples who merely expanded nature and by
those who formed a style, then we find at the beginning the union of
both principles in a people coming from the north which stormed
the Pelasgian castles, the walls the Cyclops built of stones, each stone
of a size that would gainsay even the smallest being moved from its
place by a team of mules, as Pausanias writes, which tore down these
walls, flattened the beehive tombs, and which in poverty, on variable
terrain, largely infertile, to take immeasurably Panic possession of it,
began the development of a style.

It is the post-Achaean epoch. The octagonal cowhide shields and
leather tunics of the early Iliad songs give way to round shields and

413

armour made of metal, the Iron Age begins: on the island of Samos, Rhoikos and Theodoros discover how to cast metal ore in moulds, and a man from Chios how to soften, anneal and weld it. Ships grow in size, the whole of the Mediterranean is navigated, the fifty-oared vessels of the old poems develop into galleys with two hundred. Temples are still made of coarse-grained limestone, but in about 650 Melos of Chios makes the first marble statues. The Olympic Games begin, the orchestra appears, gymnasia become publicly regulated institutions; music adopts five new modes in addition to the Lydian and Hypodorian, the mere four strings of the cithara become seven; strings made from flax and hemp on the old instruments are replaced by gut and sinew and the tendons of large animals. This happens in small states. Argolis is eight to ten miles long and five wide. Laconia is about the same size. Achaea is a small strip of earth on the flanks of a mountain sweeping down to the sea. The whole of Attica is less than half the size of our smallest provinces. The region of Corinth, Sicyon and Megara can be crossed in an hour. In general, and especially on the islands and in the settlements, the state is no more than a town with attached coastal development or circle of farms. Athens at the time of its greatest flowering took three hours to walk around; if you left the starting-point for torchlit processions in the Academy at nine, you would return to its plane-trees at midday, having passed the Theatre of Bacchus, the temples, the Areopagus, both harbours and the ghostly white forest of the Propylaia.

A world in a light that is often described. It is morning, the North wind is blowing, driving the Athenian barques towards the Cyclades, and the sea takes on the colours of wine and violets, as in Homer, and breaks gently against the rusty cliffs, everything is transparent, at least in Attica, everything is in colour, the Olympians too, Pallas the white and Poseidon the azure god. Yes, transparent, that is the word; whatever a Greek makes is in its space, brightly lit, three-dimensional, pure object; his centuries enriched the Peloponnese, filled the hills and islands, settled a little beyond the fields of pasture, raised them geographically above sea-level; all this with something which had achieved expression: life lived, carved by the will and the experiences of the race; porphyry, worked by dream, criticism and highest reason; clay, and on it the lines of human movement, ways of behaving, gestures, spatial structure.

A public, a physiological world. Reading is done aloud, which addresses the functions of ear and larynx, a period was a bodily unit: what could be said in one breath. Reading – the whole organism worked at it: the right hand holds the closed scroll, the left pulls the columns of text towards itself, one after another, slowly, delicately, so the document does not unwind and the threads do not split, the shoulders and the arms are always tensed, and writing too is done on the hand. But above all making speeches, which reflects their constitution! Speech is tied to the moment, does not bear being broadcast far away, here someone stands, wants to make an effect, is present, can convince, uses any means to advance his position and put down his opponent, and, even knowing himself to be in the wrong and that his listener assumes so, is permitted to use all the arts of rhetoric. The earliest occasions were concrete, speeches in court: theft, stolen leather or corn; the public, which meant refined listeners, had to be informed, enlightened, won over. Next came celebratory speeches, advertising speeches, speeches against membership. Then 'magic' was added, symmetrical sentence-construction, assonant, almost rhyming words, periods with similar endings; dedicated groups were formed, public circles and schools to teach style and imagery, refinements, fictitious debates: 'in praise of flies' or 'Hercules at the crossroads' or 'plague' or 'fever' or 'bedbugs' – and this talent developed over three centuries, aimed wholly at effect, victory, mockery, laughter, superiority, deepened a feeling for disposition, conscious arrangement, also structure and the playful and lovely freedom to work on constructs of the mind.

A physiological world: the limbs of the human body are the basis of its measures: the foot, that is four handbreadths, the ell six handbreadths, the finger a quarter of a handbreadth, a span three handbreadths, and so on to fathoms and stadia. A stadium is six hundred feet, which happens to be the length of the race-track. The 'Attic foot', standardised in the time of Pericles of Athens, can be deduced from many buildings, three hundred and eight millimetres, and then spreads with Philip and Alexander throughout Asia. Their measure of volume is the tall jar for wine and oil, for drinking and anointing, divided into twelfths.

Day has broken, its light penetrates the whitewashed house, the walls are painted with colours, and thin, a thief could knock them in. A bed with a few blankets, a chest, a few beautifully painted vases, weapons on hooks, a lamp of the simplest sort, all at ground level, that was enough for an Athenian of standing. He rises early, puts on his sleeveless Doric chiton, fastens the front to the back with clasps at the shoulder and the right, he does not leave his upper arms bare like a working slave, throws on his white cloak, drapes it, it is made of thin wool, it is summer. A signet ring on the fourth finger of his left hand to make impressions, it is a deforested land but full of bees: honey goes into wine, honey into bread, and sealing-wax to close up documents. He wears no hat, carries no stick, turns round in the doorway, the house-slave must put a new wick, made from the leaves of the special plant, into the hollow of the clay lamp, and push the amphora with its pointed foot deeper into the earth, it fell over in the night.

Now he looks southwards, the triremes are beached, the sea-going ones too, at most two hundred and sixty tons, they sail without compass, charts, lighthouses, close to the shore and amongst pirates. It is the great merchant fleet of the Mediterranean which displaced the Phoenicians, the bringer of corn and victor at Salamis and Himera. Now he is in the market-place. On the counters, mostly surrounded by a crowd of men, heaps of garments, gold chains and bracelets, needles and brooches, wine in skins, apples, pears, flowers and garlands. Then there are textiles, woven, the best flax is grown on the plain of Elis, the finest work comes from Patrai, coloured silk from the islands too. He wants to go on, but has to wait: mules are pulling a cart with silver ore from the Laureion and tribute money. At last the way is clear, the one leading back from Eleusis, how often has he seen it on festive nights in the smoke and light of torches, that is where the potters live, peasants of the old school, and glaze their vases, brown and black on a yellowish ground leaving the lower parts unglazed and only simply decorated, but the neck and shoulders with straight lines, zigzags, triangles, checkerboard patterns, crosses and swastikas, simple and complex meanders. Individuals add a few local variants, vernacular, affecting the shape and linkage of ornaments, soon rows of little animals appear between the lines, not lions or fabulous beasts as in Aegean art: domestic animals, garden fauna, all lined up in rows, hard, clear, sure – the Doric octave. They live along the Piraeus road by the two-pylon gate and along the sacred way, the potters' town.

And there the purple-sellers live, always exciting enormous interest, there lie the snails with the little white blood-vessel at their

416

mouth, which excrete half a nutshell of juice, white, green, violet, if they are quickly killed with a single blow. The rock ones are better than the seabed variety, trade in purple is still permitted, later it is prohibited, being then the colour for kings and the gods alone.

Outside the city a theatre is being built, that is where he is going. A theatre, that is the edge of a hill into which rows of semicircular steps are cut, divided into two, the lower to sit on, the upper for the feet of the row behind, in between a stairway: steep slabs with grooves. Down below in the centre stands the altar, the great smooth-cut wall to reflect the actor's voice is also finished. The sun provides the lighting, the sea the backdrop, or, further away, the mountains bathed in a satiny haze. He glances at all these things, theatre is not sensational, no feast for the ear and the senses. He is thinking about that place by the Alpheios where everyone was so thirsty, in the sun by day and in tents by night, five holy days and nights with a full moon. The river has dried to a murky trickle, but the Hellanodikai had been exercising in Elis for ten months and were now in competition, far-flung towns contending with each other, immense tension, immense seriousness lay upon this masculine world, and there was no Hellene who, amidst the fights and songs, did not again and again seek out with his eyes the table made of gold and ivory on which the victors' garlands lay, and the olive-tree between the temples from which branches were broken.

II. *It rested on the bones of slaves*

Ancient society rested on the bones of slaves, it discounted them, the city blossomed above their heads. Above were white four-horse chariots and fine physical specimens with the names of demigods: victory and force and oppression and the names of the great sea, below was a clanking noise: chains. Slaves were the descendants of the indigenous people, prisoners-of-war, the abducted and purchased, they lived in stables, herded together, many in shackles. Nobody thought about them, Plato and Aristotle consider them lower beings, a naked fact. A substantial import from Asia, market day on the last of the month, the cadavers stood in a ring for inspection. They cost from two to ten minai, as much as one hundred to six hundred marks. The cheapest were mill-slaves and mine-slaves. Demosthenes' father had a steel factory run by slaves, and based on the above purchase-prices

417

their labour brought him a profit of twenty-three per cent, in a bed-frame factory he owned, thirty per cent. In Athens the proportion of citizens to slaves was one to four, one hundred thousand Hellenes to four hundred thousand slaves. In Corinth there were four hundred and sixty thousand slaves, in Aegina four hundred and seventy thousand. They were not permitted to wear their hair long, had no names, could be given as presents, pawned, sold, beaten with rods, belts, whips, shackled with foot-blocks, iron collars, branded. The murder of slaves was not an offence in law, there might be a mild religious penance. They were beaten regularly once a year for no reason, made drunk to look ridiculous, were not allowed any sort of dignity, if one rose above his slavish appearance he was killed and his owner punished for not keeping him down. If there were too many of them, they were murdered at night, as many as was appropriate. In Sparta, at one critical moment in the Peloponnesian War, the two thousand most able and most hungry for freedom were identified by a trick and murdered – a great sacrifice of capacity. There too it was part of education from time to time to set growing boys in hiding-places by roads outside the city from where they had to attack and kill slaves and helots returning home late, it was educational to get used to blood and to get one's hand in at an early age. Through this division of labour, space was created for weapons training and games, for battles and statues, Greek space.

If one considers this space with the eyes of modern civilisation, much seems ambiguous. Themistocles, the hero of the Persian Wars, let himself be bribed with thirty talents by the Euboeans to fight the battle off their island, and in his turn used five of these talents to bribe one of his sub-commanders. After Salamis he extorts money from all the islands and cities without the knowledge of his co-generals. Before Salamis he is in contact with Xerxes, and after Salamis too. For years his vassal Sikinnos mediated between them. In all his deeds and speeches, says Herodotus, he acted in such a way as to create a fall-back position with the Persians in case the Athenians did anything to him. Pausanias, leader of the confederate navy, victor at Plataea, Regent of Sparta, is dealing secretly with the Persian King during the war to have Sparta and all Hellas delivered to him. Leotychides, King of Sparta, allows himself to be bribed by the Aleuadae during the 476 campaign and abandons the war against Thessaly when it is going well. All these are the heroes of the fifth century, two generations before Alcibiades, who changed sides systematically, handsome and treacherous.

Bribes on the one hand, cruelty and revenge on the other. Panionios of Chios had abducted Hermotimos, castrated him and sold him into slavery. Later, Hermotimos rises in status, becomes wealthy, visits Panionios and invites him and his sons to his house as guests. There he attacks them, first the father must castrate his four sons, then the four sons the old man, and then he sells them all together. This is related objectively by Herodotus. The six sons of the King of the Bisaltae go to war without their father's permission, when all six came home well and happy, writes Herodotus without further comment, their father tore out their eyes for their transgression, that was their reward. The same pious founder of historiography writes elsewhere about a regent who was involved in necrophilia. We learn of this incidentally, in a subordinate sentence, as follows: The messengers came back from Delphi and Aha! cries the regent in question, his interest aroused, that will be what the oracle meant by my 'shoving bread into a cold oven'. A race full of deceit and guile in military and ritual matters. The people of Phokis paint six hundred of their bravest men white, both their bodies and their shields, and send them into the enemy camp by night with orders to strike down anything not white. Complete success: the camp shudders, paralysed by fear, and four thousand are annihilated. But then the counter-ploy: the enemy forces, behind a pass, dig a large ditch, put empty jars into it, cover them with debris and restore the surface level. Now the people of Phokis attack and fall into the jars, their horses break their legs and the men struggling on the bottom can easily be killed.

Guile at the conquest of Troy, guile at the theft of Philoctetes' bow, but guile too as a triumph on the east pediment of the Temple of Zeus in Olympia, which represents the original mythic image of a chariot race with teams of four horses, in the battle between Oenomaus and Pelops; the King promised the victor his daughter, the loser death. The hero Pelops gains victory through the treachery of the charioteer Myrtilos, whom he had bribed to hammer wax pegs into the King's chariot, the chariot shattered: when Myrtilos demands his reward, Pelops drowns him in the sea; but – whether treachery or achievement – it was certainly victory which obliterated everything else, which was divine and worthy of elevation in purity onto the pediment of the supreme holy place of the Greeks.

There was only a single moral code, which, directed inwards, was identified with the state, and outwards, victory. The state is the city, remains the city, no-one thinks beyond that. Let us examine one particular year in Athens. Looking inwards: all who have non-Athenian parents are deprived of citizenship, ten per cent are struck off the lists, their property is confiscated in order to concentrate land and wealth, which is radical racism, city racism. Looking outwards: the Delian-Attic Federation is formed, of Hellenic states, be it noted, but a federation! Athens has the power! Now all federal cities have to go to court in Athens, to pay tribute money as determined by Athens, cities that are suspect or not secure, Greek cities, federated cities from the Persian wars, are given Athenian garrisons and commanders, triremes control the sea, fleets blockade Hellenic harbours, walls are destroyed, weapons seized, captives branded like barbarians, neighbour cities, neighbour islands destroyed. At the Dionysia the representatives of the cities must carry past the Athenians tablets bearing the amounts of their tribute money. These tributes are shown as gold and silver *in natura* to the Athenian citizens and their guests. All this in the civilised age of Greek history. But now we find ourselves faced once again with the contrary movement: in the same procession everyone stands as the orphans of citizens who fell for Athens pass by, looked after at state expense.

The following incident casts an unusually interesting light on the psychology of this upper stratum: after the victory at Salamis and after the division of the spoils, the Hellenes sailed to the Isthmus to award the prize to the Hellene who had most distinguished himself during the war. And when the commanders arrived, they were called upon to vote at the altar of Poseidon to determine the first and second places overall. But each one voted for himself, because each one believed himself to be the best. Better than Themistocles, better than Eurybiades, better than Leonidas! And we should also mention that during the battle, when their ships passed each other, they exchanged insults, slanders, accusations –: from such characteristics grew their great victories.

Just as laws were passed against harmful predators and snakes, the same should also apply to human enemies of the state, wrote Democritus, and Protagoras has the Father of the Gods say: Make in my name a law that a man without moral conscience and a sense of justice should be destroyed as a cancer in the community –: from this the fifth century emerged, the greatest flowering of the white race, the model, the absolute standard, not merely restricted to the Mediterranean, in these fifty years after Salamis, everything takes its place around this naval battle: Aeschylus fights in it, Euripides is born during it and on the island, Sophocles dances the victory paean with the most beautiful youths. Here 'the victory of the Greek man' reaches perfection: power and art, here Pericles reaches perfection, before plague came, and the tyrants, the two generations from which, in all documents, two things are always bursting into view, both for carrying and swinging: torches and garlands.

III. *The grey column without a base*

Behind this silhouette of Greece, a pan-Hellenic mixture, stands the grey column without a base, the temple of hewn stone, stands the camp of men on the right bank of the Eurotas, its dark choirs –: the Doric world. Dorians love mountains, Apollo is their national god, Heracles their first king, Delphi the sacred place, they reject swaddling and bathe their children in wine. They inherit high antiquity, the ancient language, the Doric dialect was the only one still left in the age of Imperial Rome. Their dream is breeding and eternal youth, equal gods, great will-power, conviction of racial aristocracy, concern beyond the individual for the whole kindred. They inherit ancient music, the old instruments: the cithara-player Timotheus of Miletus had his instrument taken away because he had raised the number of strings from seven to eleven, he was hanged. Another player has two strings of a nine-stringed instrument struck off with an axe, the old seven only are needed. 'Into the fire the spittle-spraying pipe' cries Pratinas of the flute because, instead of following the choir as before, it was trying the new fashion of leading.

They hang chains and fetters for their enemies in their temples, they pray to the gods to win their neighbour's entire country. Their kingship is exercise of power beyond all measure, they can wage war against any country they like, a hundred selected men change the guard by day and night, of everything slaughtered they get the skin and back, they are served first at meals, and they get twice as much of everything as the others. Kingship is hereditary, the Heraclids ruled for nine hundred years, even enemies no longer dared to touch them in battle from fear and terror of the gods' revenge. Riders carry news of their death throughout the land of Laconia, but in the city women run out beating a cooking-pot.

The Doric world, that is, to be armed at all times, meals in common, fifteen men, and each brings something: barley flour, cheese, figs, the kill from the hunt, and no wine. Education has only one aim: slaughter and subjection. Boys sleep naked on reeds which they must pull from the Eurotas without knives, eat little and quickly: if they want to add something to their meagre diet they must steal it from houses and farms, because soldiers live off the land. The country divided into nine thousand lots, hereditary property, but not a private possession, not for sale, all the same size. No money apart from iron currency, which with its great weight and mass had so little value, that to keep in the house even a sum of ten minae (six hundred marks) required a separate room and to move it a cart drawn by two horses. All the surrounding states had silver and gold currency. And even this iron made good for nothing else: dipped red-hot into vinegar and thus softened. The line of kings lasted nine hundred years, for the same period cooks' and bakers' recipes remained unchanged. Journeys abroad prohibited, foreign immigration prohibited, old men revered. In the time of kings, the army comprised only infantry with immense force: hoplites, heavily armed lines of foot-soldiers with lances.

Nine thousand Spartans ruled over the ten times greater aboriginal power, later still over the constant revolts of the Messenians. The death penalty was applied to one Spartan together with ten helots. The whole country was a camp, a swiftly deployable army, when shields clashed against each other and helmets rang from sling-stones, that was military music. The number of the fallen was never given, not even after victories. Woe to those who had 'trembled'! Aristodemos, who had 'trembled', the only one to survive the Battle of Thermopylae, performed deeds of the highest heroism at Plataea, fell, and remained in disgrace, because he 'had had reason' to seek his own death.

Every kind of anti-feminism is Doric. Doric, the man who locks up supplies in his house and forbids women to watch the games: she who sets foot across the Alpheios is thrown off a cliff. Doric the love of boys, so that the hero stays with men, campaigning love, such pairs stood like a wall and fell. It was erotic mysticism: knight embraced boy as a husband his wife and imparted his *arete* to him, joined him to his virtue. Doric too the rape of boys: the knight abducts the boy from his family, if it opposes him that is a dishonour, and he takes bloody revenge. But for a boy it is a disgrace not to find a lover, that means not being called to be a hero. The union takes place in a sacred spot, a sacrifice is made, the knight presents him with armour and goblet, and protects him until his thirtieth year, acts for him in legal matters; if the protégé acts dishonourably, the knight is punished, not the boy.

The Dorians work in stone, it remains unpainted. Their figures are naked. Doric, that is skin, but skin moving over muscles, masculine flesh, the body. The body, tanned by the sun, oil, dust, the strigil and cold baths, used to fresh air, mature, beautifully toned. Every muscle, the knee-cap, the positioning of joints, dealt with, assimilated, integrated, the whole warlike, yet very choice. The gymnasia were the schools where this began, and then spread across Greece. Plato, Chrysippos, the poet Timokreon had been wrestlers originally. Pythagoras was said to have won a prize in boxing, Euripides was garlanded as a wrestler in Eleusis. The body demonstrated it: servitude or rank. One day Agesilaos, the great Spartan, to encourage his troops, had the Persian prisoners stripped. At the sight of their pale, slack flesh, the Greeks began to laugh, and marched on full of contempt for their enemies. The Doric seed across the whole of Hellas: *beautiful* bodies: all religious festivals, all great celebrations included a beauty competition. The most beautiful elders were selected to carry the branches in the Panathenaea, in Eleusis the most beautiful men to bring the goddess the consecrated objects. *Big* bodies: in the gymnopaidia in Sparta, the commanders and famous men who were not big enough in stature and outward nobility were assigned to the subordinate ranks of the choral procession. Theophrastus said that the Lacedaemonians imposed a penance on their king Archidamos because he had married a short woman who would bear him doll-kings and not real ones. A Persian, a relation of Xerxes, who had been the tallest man in the army and who died in Greece, was revered as a demigod by the local inhabitants who made sacrifices in his honour. There were giants among the wrestlers celebrated in verse by Pindar; one carried a steer on his shoulders, one dragged a chariot and its team of horses to a halt from behind, another threw an eight-pound discus ninety-five feet, their local communities wrote it on their statues and memorials. Bodies *for breeding*: the law prescribed the marriageable age and selected the favourable time and the favourable conditions for impregnation. As in a stud-farm, birth failures were destroyed. The body for war, the body for festivals, the body for vice, and finally the body for art, that was the Doric seed and the history of Greece.

Doric is the Greek concept of fate: life is tragic and yet assuaged by measure. Doric in attitude is Sophocles: 'it is good for mortal man not to wish for what is beyond human capacity'. Doric is Aeschylus: Prometheus is Titanic, with curses and oaths he tears himself away from the universe and the ether, steals from the gods and yet remains a victim of moira, his destiny, measure; *balance* holds and forges him, the Parca is never absent. Mankind begins in Euripides, Hellenism, humanity. In Euripides the crisis begins, time begins its decline. The myth is exhausted. Life and history become the theme. The Doric world was masculine, now it becomes erotic, love-affairs come into question, women's plays, women as titles: Medea, Helen, Alcestis, Iphigenia, Electra, this series ends with Nora and Hedda Gabler. Psychology begins. The gods begin to grow small and great men weak, everything becomes everyday, Shavian mediocrity. In *The Frogs* of Aristophanes, Aeschylus accuses him of teaching gossip and verbal fluency, of emptying the wrestling-hall, stuffing men and sailors with words and making them disobedient; when I was alive, by heaven, they never dreamed of demanding cakes and being work-shy! But today, and thanks to you, Euripides: 'running with a burning torch, who can still do that when gymnastics are so in decline?'

The decline of gymnastics – accompanied by the decline of the Doric world. Olympia, the grey column without a base and the oracle which favoured the master-stratum. Euripides is sceptical, individual and atheistic, in his works we already meet isolated general concepts: 'goodness', 'justice', 'virtue', 'education'; he is a pacifist and anti-heroic: peace above all and no Sicilian expedition, he is torn and genial, thoroughly pessimistic and undoubtedly demonic, identical with the greatness and spirit of the deep Hellenic nihilism which began at the end of the Periclean period, the serious crisis before the end of Greek civilisation: from the Pentelic marble on the citadel, under the blows of Phidias, in the whiteness and luminosity of the calla blossom, the never equalled, the perfect, the high classical style descends in the form of Pallas, yet in the now cosmopolitan citizens' houses apes are kept as pets, colossal pheasants and Persian peacocks entice the Lacedaemonians to the bird-sellers' shops, and quail-fights in place of the mysteries entice the freemen and legal immigrants into the theatres.

Doric world represented the greatest Greek propriety, antique propriety, that is to say victorious order, and power derived from the gods. Their sagas know nothing of buried treasures, hollow mountains, their desires are not for gold but for sacred things, magical weapons from the hand of Hephaistos, the Golden Fleece, the necklace of Harmonia, the sceptre of Zeus. Sparta, that was also an inescapable destiny. People who were different from the rest of the Greeks and had as little to do with them as possible, mentally very alien. This hardness glowed everywhere: their god of war was represented in fetters so that he would stay true to them, Athens expressed the same thing by showing Nike without wings. The commanders of nearly all Greek armies were probably Spartans, but a Spartan felt very uncomfortable abroad and anywhere he could not appear as a victorious warrior. He was a man of the middle period, brought up 'in the Lycurgan manner' and forbidden to test the laws, the man from the guardroom, the co-athlete, therefore: Spartam nactus es hanc orna: Sparta is your homeland, crown it, care for it, you and Sparta are both alone in the world of Greeks.

Let us hear another story from Herodotus about this Doric virtue, so distant and alien to the Orient and the whole of pre-history: After Thermopylae, some renegades, men of Arcadia, joined the Persians. The Persians led them before their king and asked what the Greeks would be doing now; the men answered that they would be celebrating the Olympic festival and watching contests on foot and in chariots: the Persian asked what prize would be awarded in the contest; they answered, the victor would receive a garland of olive: then a Persian notable said something the king interpreted as cowardice; namely, when he heard that the prize was a garland and not something of value, he could no longer remain silent, and said so that all could hear: 'Woe to you, Mardonius, against what kind of men have you led us into conflict, who do not hold their contests for money, but for excellence'. This excellence, this garland, this festival contest between great battles, was, behind the Panhellenic silhouette, the Doric world.

IV. *The birth of art from power*

For a century we have been living in the age of the philosophy of history; when we try to sum it up, it is nothing but a continual feminine interpretation of relationships of power. We have been living for some time in the age of cultural morphology, the blossoming of high capitalism, romanticism intended to finance expeditions to savage peoples. The liberal age could not look peoples and people in the eye – 'look', in its vocabulary that was already too violent a verb – , it could not see power. Of Greece it taught: Sparta was a sad horde of warriors, a caste of soldiers, without cultural mission. A brake on Greece, 'everything came into being in opposition to power'. The modern theory of anthropological principles, a newly emergent science, saw precisely in power and art the twin spontaneous forces of antique society.

Greek antiquity teaches at any rate the following: the art of statuary develops at the same moment as the public institutions which formed the perfect body, and these begin in Sparta. It is the moment in which the head receives no more attention than the torso and the limbs, the face not yet pulled about, refined, worked in detail, its lines and planes merely complete the other lines and planes, its expression not thoughtful, but unmoved, almost drained. A generalised pose and overall motion, that is to say nature, is the meaning of the figures, statues are of mere limbs, they hardly yet include the spiritual element, they are the limbs of the gymnast, the warrior, the wrestler. Such a statue is fixed, its limbs and the torso have weight, one can walk around it, and the onlooker becomes conscious of its physical mass; the bodies are naked, here comes a crowd from bathing and from running, also naked, comparisons are made, that is formative.

It is the moment in which the orchestra, a hitherto ill-defined kind of performance at burials, youth marches, composed of improvised songs, festival songs, revenge songs, combines with gymnastics, the seed from which spring contests and lyrico-musical poetry: this happens amongst the Dorians in Sparta. It grows together here, imprinted and unified by the military ethos. Starting from here, it spreads with the commanders to the rest of Greece. Choruses, statues, but also music. The Dorians were naturally very musical, had an immensely sensitive ear, sang freely and moved as they sang. Amongst the people there were certain constant types of melody, the

426

so-called *nomoi*, ancient songs, corn-grinding songs, songs sung by women weaving, wool-spinners, mowers, women giving suck, agricultural day-labourers, women stamping out the corn, cowherds. Ancient dances joined them, one called 'winnowing corn', another 'lifting shields', another 'the owl'. The majority of ancient music comprising a metric and melodic mingling of words and notes cannot now be fully reconstructed, it was a strange union of music and gymnastics, dance and mimetic movement, called gymnopaedia, which was raised to pan-Hellenic practice by Thaletos of Sparta in the 28th Olympiad. There were poems for choruses accompanied by movement which were the starting-point of more refined lyric poetry and tragedy, and even if we no longer understand it in detail, it is nevertheless very significant for us that it began in Sparta. Sparta was called 'the Hellenic city richest in song', it was definitely the musical centre, here in 676 music was included in competition as the Muses' *agon*, here the melodies of the various popular songs of individual Doric regions were collected and put in order according to artistic rules, here a universally valid system of scales was instituted. From 645 onwards there was a lawgiver for music here, music was taught as a compulsory subject and had to be practised by all inhabitants until they reached the age of thirty, everyone had to play the flute, laws were passed down to new generations by means of poetry and song, and marching off to battle was accompanied by the sound of flutes, lyres and citharas, 'splendid playing on the cithara goes before the sword', as Alcman sang.

And the soldier city took it with its armies across the whole of Greece: Doric harmony, high religious poetry, dance-tunes, architectural style, tight military discipline, wrestling completely naked, and gymnastics raised to a system. In the ninth century, the movement began to spread, the games were reinstated after a break, from 776 onwards Olympia served as the beginning of a new period, a firm date to which the chain of years might be tied. Sport, music, poetry, stadia, contests and the statues of victors not to be separated from one another, that was the Spartan mission, and Lacedaemonian customs drove out Homeric ones. Soon there is not a single city without a gymnasium, that is one of the signs by which a Greek city can be recognised. Out of a square space with pillared halls and avenues of plane-trees, usually near a spring or near a brook, the academy emerged, and great philosophy was born in it. In the late

Greek period it was even maintained that the Spartans had saved fallen Greek music three times, and Sparta was represented allegorically as a woman with a lyre. It is also Sparta where the first building for musical and dramatic performances was created, a round building with a tent-shaped roof, since the 26th Olympiad shown in cameos. Later other cities followed, but this was the model, also in Athens for the next two: the Odeion and the Theatron.

But the Spartan-Apollonian spirit is strongest in plastic art. Statuary, first in wood, then in bronze, ivory and marble, accompanies slowly, step by step and at a distance, the breeding of the beautiful body, that is the development of the Doric-Hellenic world. At the beginning purely naturalistic, it arose from commissions and orders. Then more and more deriving laws from the material, the eternal material, stone. The anatomy of a naked man, studied in gymnasia and wrestling-grounds, has long been possessed most precisely by the eye, now the inner eye loosens reality from everything circumstantial, and the outline of victors and gods arises freely. Greek antiquity becomes ever mightier, more heroic, but its history, 'the tragic age', becomes more dangerous, the fate of the plastic form becomes less and less a matter of chance. It is no longer the eye at work, but law, the spirit. A relationship develops here which lasted for four hundred years of history, from open violence to art entirely without mediation, from the heroism of external attitude and deed, from the battlefields of Marathon and Salamis to the perfected form of the last Parthenon style, here it is really possible to talk of the birth of art from power, in the history of the statue and in this place at least.

This then was Sparta, so much was it the beginning, the growth cell of the Greek spirit, and the facts that have been laid out above are not contradicted by the Spartan's foreignness as a human being in the Greek world. Sparta was always what it had founded itself to be, a warrior city, while the other cities had long ago become pan-Hellenic, Sicilian or Asiatic. To keep defining and guarding the boundaries, that is probably one of the mysteries of power, and since Sparta acted in that way it succeeded in winning the final victory and having Greece finish in the city where it had begun. Moreover, a feeling for the greatness of Doric life persists throughout all centuries and in all political communities, a kind of longing for Sparta always remained alive in Greece! 'Laconizers', meaning followers of Sparta and admirers of Spartan style, were always present in Athens, in difficult times Sparta was repeatedly called 'the educator', and it is very interesting that Plato, spiritually the last Dorian, who during the dissolution once again took up the struggle against individualism, the melancholy attraction of art, the 'honeyed Muse', 'shadow art', to fight in favour of the 'community' and 'sensible thoughts', 'average life', the 'city with the blameless constitution', expresses this longing for Sparta, in the *Theages* he says of a virtuous man who gives lectures on virtue: 'In the wonderful harmony of his actions and his words one recognises the Dorian way, the only one which is truly Greek'. That was five hundred years after Lycurgus. And from here his truly Spartan words against art can be understood, words almost incomprehensible in the mouth of the creator of his extremely idealistic world-view: 'If you, o Glaucon, come across men who praise Homer and maintain that it was he who created Hellas, know that he was indeed the most poetic and first of all tragedians, but only that part of poetry which produces songs to the gods and in praise of excellent men should be admitted into the state'. Thus speaks this exalted intellectual, great artist and first to bear the burdensome chasm between body and spirit which two millennia have not been able to close up again, thus, beyond all criticism of perception and refinement of artistic dialogue, in this profound and transcendent late-comer is heard once again the camp of men on the right bank of the Eurotas, Sparta, power.

We thus derive Greece from Sparta, and from the Dorian-Apollonian world the Greek world. Here Dionysus stands back within the boundaries in which he stood before 1871 ('The birth of tragedy from the spirit of music').[1] The Greeks were a primitive people, that is to say close to intoxication, their worship of Zeus had orgiastic traits; great waves of excited intoxication occurred amongst them periodically, in Sparta too, they had taken over much that was cathartic from the Cretan cults. But meanwhile we have learned from travel literature and films of primitive peoples, especially negro races, whose existence seems to be a succession of intoxicated states, without art having emerged from them. Sparta must step between intoxication and art, Apollo, the great force of breeding. And since today we are no longer so excited by Wagner as to try and prove that Tristan already existed in Thrace, we look towards the Doric, not Dion, we ask questions of the Greek world.

1   Nietzsche's *Geburt der Tragödie aus dem Geiste der Musik.*

429

V. *Art as progressive anthropology*

Let us sum up and try to establish a perspective. We see the many-sided Hellenic empire, built up of individual cities and states, and in each of them we see the most monstrous level of power-hunger, cruelty, bribery, Camorra,[2] dishonour, savagery, murder, conspiracy, exploitation, blackmail. We see amongst the greatest men the most criminal types like Alcibiades, Lysander, Pausanias; the most frightful like Clearchus; liars as saviours of the state driven garlanded on a chariot into the Prytaneum and feasted there like Diocleides, the denouncer of the blasphemy committed on the herms, which he immediately confesses was a lie. We see deceit, prettified; the stamps on sacks of state monies were not noticed and three hundred talents removed; blatant: embezzlement; publicly legalised, capitalistic: 'a golden handshake for platform speakers', that was a saying, meaning 'the silent purchase of state orators'. We see bribable judges: 'not guilty' when they see the dagger-handles, the selling of verdicts, sycophants (professional and officious denouncers) and counter-sycophants, who 'slip to and fro on the agora with stings raised', whole generations, whole systems –: 'I am a witness in island cases, a sycophant and smeller-out of things, I don't like digging, my grand-father lived off calumny in his time too', says a figure in Aristophanes. We see the signs of modern public life, the modern state, modern power.

It cannot be said, that is a long way off, antiquity. Not at all! Antiquity is very near, is completely inside us, the cultural cycle is not yet completed. The idealistic system of a modern philosopher is closer to Plato than to the world-view of a modern empiricist; modern relativist nihilism is wholly identical as a natural tendency with the so-called Pyrrhonic scepticism of the third century before Christ. Anaximander's pessimism, that oft-repeated saying: 'things have their origin from the place where they must also of necessity perish, for they must pay the penalty and be condemned for their injustice according to the order of time' – ; in an essay Nietzsche links that directly to Schopenhauer. The problem of the thing in itself arises and remains unsolved to this day. The problem of development begins its history and grows ever more confused in our day. Du Bois-Reymond's *ignorabimus* extends back across the French sixteenth

2 Neapolitan mafia.

century's *Quoad nihil scitur* to the leitmotif of the whole Greco-Roman epoch. Or let us take politics: the whole range of statecraft expressions is already there in the fifth century: 'the public good', 'the equality of citizens', 'political parties'; factually the opposition of poor and rich, of the mob and aristocracy, of democratic and oligarchic government, of monarchy and the rule of the people. They knew popular festivals, national holidays, festivals for Greeks from abroad. They speak of exported fronts: northwards went the bold and free but barbaric states, to Asia went the educated but cowardly and slavish, – that is exactly where we are in our own political principles.

If all this is considered not under moral, sentimental, historico-philosophical points of view, but according to anthropological principles, we see on the one hand power and beside it the other outburst of Hellenic nationhood: art. How do these two behave towards each other, what were their relationships? Let us forget that many artists left their native land, embittered, as enemies, disappointed, those are individual traits. Let us also forget that Phidias is believed to have died in prison, under suspicion of having stolen ivory. Let us not consider individual crises and disasters, the rivalry of individual schools and formations, but let us concentrate on the gradual, centuries-long self-adjustment to the definitive, final, classical style, its appearance during the dissolution, and then its end. If we concentrate on that, we see Dorian culture under the protection of its militarism giving the Greek practice of art a place in the state and carrying it across the whole of Greece – and this contribution of power is enormous – ; but the fact that it was there at all, that it could develop in this way, was naturally a fact of race, of species, of the free play of the gene, that was *in toto* such an enormous outburst of a new human element, that it can only be considered absolute, with its own laws, self-ignited, called into being by nothing, by no gods and by no power. The two can be looked at side by side, power and art, it may be a useful exercise for both: *power* as the iron grip forcing the social process, whereas, in the natural *bellum omnium contra omnes*, without the state society cannot put down roots on a larger scale beyond the realm of the family (Nietzsche). Or, to follow Burckhardt:[3] 'Only on that basis, on a ground made safe by power, can cultures of the highest rank flourish'. He also has a particularly splendid passage relating to

3 Jakob Burckhardt (1818–97), Swiss cultural historian.

Sparta: 'It has never been a gentle affair when a new power was establishing itself, and Sparta at least truly became one when compared with everything existing round about; this comparison also managed to compel the attention of the whole developed world until the evening of its days, so great is the magic of a mighty will, even over later millennia, even when no sympathy can play a part'.

It can perhaps be expressed thus: the state, power, purifies the individual, filters out his sensitivity, makes him cubic, creates surfaces, makes him fit for art. Yes, that is perhaps the way to put it: the state makes the individual fit for art, yet power can never pass over into art. Both can have common experiences of a mythic, popular, political kind, but art remains aloof as the lonely higher world. Art keeps its own laws and expresses nothing but itself. For if we once turn to the nature of Greek art, the Doric temple expresses nothing and cannot be understood, and the column is not natural, they do not incorporate a concrete political or cultural will, they are parallel to nothing, but the whole is a *style*, that means, seen from within, a certain feeling for space, for spatial panic, and seen from outside there are certain predispositions and principles within which to represent that, to express it, in fact to conjure it up. This principle of representation no longer comes directly from nature like politics or power, but from the anthropological principle which came into being at a later stage, and not until the natural basis of creation was already present. One might also say, it attained consciousness as a principle in a new act of creation, became the human entelechy, after, as potentiality and activity, it had already fostered the formation and division of nature. Antiquity is then the new direction, the beginning of this principle of turning into a counter-movement, of becoming 'unnatural', a counter-movement against mere geology and vegetation to become fundamentally *style*, art, struggle, the incorporation in material of ideal being, deep study and then dissolution of material, the isolation of form as a step upwards and elevation of the earth.

It becomes *expression*, and all who made and interpreted Western culture understood antiquity in this sense and took their direction from it: Nietzsche entirely: the titanic raising up of the heavy natural blocks of science, morals, attitude, instinct, sociology, all these 'German diseases of taste', into the empires of Helle, of Gaia, into the school of healing in the most spiritual and most sensual aspects; of national introversion, of the politically opinionated into realms of space and empire, one might also say of power, of the Dorians; the raising up of the religious from the puritan and passive schools into the ordered and ordering aesthetic one, one might also say in geographical terms: of the Nazarene into its favourite interpretations: the Provençal and Ligurian; the purely eugenic utopia as a late flower of the declining moral world into the form-conscious, spiritually imprinted, disciplined utopia. And in this process, form never as a tired last resort, tenuous, empty in the German bourgeois sense, but as the enormously human power, pure power, victory over naked facts and civilisatory matters simply as what Western culture has achieved, super-eminence, mind as a real category of its own, the balancing and collecting of fragments. The whole of Nietzsche in one sentence, his deepest and most forward-looking, of course: 'Only as an aesthetic phenomenon are existence and the world justified for ever'. But that is Hellenic.

And we see Goethe standing here too. His Iphigenia is phenomenologically and politically absolutely unnatural.[4] To find someone sitting in Weimar amongst courtiers and the local bourgeoisie and writing those superlative verses on the way of death, the Song of the Fates and the frightening summoning-up of the Tantalids, there is no word for that level of unnaturalness. No national tradition has shown the path to it, no current problem leads up to it, no naïve causality stands behind it, here distant, inner, sublime laws are at work which since antiquity have been categorised as aesthetic. That they are the ones which go on to victory, shining and outlasting the ages, has its basis in their centrality to the anthropological principle, in the character of their main preoccupation, in their character as an axis, the spindle of necessity: man is the race which has style. Style is superior to reality, it carries within itself the proof of existence. Truth must be tested, a battery of instruments for progress. 'Thought is always the product of necessity', says Schiller, in whom we notice a very conscious repositioning of the central pivot from the moral to the aesthetic worldview, he believes that thought always stands close to the serviceable and the satisfaction of instincts, with axes and spiked cudgels, it is natural, but in form is distance, is duration. Where the tree of knowledge stands is always the fall from grace, this worldview supposes, division, termination, exile –: art is the preservation of a

---

4   Goethe's poetic drama *Iphigenie auf Tauris* (1786).

433

people's species, its definitive inheritability. The extinguishing of all ideological tensions with one exception: art and history, the Romantics saw that too, Novalis[5] left us the extraordinary statement: 'Art as progressive anthropology'.

Historical periods end with art, and humankind will end with art. First the dinosaurs, the lizards, then the species with art. Hunger and love, that is palaeontology, and every kind of authority and division of labour is already to be found amongst insects, but *these creatures* here made gods and art, then only art. A late world, built on previous foundations and early forms of being, everything is coming to fruition in it. All things turn around, all concepts and categories change their character in the moment they are considered as art, when they confront it, when they are confronted by it. Man, the mixed form, the Minotaur, by nature always in the labyrinth and a refined cannibal, here he is pure harmony and monolithic in the heights, and twists creation out of the hand of that other one.

We look back at the Doric world, the peoples with style, we listen to them, even if they have passed away, their time fulfilled, the great families gone and the sun on their columns gone to shine on new earths, while on the old only the fields of asphodel bloom; once again from the depths, from fragments, bits of wattle-and-daub, bronzes covered in sea-shells recovered from the wrecks of raiders by grubbing in the mud at the bottom of the sea, they call out to us late-comers the law of outline, a law which speaks to us nowhere more overwhelmingly than from the stele of the dying runner, end of the sixth century, Attic, Athens, Theseion, from his biologically impossible movements which can only be stylised in Parian marble. A law opposed to life, a law only for heroes, only for the man working marble and the man casting helmeted heads: 'art is more than nature, and the runner is less than life', which means, all life wants more than life, wants outline, style, abstraction, a profounder life, spirit.

All joy longs for eternity, said the last century, the new one continues: all eternity longs for art. Absolute art, form. Yet 'all beauty is difficult, and whoever draws near to it must wrestle naked and alone with his creatures' – that is the first Doric verse, the second: he must also perish. What remain are the laws alone, but they outlast the epochs. And we are reminded of a great writer from a foreign

---

5   Novalis was the pseudonym of the German poet Felix von Hardenberg (1772–1801).

post-Hellenic people, who believed in the norms of beauty, which are like the commandments of a god, which preserve eternity in what has been created. The sight of a few columns of the Acropolis, he said, gave him an inkling of what imperishable beauty might be attainable through the ordering of sentences, words, vowels.[6] For in reality he did not believe that there is anything external in art.

6   This sentence, paraphrasing Flaubert, is quoted from the third part of Heinrich Mann's essay on the French novelist published in the journal *Die Zukunft* in 1930. In 1905 Mann had published a more accurate translation of Flaubert's words from a letter to George Sand of April 1876.

An extract from *Writing needs inner latitude*

1934

… As to the future, it seems obvious to me that no book contemptuous of the new state should be allowed to appear in Germany. The more strictly, single-mindedly, inexorably this principle is applied by publishers and booksellers in the political direction, the more breadth of heart one will be permitted to demonstrate intellectually. And the arts will be allowed the inner latitude their nature demands. Writers need a certain licence to experiment. The sciences are granted without question the use of manpower as well as public resources for years of experimentation, even if it is unknown at the outset whether there will be any result, indeed, there is no criticism, if at the end it emerges that all the effort has produced nothing of substance. Art has an even better case than this. Its nature is problematic, lacking the directional focus and purposiveness of science, and comprises the development, breakthrough, fateful play of incipient, unsolved, fragmentary forces. It is certainly political too, even especially so, but in a different sense from all other cultural and political expression. It is political within those profoundest layers of being in which true revolutions come into being, there it reformulates and makes any step backward impossible. The total state, this great and new concept, cannot mean that art's content and theme should not be allowed to encompass anything else. The total state itself is only a reflection of that world totality, that substantial unity of all appearances and forms, that transcendent completeness of being at rest in itself, that logos, that religious ordering towards which art is always striving, of itself and with its constructive means, that is to say applying its own positive, thrilling and purifying principle which makes it real, which was what first made it manifest to humanity at all … I represent the view that in future all art will possess more of man, of the people, indeed of the whole new race than before; it will take over the functions of religion, philosophy and of politics, and again become the primary anthropological unity of the Nordic and Hyperborean world which it once was. It should therefore be subject to less restraint, and left to its own intuition and way of fashioning the world.

An extract from *Pallas*

1943

… What lives is different from what thinks. This is a fundamental fact of today, we must learn to live with it. Whether it was ever different once, whether a sidereal fusion of the two is shimmering towards us from afterworlds, at this moment at any rate it is not happening. Not merely live with it: recognise, defend the Oresteian epoch, the world as a spiritual construct, as transcendent apperception, existence as something made by the mind, being as a dream of form. All this was dearly won, suffered for, this and more. Pallas invented the flute – reed and wax – , a little thing. Our brain too is faced with limitations of space. We can only form restricted partial centres; an ability to develop perspectives long horizontally and temporally has not been given to us. Tending small spaces, chiselling on a handsbreadth scale, narrow summarising, concise theses –: anything more lies beyond the epoch.

A celebration of Dionysus, of wine not the ear of corn, Bacchus not Demeter, phallic congestion not nine-month magic, the aphorism not the historical novel! Some thing has been written, paper and typewriter, thoughts, sentences, it lies on the table. One returns from other spheres, human circles, professional surroundings, charging the brain with facts, overspill, repressing every flight and every dream – hours later a return and a sight of the white strip on the table. What is that? A lifeless something, vague worlds, brought together and thought together with pain and effort, regrouped, tested, improved, left in wretched state, disjointed, unproven, weak – ripe for the fire, a decadent nothing. The whole thing misguided, a racial sickness, a dark scar, connections gone astray? Then Pallas approaches, never disconcerted, always in her helmet, never impregnated, slim childless goddess, born of the father without sex.

The law of coldness, of scant community, is approaching. Animals renew themselves from blood, nature exhausts itself from the loins: after nature – and before it in the cycle of hours – appeared the mind, broke out for the first time in a created being and filled it with the dream of the absolute. Dreams too generate, pictures weave, concepts burn matter and thing – ash the earth, cinders we. Nietzsche says the Greeks repeatedly regenerated and corrected themselves through their physiological needs, that preserved their life – perhaps it was so, but his own physiological needs were cognition, that was the new biology demanded and created by mind. Out of the sense-lessness of material and historical process arose a new reality, made by the agents of formal reason, the second reality, made by the slow collectors and inducers of thought decisions. There is no going back. No summoning of Ishtar, no retournons à la grand'mère, no invo-cation of the Mothers' realms, no enthronement of Gretchen[1] above Nietzsche can change anything about the fact that there is no longer a state of nature for us. Where man does exist in a state of nature he has palaeontological and museum character. The last white one is no longer nature, he has trodden the path he was forced to take by that 'absolute reality', gods, pre-gods, Ur, pre-Urs, ens realissimum, natura naturans, in a word: the heart of darkness[2] – he has stepped outside nature. His goal, or perhaps only his transition, in any case his existential commission is no longer natural nature, but worked nature, nature in thought, stylised nature – art.

The world of expression! Before it stands Pallas, childless goddess, is silent about the grandchildren of Demeter and all embryonic jelly, that may rest in primal silence, on the knees of the gods. These, eternal breath-blowers and clay-kneaders, millipedes and millidyers, who will overtake time and space again, and the fission-fungus and the spectres, these will not allow even the grandchildren too little play and suffering – some day! But I see the Achaeans around me. Achilles, sheathing his sword: *not yet* – or I will drag you by your golden hair; – Odysseus, defeated, there lies the island, you will collect the bow of Philoctetes. *Today! This!* Not Oceanus, not the massive wastes of the tide; where the ships sail, the Aegean and the Tyrrhenian Sea – *there*! Grandchildren! There are already sources of nourishment from the Gulf Stream, meteors deliver tasty and cultivated tillage – mollusc milk is secured – you, turn – get the bow – you alone!

Pallas stops, it is evening, she loosens her armour, taking down the breastplate with the Gorgon's head, this head in which the Babylonian dragon Tiamat and the snake of Apophis from Egypt live on, but beaten and conquered. It is evening, there lies her city, stony land, the marble mountain and two rivers. Everywhere olive

1 The redeemed soul in Goethe's *Faust*.
2 Benn had certainly read Joseph Conrad (in translation), and admired him.

438

tree, her work, great groves. She stands on the place of judgement in those days, the hill of Ares, the old fortress of the Amazons which Theseus the stone-raiser destroyed. Before her the steps of the altar on which the judgement was decided. She sees the Furies, she sees Orestes. She sees Apollo, companion of the scene, and she recalls the remark of Proteus, master of the sea-calves, that on this place, not far into the future as reckoned on the gods' timescale, another would stand to proclaim the resurrection of the dead. Clytemnestra – Agamemnon; murder of a spouse – of a mother; father-idea – mother-idea – ; the slaughtered and the resurrected: all merely murmurs, all ideas – ideas too are as senseless as facts, just as chaotic, because they too bring order and illumination to only one part of the aeon; only finished formations are valid, statues, friezes, the shield of Achilles, they have no ideas, say only themselves and are perfect.

There under the stars she saw the horn of Amalthea, the Cretan goat which suckled her father when he was a boy, doves brought him nourishment, gold-coloured bees brought him honey. He then eradicated what was unformed, without shape, without bounds, and the Titans and giants, anything unlimited. This star had a bright green light, it was purer than Ariadne, next to it, whom Bacchus under love's influence had hurled aloft. She remembered her father. Rhea, his mother, had saved his life with a stone wrapped in goat's hair. She gave it to Saturn to swallow instead of the newborn divine child. This oft-mentioned stone! What had life and form had won time to steal into the light! Then his rule began, and the course of things entered his track. This land, in which poverty was at home and the custom inherited from the fathers of winning advantages only through work and insight – there now the statues of the gods made of ivory and gold, there now the ghostly white procession of the Propylaea. In it a people recognised and created itself. How long has it been since the rays of Helios touched not only the backs and fins of creatures gazing downwards, but encountered an answering fire, since a mortal man walking upright attained a view of himself, found meaning in himself, thought, and, turning inward, returned his innermost being to himself in utterance and works: now – here! Pallas turned and strode to the city. It was shining with olive branches and red thistle-heads; tomorrow's competitors surged through the streets, crowds of pilgrims and the mass of onlookers. It was the evening before the Panathenaia. People from the sources, people from the

439

mountain terraces, people from the grave-mounds in the marshes around Marathon; people from the sea came, had sailed for the flashing lance of Athena Promachos, that had been their beacon fire. Tomorrow they would step before the images and the statues and the masks made for the play. All the Hellenes! The Hellenes from the plane-trees, those carrying chisels, the Oresteian Hellenes! Pallas now disappeared amongst them, motherless goddess, armed again and alone.

Extracts from *On the theme of history*

probably 1943, published 1949

... Worship of power, no matter whether it represented the most stupid, jackal-like disposition, as long as it was power: Führer lead, we follow! Born scoundrels and trained murderers, – any part of them not covered by these two descriptors is just greenery, decorative arabesques ...

Germany has let its beasts rise to the top, wrote Heinrich Mann[1] shortly after his emigration ...

And the attitude of its leading men, even in the years of peace, proves Heinrich Mann to be right. There they sit in a celebratory meeting of the German Academy, at Goebbels's invitation. The great conductors, the professors of philosophy or physics, honorary senators from the old respectable years, Pour-le-mérite holders (Peace class), presidents of the Reichsgericht, imperial excellencies, publishers, 'permitted' novelists, Goethe-scholars, keepers of monuments, actors from the state theatres, theatre directors, the honest merchant, and all without exception allow the minister's anti-Semitic babble to run over them without a murmur ... all without exception see the lorries into which Jewish children, taken from their houses in public view, are thrown, to disappear for ever: the work of this minister –: they all move their arms and clap this Goebbels. There they sit: the scions of the old families which gave birth to Novalis, Kleist, Platen, Droste-Hülshoff,[2] side by side with the children of the many great families of parsons who had preached the commandment of love fifty-two times a year for four centuries, shoulder to shoulder with the honest merchant whose word was his bond and commitments a matter of honour, and with them they beat Jews to death and enrich themselves with the property left behind, attack small countries and take the last of their possessions as a matter of course – and see that their cultures are purified 'thoroughly', 'finally', and 'fully and completely'. No-one feels in duty bound to any tradition, any history of family or intellectual nature, any attitude to the forefathers and their inheritance – , but they call the whole thing *race*.

---

1 Heinrich Mann (1871–1950), novelist, brother of Thomas Mann, emigrated from Germany in 1933.
2 German writers of the eighteenth and nineteenth centuries from aristocratic families.

The German Academy! Not one stands up to spit on the floral arrangements, kick the potted palms, and declare it is inadmissible to maintain that this evil popular rabble-rousing can possibly give birth to some dim national essence ... they all clap ...

No, one has to admit, it was not the beasts, it was Germany that put its identity on show in this movement ...

Until 1933 the German army was the last elite and the last kernel of substance in Nazi Germany. Joining the army was, as I said at the time, the aristocratic form of emigration. The end began with the expulsion of Baron Friedrich [*recte* Werner] von Fritsch as Commander-in-Chief.[3] Those who now stayed in place or rose to the surface were creatures ...

... I personally do not believe in Darwinism, I do not believe that he has given a factually satisfactory explanation for even one section of life. Instead, I see that in nature there are just as many signs suggesting maintenance of peace and conditions that last, and non-military means of arriving at a settlement between the individual and his surroundings. This thought is far from new ...

... Every definition which emphasises the animalistic in defining man fails to take account of what is characteristic and essential to his existence. Man is a being who must be carefully watched, both for himself and for his ideas, but precisely because he is not an animal. This observation arises not from biological, but from intellectual principles, only where the spirit of the social and moral environment is incapable of doing that, where it has not attained the potential heights of anthropological existence, do the methods appropriate to beasts arise. Not eugenics, but education is the law to take account of that.

... In a universal perspective, we have not the faintest idea who or what we are, from where or in what direction we are headed, how to establish a connection between work and success, or life and death ... What rises to the surface is always merely the confused play of hidden forces. Thinking about them, embodying them in a material placed in our hands by the earth, in 'stone, verse, flute-song', in discrete, heritable forms –: this work on the world of expression, without expectations, but not without hope –: the present hour has nothing else for us.

3   Baron Werner von Fritsch (1880-1939), Commander-in-Chief of the German army under
    Hitler until his dismissal was engineered by the Gestapo in 1938.

A game of the Aeon, a game of the Parcae and of dreams! Whatever multitudes have won the victory in world history, they have never destroyed this doctrine! The doctrine of the world of expression as victor over nationalism, racism, history, but also over the grief of humanity and the individual which is our birthright. To work at some inner commission, or to be silent at some inner commission, alone and inactive, until the hour of disclosure returns. I have seen no-one greater than the man who could say: grief and light, and worshipped both; and whose being measured itself on the scales whose pans move against each other, sinking and rising, but which never weighs itself.

... Nihilism is an inner reality, precisely a determination to move oneself in the direction of aesthetic interpretation, therein history can have no result, no possibility. This direction is intended in the sentence from *Illusions perdues*: 'a word is weightier than a victory'.[4]

Wishes for Germany: New interpretation of the concepts hero and honour. Rejection of any person who during the next hundred years says Prussianism or the Reich. History to be left to the management of middle-ranking officials in the civil service, but publicly subordinate to a European executive in direction and principle. Children from six to sixteen to be educated at public expense, as their parents choose, in Switzerland, England, France, America, Denmark.

4   Balzac's novel of 1836–43.

Three extracts from *The phenotype's novel*

Ambivalence

The phenotype[1] of the twelfth and thirteenth century celebrated courtly love, that of the seventeenth spiritualised pomp, that of the eighteenth secularised cognition, that of today integrated ambivalence, the merging of everything with its opposites.

On the one hand bound to the mind and its standards down to the very last fibre of the body – *on the other* sceptical towards this mind as a regional, geographical-historical offspring of the race. On the one hand fighting for expression to the extent of anguished peculiarities, destructions of form to the extent of bizarre word-play – on the other smiling bitterly at this expression as it is being minted, with its features of chance and transition. On the one hand occasionally feeling conditioned by powers that rule afar and spin the threads according to one's apportioned share (Moira), and on the other being directed and urgently demanding oneself to deny it, as if one were in charge, standing in heaven, and while yawning and chewing could grind the spindles beneath one's heels. On the one hand in fear of the dead, their palpable glance eternally examining further, in a certain conviction of the power and frightfulness of the psyche, of the psyche which has gone too, and of shadows – on the other attending with satisfaction to the plaudits of the press, white spats, the great prizes, chamois-hunts. On the one hand tradition – on the other congenital caprice. On the one hand touched by what is gentle and pliant – on the other full of hate for whoever stands beside it. On the one hand facing the universe as the pompous conqueror of minted forms – on the other facing eye and nose, forehead and eyebrows, mouth and chin as the only form, the only one we know. On the one hand casuistic and subtle – on the other suspecting the final linking of all causes in quite other regions. On the one hand deeply marked by the factual knowledge of the last four thousand years in a new historical understanding reserved for one's generation, by what this nourishes, a constant flood of sublime time-sensuality, a sense of time-transience, time-destruction – on the other with a public and private weakness for imperialist, for Caesarean things, as the bourgeois understands

46 Phenotype: the observed properties of an organism. (Genotype: its hereditary makeup.)

444

them gigantic, 'global' things; while losing a perception of space: a longing for the validity of time and duration. On the one hand glassy – on the other bloody. On the one hand exhaustion – on the other ski-jumping. On the one hand archaic – on the other up-to-date with a hat from Bond Street and a pearl tie-pin from the Rue de la paix. On the one hand bright in the evening – on the other groundlessly cast down the next morning –: thus, half in play and half in suffering – forty per cent Adam and Eve, thirty per cent antiquity, twenty per cent Palestine, ten per cent Upper Asia – , strides the phenotype, generally euphoric, through the continent-destroying hour of the great battles.

The city park

On another plane, the city park. It comes into view without more ado (more ado?), maybe as seen from the bench placed to provide certain horticultural views by the society for the improvement of urban scenery. A sky hangs above it too, not the pale-blue Texas sky and not the cloudless one of the Midi which out-arches the pines, but still a sort of conclusion on high for experimental glances. Various kinds of paths lead to it, that is traditional, but immensely striking the *swan motif.* Swans – how stylised! Nonsensical, putting a water-bird's head so far above the surface on an apparently glass-blown neck! No logic there, arranged purely for effect. The willows too, hanging into the ripples, moving unsatisfied longings, melancholy, bionegative matters away into the farmers' city, immediately, as everyone appreciates, intended for effect.

A world of contradictions, yet the world has already seen so much: catamites crowned, a white horse honoured as a god, a mausoleum erected to the Manes of a drinking-cup, a beautiful tree decorated with jewels – and now this fragmentation! Yet our position is not favourable. Everything one hears about life, about the mind, about art, from Plato to Leonardo and Nietzsche, is not crystal-clear, contains subterfuges – there is already quite open talk about the loss of the object! Yes, indeed, we doubt the substance which gave rise to these words, we doubt its experiences and its happinesses, we doubt its method of self-presentation, we doubt its images. We have scarcely two footfalls of earth before us, very little earthly at all, everything is very narrow, everything must be weighed up with great care, we look

445

pensively at the veined chalices of large flowers into which moths sink in such intoxication. The Reich is only one page in size or a painted hat with a feather or a fugue – and out there is the surge. It is March, the park has a feel of uncleanliness, even in this plain, in this hollow, the liliacea bear themselves tensely, they open in a sudden florescence, yesterday still closed, they burst in a sort of self-deflowering, in a blue leap up against the light, they appear hard and sharp as weapons – beside them are other weapons: bells, catkins, bursting out to the limit, sure of form to the very violet, bee-brown rim – , weapons of an enemy power, a super-power on which everything shatters – nature. Against it one must assemble all one's strengths.

Our position is not favourable. The senses are in retreat. Has anyone considered the fact that Nietzsche wore lenses of diopter strength fourteen, usually two glasses, boys had to lead him up and down steps. And we no can no longer hear across great distances, hunters in the great snowy peaks could hear further. So cast up your fountains in yourself, erect your own echo-walls! Our ears have not been licked by Cassandra's snake, which opened up voices in the air and the earth's melodies, we did not sleep on the marble where this reptile coiled. But millennia live in our souls, lost things, silent things, dust; Cain, Zenobia, the Atridae swinging their thyrsus wands. And the pool there! Water! Water is darker than earth, you could watch it for hours, stay on its banks –: *become* water – transform yourself, transformations and depth under waves – ah, an hour on *one* plane, in *one* happiness – !

Summary
The foregoing are the phenotype's impressions, memories and deeds during one quarter of a year, from 20.3.1944 to 20.6.1944 – a period sufficient to describe his behaviour. He lived in barracks in the East, on army rations, two Kommiss-loaves a week, adequate margarine, twice a day a bowl of soup or cabbage stew, so he was well looked after, his room overlooked the parade-ground on which the generality performed its ideas.

He was growing to feel his age, the days of overview, the hour of certainty that no-one else would come to explain and advise, nothing else to clarify what he had failed to clarify himself. Everything was stepping into a bright light, into established conditions, connections

446

which were valid within the framework of their situation – only within that framework: for in the background stood huge disharmony as the universal law.

Into this pure projection of an abstract intellect, seemingly foreign and one of those mutations in which the background, 'absolute reality' as modern physics calls it, occasionally moves on, into these tensions and splits in the zone of transformation, there entered geographically something of the wide plains flowing across towards Asia, the plains in which he was living at that time, something of their forests and desolate rivers, the first which hum so blue-white at the rim and the last whose sedge stares so monotonously – this crumb betrayed something of their repetitions, so old and never tiring. Something immobile entered him, emerged, since it had probably always been there, an invisible and unnameable god belonging to country people, since he remained in ploughed fields, harvest fell, without his making a move, onto his shoulders, his hollows lay nearby, not unreachable were the entrances to nests and ravine. He also had leisure, measure, to consider mystic disappearances in running water, spiriting away by a river nymph, a naiad, foam-births, graves in the swell. He stopped there: he left his rod unused, the waters moved on their way, yes, whole days watered by in enraptured silence, without impatience, with that honey in the hours which comes after blossoming, after much blossoming, from fields of snow and purple.

And in Normandy began the great battle which would give him back freedom, not the only true, absolute freedom, but the freedom he had grown up in, and the companions with whom he had begun his life. At the same time he did not see Ararat and a rainbow when he looked out of the ark. As far as the future was concerned, he was sure of only one thing, 1948 would see the fiftieth anniversary of the machine-gun, Sudan would rise up, dervishes storming, wonderfully multicoloured targets for the Maxim-Nordfeld guns, the black banner sank, the light green, the dark green – and now was the moment for the famous attack of the 21st Lancers under Major Kitchener – spring 1898 – , and now all the lions and eagles from all the great wars, victors and vanquished, would stream together, celebrate and be celebrated, all these richly experienced experts on rocket development and flame-jet bombs, keen on points of breach and gaps in the front, and there would be no end of vivats and evvivas. Once again he entered the ambivalence of things which had revealed itself

447

to him so determinatively. On the one hand the freeing of the mind through the battles, and on the other the mind's categorisation of all such events as part of animalistic motions, of geology – this antinomy had no end. This dovetailing of history and the world of the mind was one of the questions which his epoch could not answer, even in Nietzsche's remark about the mysterious hieroglyph between the state and genius he omitted to describe this hieroglyph more closely; it remained an open question, which would stay open until it answered itself and then disappeared.

But one day it would answer itself, in circles of that never-ending motion which was only ever self-referential. He classed it among these distant encounters. And once again it entered his field of vision: a brook hurtled down from high snow-fields, a wood of grey olive-trees melted up from the depths – mourning and light were both worshipped as all that rested quietly within him, and then summer ending with the violet of thistles and the sulphur-yellow, the hot, sweet rose Diane vaincue.

An extract from *Marginalia*

first published 1949

Lyric poetry

… The lyric poet moves in a laboratory, a laboratory for words. Here he models, fabricates words, opens them, explodes, shatters them, in order to load them with tensions which persist for a few decades. The troubadour returns: trobaire or trobador = finder, that means inventor of words (eleventh century, between the Loire and the Pyrenees), that is to say: artist. Whoever knows the dance enters the laboratory. Gauguin writes once about Van Gogh: 'In Arles, everything – quays, bridges and ships, the whole of the South – became Holland for him'. In this sense, for the lyric poet, everything that happens becomes Holland, namely: word, word-root, sequence of words, linking of words; syllables are psychoanalysed, diphthongs re-educated, consonants transplanted. For him the word is real and magical, a modern totem …

Extracts from *Double life*

1949

... Actually all that my generation discussed, thought out inwardly, one might say: suffered, or expounded – all that had already been expressed and exhausted, found definitive formulation by Nietzsche, anything more was exegesis. His dangerously stormy, flashing style, his restless diction, his self-denial of any idyll and any generally valid basis, his proposition of instinctual psychology and constitution as motive force, physiology as dialectic – 'perception as affect', the whole of psychoanalysis, of existentialism, all this thanks to him. He is, as is emerging ever more clearly, the far-reaching giant of the epoch after Goethe.

... In the beginning was the word. Amazing, the cause of much reflection on my part, that it was so. In the beginning, when animism and totemism and cave-making and animals and magic masks and rattles maintained the field, the world – the Jews were probably very ancient when they said that, and knew a great deal. Indeed, the earth collects itself in the word, there is nothing more treacherous than the word. I always found it immensely interesting to observe how specialist scholars, and deep philosophers too, suddenly found themselves face to face with the free word, the word that can bring no historically secure tirades and systems and circumstances gleaned from external observation, not commentaries, but: form. And what do they do? Collapse utterly! Little idyll-makers, little home-makers, yokels. In the beginning, in the middle, and at the end, is the word.

Additional note: Today it is actually the case that there are only two instances of verbal transcendence: mathematical theorems and the word as art. Everything else is business language, ordering beer.

... The ages end with art and the human race will end with art... A new attitude, a new affectation. From Homer to Goethe is one hour, from Goethe to today twenty-four hours, twenty-four hours of transformation, of dangers that can only be met by the man who is putting his own rules into practice. Nowadays one often hears the question of what is a 'correct' view of Goethe, there will be no such thing, one must be content with the thought that something has started flowing in a way that is confusing and not to be understood, but that scatters seeds on banks that had become deserts –: that is art.

Extracts from *Problems of lyric poetry*

1951

… in lyric poetry, mediocrity is absolutely forbidden and unbearable; its field is narrow, its means very subtle, its substance the *ens realissimum* of all substances, and so its standards must be extreme. Mediocre novels are not as unbearable, they can entertain, inform, excite, but lyric poetry must be exorbitant or nothing. That is part of its nature.

Also part of its nature is something else, the poets' tragic realisation about themselves: none of the great lyric poets of our time has left more than six to eight perfect poems, the remainder may be interesting from the point of view of their author's biography and development, but very few are serene, luminous, full of long-lasting fascination – and so these six poems are the reason for the thirty to fifty years of asceticism, suffering and struggle.

Next I should like to describe one process more directly than is usually the case. This is the process of bringing a poem into being. What does the author intend? What conditions are present? The conditions are as follows: the author has at his disposal: firstly, a sense of a creative seed, psychic material; secondly, words, at hand or usable, familiar, malleable, he knows his words. There is a phenomenon which can be called the allocation of words to an author. Today, perhaps, he has come across a particular word that preoccupies him, excites him, that he believes he can use as *leitmotif*; thirdly, he has an Ariadne thread which can lead him out of this bipolar tension, lead him with absolute certainty, because – and now comes the mystery: the poem is already complete before it has begun, he just does not yet know its text. The poem cannot sound different in any way than it does when complete. You know exactly when it is complete, and naturally that can take a long time, weeks, years, but until it is ready, you do not let it go. You keep feeling it around, its individual words, its individual lines. You take the second stanza by itself, consider it, wonder if the third stanza is the *missing link* between the second and fourth, and so, for all your self-control, your self-examination, your self-criticism, you are led by something inside you through all the stanzas – a perfect example of that freedom led by necessity discussed by Schiller. You might also say, a poem is like the Phaeacians' ship described by Homer sailing straight into harbour without a

451

steersman. Recently I read in the magazine *Das Lot* a remark by a young writer, Albert Fabri, whom I do not know, nor whether he writes lyric works, a remark which portrays exactly this state of affairs, he says: 'The question of who wrote a poem is always irrelevant. An unknown, irreducible X takes part in the authorship of the poem, in other words, every poem has its own Homeric question, every poem is by several people, that means is by an unknown author.'

This state of affairs is so remarkable that I should like to express it once more in a different way. Something inside you hurls out a few lines, or gropes its way forward in a few lines, something else inside you immediately takes these lines in hand, puts them into a kind of observation machine, a microscope, tests them, colours them, searches for pathological places. If the first is maybe naïve, the second is something quite different: refined and sceptical. If the first is maybe subjective, the second brings in the objective world, it is the formal, intellectual principle.

I do not intend to speak about form in a profound and exhaustive way. Form, in isolation, is a difficult concept. But form itself *is* the poem. The contents of a poem, let us say mourning, a feeling of panic, a flooding sense of finality, everyone has those moments, that is the human lot, its possession in more or less multifarious and sublime measure, but lyric poetry can only be made of it if it is embodied in a form which makes this content autochthonous, makes words into fascination. A form in isolation, in itself, does not exist. It is being, the artist's existential mandate, his goal. It is probably in this sense that we should understand Staiger's sentence: Form is the highest content.[1]

… the author possesses a dim creative seed, psychic material. In other words, that would be the subject to be made into a poem … In Hofmannsthal, who at least in his last period consciously took up the connection between cult, education and nation, I found a very radical remark: 'No direct way leads from poetry to life, none from life into poetry' – which can only mean that poetry, that is, the poem, is autonomous, is a life of its own, as his next words confirm: 'Words are everything'. Most famous of all is Mallarmé's maxim: a poem does not arise from feelings, but from words. Eliot takes the most remarkable standpoint, a certain measure of *impurity* must be retained

---

1   Emil Staiger (1908–87), Swiss Germanist.

even by *poésie pure*, the subject must in a certain sense be valued for itself, if verses are to be felt as a poem.[2] I would say that it is impossible not to see the author behind every poem, his nature, his being, his inner situation, even the objects appear a poem because they were previously *his* objects, he remains in every case that impurity in Eliot's sense. I therefore think that there is no other subject for lyric poetry than its author.

… There are colours and sounds in nature, but no words … one's relationship to words is primary, this connection cannot be learned … you either know how to place words in a fascinating way or you do not. The word is the mind's phallus, centrally rooted. Moreover nationally rooted. Pictures, statues, sonatas, symphonies are international – poems never. A poem can be defined as the untranslatable. Consciousness grows into words, consciousness transcends into words … Words hit home beyond their reporting and information content, on the one hand they are spirit, but on the other possess the essence and ambiguity of natural things.

… Now we must look directly at the cause of these things, the lyric self, face to face and with a sharper focus. What is the nature of lyric poets' psychology, sociology, phenomenology? Firstly and contrary to the general opinion, they are not dreamers, others may dream but they interpret dreams, and they have to be brought from dreams to words. Nor are they really spiritual beings, aesthetes, they make art, that means they need a hard, massive brain, a brain with canine teeth which can pulverise resistance, including their own. They are *petits bourgeois* with a special urge born partly of vulcanism and partly of apathy. Within society they are of no interest … [The artist] stands alone, subjected to silence and ridicule … He works alone, the lyric poet especially alone, since in every decade there are always only a few great lyric poets, distributed across the nations, writing in various languages, mostly unknown to each other – those *phares*, lighthouses in French, those figures who illuminate the great creative sea for a long time but remain in the dark themselves.

… This lyric self stands with its back to the wall out of defensiveness and aggression. It defends itself against the middle ranks which are approaching …

2   Hugo von Hofmannsthal (1874–1929), Austrian poet and dramatist; Stephane Mallarmé (1842–98), French poet; T.S. Eliot (1888–1965), American/English poet and dramatist. Benn was fluent in French, but had to read English writers in translation.

… The lyric poet cannot know enough, cannot work enough, must get close to everything, must find out where the world is today, what time the earth is living this afternoon. The great matadors say one must fight close to the bull, then there is a chance of victory, Nothing in a poem must be there by chance …

Out of all this comes the poem, which may collect together the fragments of one hour –: the absolute poem, the poem without belief, the poem without hope, the poem addressed to no-one, the poem made of words which you set up in a fascinating way. And … whoever claims to see behind this formulation only nihilism and lasciviousness fails to see that behind fascination there lie enough darknesses and abysses of being to satisfy the deepest thinker, that in every form which fascinates there live enough residues of passion, nature and tragic experience. But naturally that requires a decision, you are leaving religion, you are leaving the collective and crossing into uncharted fields. But what is the point of having to listen to the eternal discussion of a fundamental crisis and catastrophe in our culture, if you are not prepared to see what is at stake, even if you take no decision?

But you do have to take this decision! The species which do not accept their law and their inner order lose the tension in their form and sink back. Our order is the mind, its law is expression, imprint, style. All else is annihilation. Whether it is abstract, atonal, surreal, it is the law of form, the Ananke of expressive creation, that governs us. That is not a private opinion, a hobby of the lyric self, all those active in this territory have said so – 'a word is weightier than a victory!' This poem without belief too, this poem without hope, this poem addressed to no-one, is transcendent, it is, to quote a French thinker on this question: 'the co-performance of a development special to man, yet surpassing him'.

An extract from *Speech in Darmstadt,* delivered to the Deutsche Akademie für Sprache und Dichtung on receiving the Georg-Büchner-Prize, 21 October 1951

… Before I travelled here, I re-read *Woyzeck.*[1] Guilt, innocence, poverty, murder, confusion make up the action. But when one reads it today it has the peace of a cornfield and seems like a folksong with the hearts' grief and the sorrow of all people. What power has passed over this gloomy human material and so transformed it and preserved its capacity to thrill?

We are touching the mystery of art, its origin, its life under the pinions of daemons. The daemons do not ask for respectability and refinement of manners, their hard-won nourishment is tears, asphodels and blood. They fly at night above all earthly security, they tear hearts, they destroy happiness and property. They are linked to madness, to blindness, to betrayal, to the unattainable seeking fellows. He who is delivered up to them, whether twenty years old or sixty, knows the features of their red heads, feels their blows, expects damnation. Generations of artists come and go – as long as they live, the fleeting ones with the susceptibility of the disturbed and the sensitivity of haemophiliacs, only the dead are fortunate, their work has come to rest and shines in fulfilment.

But this shining in fulfilment and the dead's good fortune do not deceive us. Ages and zones lie close to each other, in none does the light shine, and only retrospectively does it seem as if the words had come on the feet of doves. When the epochs are at an end, when the peoples are dead and the kings at rest in their chamber, when the kingdoms lie accomplished and ruins crumble between the eternal seas, then everything will look ordered, as if they all had simply needed to reach up and bring down the great, shining, completed garlands, whereas once everything had been equally fought for, hung with blood, expiated with sacrifices, torn from the underworld and disputed with shadows.

The living and the dead, generations come and go – only from a distance is it possible to see interconnections. We travel through cities,

---

1   Georg Büchner (1813–37), German dramatist. He began writing his play *Woyzeck* in 1836, but it was unfinished at his death.

see lights in windows, bars glittering, dancing pairs interweaving, and in one house, at the back, lives one of these fleeting figures, wrapping the world around him like a coat to keep it quiet. Even if not everyone transports his work into security and purity, like Büchner with his *Woyzeck*, even if many lack finish, even if, in Jeremiah's words, they dwell in the rock and are like the dove that maketh her nest in the sides of the hole's mouth – they do nest in the kingdoms where the inextinguishable burns with neither light nor fire, which is as senseless as space and time and the thought and the unthought, and yet alone on that reflex of immortality which rises from the *form* of a vase or a rescued line of verse, untouchable and perfected above sunken metropolises and collapsing empires.

Extracts from *Speech in Knokke*[1]

1952

... Against this background rises the modern lyric self. It steps into its laboratory, the words laboratory, here it models, fabricates words, opens them, blows them apart, shatters them in pieces, in order to load them with tensions, whose validity may then last for a few decades. This modern lyric self has seen everything collapse: theology, biology, philosophy, sociology, materialism, idealism, it hangs for dear life to one thing only: its work on the poem. It has secluded itself from every train of thought connected with belief, progress, humanism, it has restricted itself to words that it has bound together to make the poem. This self is utterly unhistorical, it feels no historic errand, neither for half a century nor a whole one, of no use is the prospect, the promise of alleged spiritual connections, ideas that fructify, ramify, integrate or resurrect, it measures out its own circle – moira, the part reserved for it – it does not look beyond itself, it denies itself this relief, it will attain the age of seventy at most, by then it must have described its morphology and found its words. Six to eight perfected poems – even the great writers have not left more than that – around this half-dozen rages the battle.

... I must admit that this lyric self feels no moral duty, whether to make men better or to educate the young, or to provide leisure entertainment, it does not wear wigs of that sort. Not because of amorality, on the contrary, because it considers the process set in motion by art to be more educational. It is not indifferent, yet it is not brotherly but egocentric, not collective but anchoritish, not religious but monomanic, it is Cain rather than Abel, and it takes into consideration that, according to Genesis 4 verse 15, the Lord forgave Cain, and that according to verse 21, it was his grandson Jubal from whom fiddlers and pipers came.[2]

Instead, this self has also a few traits which make it seem positive. It does not believe in the downfall either of the West or of humanity of all colours. There has always been a crisis, always a twilight of the gods, cultures went under and new cultures appeared, now robot

---

1 The original German typescript is dated 29 August 1952, but the speech was delivered on 12 September 1952 in French.
2 'Such as handle the harp and organ' in the English Authorised Version.

cultures will start, there has always been apocalypse, the seven-headed beast from the sea and the two-horned beast from the earth were always there.

Nor does it need historical changes of direction, thinking in such changes has already become an intellectual cliché. The absolute poem needs no historical change of direction, it is in a position to operate without time, as the formulae of modern physics have been doing for a long time. Therefore neither does the self have the fear so many write about today, the famous fear of living, it knows the periodicity of coming and going, it makes its poems, measures out its own circle, then it is finished.

An extract from *Should poetry improve life?*

1955

... Poetry does not improve, but it does something much more decisive: it brings about change. It has no historical powers of contact, if it is pure art, no therapeutic or pedagogic powers of contact, it acts in a different way: it suspends time and history, its effect is on the gene, the inherited mass, substance – a long inner journey. The nature of poetry is infinite restraint, its core making fragments, but its periphery is narrow, it touches little, but incandescently. All things change direction, all concepts and categories change their character the moment they are considered as art, when they face it, when they submit to it. It makes things flow that were petrified and dull and tired, flow in a way that is confusing and not to be understood, but that scatters seeds on banks that had become deserts, seeds of happiness and seeds of grief, the nature of poetry is perfection and fascination.

Index of Poem Titles and First Lines (English)

Titles are in italic, first lines in roman type.

824: Frauenliebe und -leben. 19

462

Index of Poem Titles and First Lines (German)

Titles are in italic, first lines in roman type.

473